Secondary Sources

This collection is one part of an Open University integrated teaching system and the selection is therefore related to other material available to students. It is designed to evoke the critical understanding of students.

AA312 Total War and Social Change: Europe 1914–1955

Book 1 *Europe in 1914*
Book 2 *The Impact of World War I*
Book 3 *Between Two Wars*
Book 4 *The Impact of World War II*
Book 5 *Retrospect: War and Change in Europe 1914–1955*

Other material associated with the course

Primary Sources 1: World War I, eds Arthur Marwick and Wendy Simpson, Open University, 2000

Primary Sources 2: Interwar and World War II, eds Arthur Marwick and Wendy Simpson, Open University, 2000

Secondary Sources, eds Arthur Marwick and Wendy Simpson, Open University, 2000

Total War and Historical Change: Europe 1914–1955, eds. Clive Emsley, Arthur Marwick and Wendy Simpson, Open University Press, 2000 (Course Reader)

J. M. Roberts, *Europe 1880–1945,* Longman, 2001 (third edition) (Set Book)

secondary sources

Secondary Sources

Edited by Arthur Marwick, Clive Emsley and Annika Mombauer

Total War and Social Change: Europe 1914–1955

Fri 12:40

This publication forms part of an Open University course: AA312 *Total War And Social Change: Europe 1914–1955*. Details of this and other Open University courses can be obtained from the Course Reservations Centre, PO Box 724, The Open University, Milton Keynes MK7 6ZS, United Kingdom: tel. +44 (0)1908 653231, e-mail ces-gen@open.ac.uk

Alternatively, you may visit the Open University website at http://www.open.ac.uk where you can learn more about the wide range of courses and packs offered at all levels by the Open University.

For availability of this or other components, contact Open University Worldwide Ltd, The Berrill Building, Walton Hall, Milton Keynes MK7 6AA, United Kingdom: tel. +44 (0)1908 858785; fax +44 (0)1908 858787; e-mail ouwenq@open.ac.uk; website http://www.ouw.co.uk

First published 2000 by The Open University. Reprinted 2002, 2007

Edited, designed and typeset by The Open University

Printed and bound in Malta by Gutenberg Press.

ISBN 978 0 7492 8546 X

Cover illustration: Otto Lehmann, *Support our Men in Uniform*, 96.5 × 69.2 cm. Imperial War Museum, London.

1.3

B/AA312_SS_e1i3_N978074928546X

Acknowledgements

Grateful acknowledgement is made to the following sources for permission to reproduce material in this book:

Text

p.7: Rendall, J. (1991) '"Uneven Developments": women's history, feminist history and gender history in Great Britain', *Writing Women's History: International Perspectives,* Macmillan Academic and Professional Ltd. Karen Offen, Ruth Roach Pierson, Jane Rendall 1991; *p.16:* Joll, J. (1984) 'Introduction', *The Origins of the First World War,* Longman Group/Pearson Education Ltd; *p.23:* Fischer, F. (1990) 'Foreign policy and the outbreak of the First World War', in Schollgen, G. (ed.) *Escape into War? The Foreign Policy of Imperial Germany,* Berg Publishers Limited; *p.25:* Gordon, M. R. (1974) 'Domestic conflict and the origins of the First World War: the British and German cases', *Journal of Modern History,* The University of Chicago Press; *p.36:* Mommsen, W. J. (1973) 'Domestic factors in German foreign policy before 1914', *Central European History,* vol.6. no.1. Emory University; *p.40:* Röhl, J. C. G. (1994) 'Dress rehearsal in December: military decision making in Germany on the eve of the First World War', *The Kaiser and his Court: Wilhelm II and the Government of Germany.* Cambridge University Press. Copyright © J. C. G. Röhl; *p.54:* Aldcroft, D. (1977) 'Introduction', *From Versailles to Wall Street 1919–1929,* University of California. Copyright © 1977 Derek Aldcroft; *p.60:* Hausen, K. (1987) 'The German nation's obligations to the heroes' widows of World War I', *Behind the Lines: Gender and the Two World Wars,* Yale University Press; *p.72:* Kershaw, I. (1998) 'Levered into power', *Hitler: 1889–1936: Hubris,* Penguin Books Limited; *p.78:* Hitler, A. (1939) 'War propaganda', trans. Murphy, J. *Mein Kampf,* Century Hutchison, by permission of The Random House Group; *p.84:* Bell, P. M. H. (1997) 'Appeasement', *A Companion to Modern European History,* Basil Blackwell Ltd; *p.102:* Koch, H. W. (1983) 'Hitler's "Programme" and the genesis of operation "Barbarossa"', *The Historical Journal,* **26,** 4. Cambridge University Press; *p.131:* Kettenacker, L. (1997) 'Drifting apart: the two republics', *Germany Since 1945,* Oxford University Press; *p.143:* Knox, M. (1984) 'Conquest, foreign and domestic, in Fascist Italy and Nazi Germany', *Journal of Modern History,* The University of Chicago Press. Copyright © MacGregor Knox.

Contents

1   JANE RENDALL, '"UNEVEN DEVELOPMENTS": WOMEN'S HISTORY, FEMINIST HISTORY AND GENDER HISTORY IN GREAT BRITAIN'

The development of women's history over the last twenty years has been uneven, marked by significant differences in the pace of change and in national experience, yet also simultaneously inspired by outstanding and creative growth, notably in the United States. The title of this article has been most recently used in a study of contested and unevenly growing ideologies of gender in nineteenth century England; but its original coiner, Marx, offered it as a means of analysing differential rates of international economic change, which incorporated the specific historical context of each nation's economic growth, yet also explained the interaction between different national patterns of development.[1] By analogy – however imperfect – we may reflect upon the dilemmas which now face those who write and read women's history within national contexts, contexts which themselves contain great variations, yet are also within an international framework.

My understanding of the massive developments in this field in the English language in this period is clearly rooted in a personal viewpoint, from Great Britain. It has been possible for me at an English university not only to be involved in the women's movement, but also to teach women's history and to collaborate with others in teaching women's studies. I have been conscious of the relative privilege of such as position, yet also of provincialism in an international context. For here women's history in almost all institutions of higher education, remains, despite prolific publication, a marginal area, lacking academic respectability, outside the mainstream, an academic extra occasionally demanded by troublesome women students and subversive temporary staff. The course of women's history has been marked by the strength and importance of approaches to history that lie outside academic establishments; in this has lain an outlook which is radical but also marginalised.[2] It is from this perspective that I would like to look at the relationship between women's history, feminist history, and the history of gender, and to consider the implications of the relationship now being forged between history and other disciplines. We should welcome the richness and liveliness of current theoretical debates: though at the same time we should be conscious of their relationship to political practice.

There is of course nothing new in the relationship between women's history and feminist history, which overlap yet are by no means identical. There is clearly no easy equation between the two. Social historians, economic historians, and historians of political movements have in certain periods located women's history as a branch of their own discipline: we as feminists have sought strength and support in the reconstruction of our own past. So successive generations of women and men have linked intellectual and political concerns. In the same way the social science of the eighteenth century might be echoed in the work of the Glasgow historian John Millar who wrote his powerful essay 'Of the Rank and Condition of Women in Different Ages' in 1771. But it was also echoed in Catherine Macaulay's *Letters on Education* in 1790 and in the writing of Mary Hays, the radical friend of Mary Wollstonecraft who turned from the advocacy of women's rights in the 1790s to the safer territory of female biography in the next decade.[3] And the generation of women who became social and economic historians at the end of the nineteenth and beginning of the twentieth centuries – women like Eileen Power, Alice Clark and Ivy Pinchbeck – reflected in their work at once the new insights of their discipline of social and economic history, the novelty of their own situation as working women, and the continuing debate over women's role in the public world.[4]

Today there is also a marked contrast between a women's history that has emerged from the new approaches to social history, and the work of feminist historians. In Great Britain there is particular awareness of such a distinction. Empirical traditions, aspirations towards objectivity, and rejection of theory are all still deeply rooted within a conservative profession. At the same time, from the 1970s onwards the close co-operation and interaction of British and American scholars working on British women's history have proved to be particularly fruitful in generating new perspectives.

It is now commonplace to acknowledge the dual origins of the growth of women's history in the political impetus of the women's movement, coupled with new approaches to social history. Social historians have seized upon the possibilities of extending their historical range, in dealing with, for instance, demography and the history of the family, or with the histories, differentiated by sex, of literacy and education, or of witchcraft and criminality. They have accepted the necessity of a social history which incorporates or even at times focuses upon the lives of women. The journal *Social History* illustrates the strength of this approach in Great Britain. Important studies have been published – to name but a few examples – on family structures and attitudes, on women's work from the medieval period onwards, and on deviance and criminality in the early modern period.[5] So it could be said, for instance, that much of the most substantial historical work relevant to women's history in medieval and early modern Britain has been done in Britain by social historians, whose interest is not specifically in women's history and who would disclaim any political purpose: there are, however, exceptions to this.[6] Regrettably, the same can be said of the writing of the history of European women's lives. Few British feminist historians have ventured into such territories, even in comparative terms.

One reason for this may be the attractions of investigating the nineteenth century paradigm, and its twentieth century legacy. I would want to suggest, tentatively, that a second reason may be more pragmatic, not unrelated to the condition of women in the historical profession. Work on the history of earlier periods or different national experiences requires some technical ability, access to specialised libraries, and time spent in other countries. In 1986–7 women, though one third of higher degree graduates, were still, at around 18 per cent, grossly underrepresented among the academic staff in the history departments of our universities.[7] Their absence from such institutions has undoubtedly influenced the kind of history that has been written. Many feminist historians working in modern British history have found their institutional base in the social sciences rather than within history departments.[8]

For the writing of women's history from a feminist perspective has drawn much of its impetus from outside our universities, from an alternative and critical viewpoint which has taken its energy from less well-funded, under-resourced institutions, from polytechnics and from adult and community education.

Informal feminist history groups, and autonomous, if struggling, resource centres - for instance, the Women's Research and Resource Centre, later renamed the Feminist Library in London – offered support and encouragement.[9] The Fawcett Library, originally the library of the London and National Society for Women's Suffrage, based in the City of London Polytechnic since 1977, provided a welcoming base for those interested in the history of the women's movement.[10] And much was owed to feminists working in both mainstream and alternative publishing, who stimulated and made possible the publication of work in women's history: the availability of such work brought the very notion of subverting the historical record to a far greater audience.

Feminist historians inspired by the concerns of the women's movement began in the 1970s to recover their own past. One way was to return to earlier models, to the lives of great women, such as Mary Wollstonecraft, Alexandra Kollontai, or Eleanor Marx. Another was to consider the constraints upon women's lives – to ask how much could be learned from prescriptions that appeared to justify secondary and inferior roles for women, from the ideologies of separate spheres? At this stage it seemed a question of recovery, of rescuing women invisible because of their class and sex, even when they could be found in familiar public settings. One important work characterising the concerns of the 1970s was Jill Liddington and Jill Norris' *One Hand Tied Behind Us* (1978),[11] which brought to light the wholly new world of the political activities of Lancashire working women neglected by previous generations of both suffrage and labour historians. Equally in evidence was a prevailing concern with the understanding of the nineteenth century form of the separate spheres of women and men, which remains for capitalist societies today such a dominating legacy. In all these illustrations of the concerns of the 1970s I think one can see the relationship between the women's movement in Britain and the politics of the left - the constant renegotiation of the relationship between socialism and feminism, the dominance of the concerns of labour history. While radical feminism existed within the women's movement it remained a minority voice among feminist historians.[12]

This then is the context from which I come to the emergence of gender as a primary category of historical analysis, and to the contrasts I want to point out. In the mid 1970s the American historians Natalie Zemon Davis and Joan Kelly, among others, wrote of the need to understand not merely a history of subjection, but the significance of gender groups in the past, of the construction of sex roles, their meaning and functions. It is interesting that both these scholars, as early modern European historians, had been exposed to those new developments in social history – the history of mentalities, of material life, and new anthropological perspectives – stressed above. Joan Kelly wrote of the displacing of separate spheres, 'the earlier split vision of bourgeois patriarchal society' by a social theory that united different sets of social relations, work and sex, or class and race, and sex/gender.[13] While these formulations were imprecise, the weight of variables – particularly that of race – still unclear, nevertheless such a programme was welcomed by those working within the marginal and radical framework I have outlined.

A most important focus for women's history in Britain until recently has been the key journal *History Workshop*. Founded in 1976 as a socialist journal, *History*

Workshop stood apart from academic establishments. Its first editorial argued that history is too important to be left to professional historians. It has remained at the forefront of our thinking about women's history, and about the relationship between history and theory. By 1982 the journal had become a journal of socialist and feminist historians, in recognition, as the editorial suggested, that it was involved not only in 'contributing to the sexual enlightenment of socialist history' but in participating 'in the construction of a new *autonomous* feminist history'. The relations of production had to be supplemented by those of reproduction. In more general terms *History Workshop* explicitly rejected the philistinism of British empiricism and called for the recognition of the importance of theoretical work drawing upon structuralist and poststructuralist debates.[14] One influential study undertaken in the 1970s by a US-based historian demonstrated how an analysis of gender relations, drawing upon both empirical research and theoretical insights, might throw new light on nineteenth-century British political history. Judith Walkowitz' work, on the regulation of prostitution in Victorian Britain and the resistances to such regulation, illuminated our understanding of sexuality and political structures alike. Its impact on feminists, teachers and students alike, cannot be overestimated.[15] In *Eve and the New Jerusalem,* an equally influential work published in 1983, Barbara Taylor pointed to the possibility of reconstructing the history of socialism in a way that took not only class but also sexual difference into account.[16]

By 1985 our index of change, *History Workshop,* had suggested that 'while rediscovering the worlds that women have inhabited is important... it can lead to a ghettoisation of women's history and to its presentation in forms which historians working in different fields find easy to ignore'. It called not only for the writing of women's history but for 'a feminist commitment to reconstructing the history of men as social group and gender category' as a part of the re-reading of the whole historical record.[17]

The possibilities of writing the history of gender have since been indicated in a work whose reverberations are still being absorbed. In the most ambitious attempt to write a history uniting the variables of class and gender, the major work by Leonore Davidoff and Catherine Hall, *Family Fortunes,* deployed the categories of gender and of class in a study of the middle classes of early nineteenth-century England, uniting feminist theory and a form of marxist analysis. They place gender at the centre of that analysis, starting 'from the premise that identity is gendered and that the organization of sexual difference is central to the social world. Distinctions between men and women are ever present, shaping experience, influencing behaviour, structuring explanations'.[18] Class is their second variable: but the very process of class formation is itself given a new dimension, because it is gendered. The modes of production, distribution and exchange are, in *this* study, integrally related to the consumption and reproduction of the household. Central to the emergence of class consciousness was its gendered identity: and only through analysis of domestic and private discourses, as well as of market and public worlds, can the creation of that powerful bourgeois culture be understood. In consequence this is a history which has as much to say of masculinity and of capitalist structures, as it does of femininity and of domesticity, in a survey as rich in cultural analysis as in discussion of material life.

So a term once purely grammatical has taken on a new meaning, a meaning which many historians have yet to discover. We should not underestimate the importance of this linguistic achievement. Those who as feminist historians have come to use the term 'gender' have done so by many routes, and not only in English.[19] And from all directions the possibilities for the future are exciting ones. The new journal, *Gender & History,* founded in 1989 and edited by Leonore Davidoff, is the first academic journal devoted to these issues.

We now have the means by which to examine all historical social relationships from a feminist perspective: this includes the study of male institutions and the construction of masculinity. The male domination of the historical record has made that construction invisible: it should now be possible to unmask it. Those who have seen only activity in the public sphere as historically worthy of study should now be challenged, as it becomes possible to explore all aspects of gender relations - political structures, cultural representations, symbolic systems. And those relations must be considered at all levels, where the most powerful are found – in parliaments, and cabinets, in international relations and in academies – and among the least powerful - in work and in play, in armies, communities, and private relationships. Those whose concern has been the descriptive, the recovery of the 'social' lives of men and women, should equally be challenged, for such descriptive work obscures the political structures inseparable from the construction of gender. We can now examine the varieties of masculinities and femininities that have been created, contested and negotiated over time: and we have to relate those varieties in their specific locations to those other variables of race, and class, ethnicity and sexual orientation. In some societies gender will provide a separation of the worlds of men and women overriding all other affiliations: in others the distinctions and boundaries of race or class may have the most fundamental effects in shaping lives.

Awareness of gender has already offered us the benefit of an interdisciplinary perspective: we are committed to the study of gendered divisions as a totality and to do that we need to draw upon the methods developed in other disciplines. The focus of the 1980s has been on the meaning of sexual difference rather than its cause, on literature and psychoanalysis rather than on social science or political theory, though the latter have had their place also.

To understand the creation of gender identity historians have begun to look at language, symbol, form, and at the challenge of the subjective. They have, for instance, begun to examine the way women construct their own lives in the differing narratives of autobiographical writing, life histories and oral histories. They have reconstructed the gendered symbolic order of revolution and republic in France. Following the work of Michel Foucault in particular, they have taken further the understanding of gendered political structures through arguments shaped by structuralism and poststructuralism. Joan Scott has persuasively argued that the radical potential of women's history 'comes in the writing of histories that focus on women's experiences *and* analyze the ways in which politics construct gender and gender constructs politics': we are offered 'multiple and mobile power relations'.[20]

And we do have work now, mainly but not only from the United States, which exemplifies the benefits of such approaches in subtle and original ways. In her work on sixteenth-century Augsburg, Lyndal Roper has studied the impact of the

Reformation on shifting patterns of gender, and the construction of heterosexuality through the close reading of criminal records.[21] A recent history of involvement with spiritualism in Victorian England becomes a reading of the subversion of existing power relationships, of the celebration of female spiritual authority, a hidden element in a female ministry.[22] Like Davidoff and Hall, Mary Poovey has addressed the middle-class world of nineteenth-century England and in analysis of the discourses of law, literature and medicine, has drawn out the significance of its dualities and contradictions, of how the masculine identity of the middle classes has depended on its construction of the Other and the subordinate, the feminine.[23] Joan Scott's critique of E.P. Thompson's *Making of the English Working Class* has been paralleled by more specific scrutiny – which still awaits much further research – of the gendering of working-class culture in nineteenth-century England.[24]

More speculative work has been published in recent years. Denise Riley has expanded discussion of the construction of gender to that of the construction of 'women' as a volatile and inconstant category discourse. She has suggested that an increasing degree of sexualisation and stress on gender boundaries in western Europe from the seventeenth to the nineteenth centuries constructed the collective category of womanhood. From that category grew both the strength and the ambiguities of nineteenth-century western feminism, torn as it notoriously seemed to be between equality and difference.[25]

But as feminists we may still have reservations about focusing upon the history of gender, diversely conceived. I should like to restate two, both of which have implications for the relationship between theory and practice.

First there are the implications of the recent stress on writing the history of gender through the analysis of discourse. Much of the work already completed in this area has drawn on the texts and symbols of the literate, reading their interesting complexities, noting those male discourses – ideologies of the public sphere, of political economy, of medicine – that explain the relations of power. These are the texts to which the attention of historians has been especially drawn. In themselves, that is admirable. Yet to study the history of gender does not and should not mean that we forget to explore the worlds of the less literate, the less powerful, of the ways ordinary men and women lived their lives. Did they absorb or ignore the public written discourse of elites, did they respect or reject the symbolic forms of power? How far should we read the culture of a society not only in terms of its public writings but of its material culture also? As one literary critic has suggested, an interdisciplinary project may have two purposes: to locate and pursue the common ground between disciplines, and to illuminate by difference and comparison.[26]

Historians need to ask questions about the location, and extent, of those constructions of masculinity and femininity as they change over time and place. They must still supplement the new skills of the reading of meaning with older historical practice. We have not only to learn from literary and psychoanalytic paradigms, but to meld those with our own. There are the archival sources historians need to demonstrate the extent and effectiveness of prevailing patterns of gender-determined authority and subordination, whether in terms of property ownership, of structures of employment or relations of marriage: so we may be talking of church courts or business records, of census materials or freemen's rolls. There is the material culture to which we should also turn our attention: the exploitation of new sources such as artefacts, the building and spatial arrangements of town and countryside, of household, neighbourhood and community, the technology of labour and the commodities of consumption. I do not suggest that one kind of source material has greater weight than others, but simply that we remind ourselves of the range that needs to be used. The history of gender should not be regarded as narrowly conceived in a single mould: engagement and debate, with marxist theory as with the historicisation of the concept of patriarchy, must enlarge our understanding.

To the best historical work cited above these points are entirely superfluous. Yet an earlier point is relevant here. In Britain what is particularly noticeable is the absence of feminist historians from so much historical territory beyond certain well-mapped paths: it has been, for instance, social historians, rooted in empiricist traditions, who appear, with one or two obvious exceptions, as the most distinguished exponents of women's history of the medieval and early modern period. That ground should be challenged by feminist historians who combine a theoretical and political perspective which deploys the insights of other disciplines, with a sufficient grounding in their craft. That is the only way in which the excitement of the theoretical insights currently being generated will successfully confront the dominant myth of objectivity. And there is still so much that remains to be done, if we have to consider the interaction of gender, race or class in those contexts of which as yet we have little or no knowledge.

My second point is related to the first, to the central political importance of continuing to write women's history. This can again be illustrated simply from one national perspective, though the point is more generally relevant. Almost all the work I have mentioned so far arises out of the characteristic concerns of a dominant white and English culture. But Britain is a multicultural society. No one has yet written the history of women in the black and Asian communities in Britain, though there is material to do so; relatively few have used the sources that exist for the history of British imperial relations to undertake that analysis of gender, race and class for which there is such need.[27] Nor should the history of gender relations in Britain focus only on England. To give one instance only: as one distinguished Scottish social historian has acknowledged, the neglect of women's history in Scotland is 'a historiographical disgrace'.[28] Very rich source materials exist from which the history of women in Scotland might be written: yet the conservatism of academic establishments has meant that such materials are in the main left to be exploited by those with few resources, outside the institutions of higher education. For those working in such areas, the process of recovery, of making visible, is still of vital political importance in all attempts to challenge a masculine establishment.

The new feminist history, and the history of gender are developing with a remarkable velocity. They need to retain a respect for a process that must remain at the heart of feminist concerns. There is very great unevenness, both across periods and between those within and outside dominant cultures. The idea of moving on from the recovery of women's history to the history of gender may seem a dangerous one, giving hostages to an already hostile establishment. As the Australian historian Marilyn Lake has written, the significance of women's history is greater than merely illuminating how men may grab and hold on to power. Our analysis of political structures, of the construction of masculinity, must not simply re-legitimate such subjects and perpetuate the absence of women from the historical record. Perhaps as yet there is little chance of that: compared to the wealth of publications on women's history there is as yet relatively little in print which has accepted the challenge of defining and constructing the history of masculinity. Lake suggests that our task is 'to transform the disciplinary paradigm by challenging the masculine model of social reality which underpins it'.[29] We may know increasingly more of the fluidity of the categories of masculinity and femininity, but let us not forget, in such knowledge, that the challenge of an alternative practice and an alternative history remain to be forged.

Notes

I am very grateful for the comments of Karen Offen and Leonore Davidoff, though they are in no way responsible for the finished product.

[1] T.B. Bottomore, *Dictionary of Marxist Thought* (Oxford: Basil Blackwell, 1983), pp. 502–3; Mary Poovey, *Uneven Developments: The Ideological Work of Gender in Mid-Victorian England* (Chicago: University of Chicago Press, 1988).

[2] See, for discussions of the situation in Britain: Jane Lewis, 'Women Lost and Found: the Impact of Feminism on History', in Dale Spender (ed.), *Men's Studies Modified: The Impact of Feminism on the Academic Disciplines* (Oxford and New York: Pergamon Press, 1981); Anna Davin, 'Redressing the Balance or Transforming the Art? The British Experience', in S. Jay Kleinberg (ed.), *Retrieving Women's History: Changing Perceptions of the Role of Women in Politics and Society* (Oxford and New York: Berg/ UNESCO, 1988).

[3] John Millar, *The Origin and Distinction of Ranks* (Edinburgh, 1776); Catharine Macaulay, *Letters on Education, with Observations on Religious and Metaphysical Subjects* (London, 1790); Mary Hays, *Female Biography, or, Memoirs of Illustrious and Celebrated Women, of all Ages and Countries* (London: 1802).

[4] On this generation, see Joan Thirsk, 'Foreword', in Mary Prior (ed.), *Women in English Society, 1500–1800* (London: Methuen, 1985).

[5] The works of distinguished social historians in this category might include, for example: Alan Macfarlane, *Marriage and Love in England: Modes of Reproduction, 1300–1840* (Oxford: Basil Blackwell, 1986); Ralph Houlbrooke, *The English Family, 1450–1700* (London and New York: Longman, 1984); Martin Ingram, *Church Courts, Sex and Marriage in England, 1570–1640* (Cambridge: Cambridge University Press, 1987); J.A. Sharpe, *Defamation and Sexual Slander in Early Modern England: the Church Courts at York*, Borthwick Papers, 58 (York: St Anthony's Press, 1980); Keith D.M. Snell, *Annals of the Labouring Poor: Social Change and Agrarian England, 1660–1900* (Cambridge: Cambridge University Press, 1985); David Levine, *Reproducing Families: The Political Economy of English Population History* (Cambridge: Cambridge University Press, 1987).

[6] See, for instance: Lindsey Charles and Lorna Duffin (eds.), *Women and Work in Pre-Industrial England* (London: Croom Helm, 1985); Mary Prior (ed.), *Women in English Society, 1500–1800* (London and New York: Methuen, 1985); Bridget Hill, *Women, Work and Sexual Politics in Eighteenth-Century England* (Oxford and New York: Basil Blackwell, 1989).

Substantial recent monographs in this area by American scholars include: Barbara Hanawalt, *The Ties that Bound: Peasant Families in Medieval England* (New York: Oxford University Press, 1986); Judith M. Bennett, *Women in the Medieval English Countryside: Gender and Household in Brigstock before the Plague* (New York: Oxford University Press, 1988); Hilda Smith, *Reason's Disciples: Seventeenth-Century English Feminists* (Urbana, Illinois: University of Illinois Press, 1982); Susan Dwyer Amussen, *An*

Ordered Society: Gender and Class in Early Modern England (Oxford and New York: Basil Blackwell, 1988).

[7] These figures are for the humanities cost-centre of the Universities Funding Council. This information was received from the Association of University Teachers, LA/3716 April 1989.

[8] For instance: Leonore Davidoff, Department of Sociology, University of Essex; Carol Dyhouse, Department of Education, University of Sussex; Jane Lewis, Department of Social Science and Administration, London School of Economics; Penelope Summerfield, Department of Education, University of Lancaster; Patricia Thane, Department of Social Policy, Goldsmiths College.

[9] See Davin, 'Redressing the Balance'.

[10] See 'The Fawcett Library: Britain's Major Research Resources on Women Past and Present', a Special Issue of *Women's Studies International Forum*, 10, no. 3 (1987).

[11] *One Hand Tied Behind Us: The Rise of the Women's Suffrage Movement* (London: Virago, 1978).

[12] The work of Sheila Jeffreys has been particularly influential. See Jeffreys, *The Spinster and her Enemies: Feminism and Sexuality, 1880–1930* (London: Pandora, 1985), and Lesbian History Group (ed.), *Not a Passing Phase: Reclaiming Lesbians in History 1840–1945* (London: Women's Press, 1989).

[13] Nathalie Zemon Davis, 'Women's History in Transition: the European Case', *Feminist Studies*, 3, nos. 3–4 (1976), pp. 83–103; Joan Kelly, 'The Doubled Vision of Feminist Theory', in *Women, History and Theory: The Essays of Joan Kelly* (Chicago: University of Chicago Press, 1984), especially pp.59–62.

[14] Editorial, '*History Workshop Journal* and Feminism', *History Workshop Journal*, 13 (1982); Editorial, 'History and Theory', *History Workshop Journal*, 6 (1978), pp.1–6.

[15] Judith Walkowitz, *Prostitution and Victorian Society: Women, Class and the State* (Cambridge: Cambridge University Press, 1980).

[16] Barbara Taylor, *Eve and the New Jerusalem: Socialism and Feminism in the Nineteenth Century* (London: Virago, 1983). Taylor does not use the term 'gender': her work 'is an examination of how a vision – the vision of women's emancipation as an integral feature of a general social emancipation – arose, became part of the ideological armoury of a popular social movement, and inspired attempts to construct a new sexual culture in a society riven with sex- and class-based conflicts' (p.xi).

[17] Editorial, 'Women's History and Men's History', *History Workshop*, 19, (1985), pp.1–2.

[18] Leonore Davidoff and Catherine Hall, *Family Fortunes: Men and Women of the English Middle Class, 1780–1850* (London: Hutchinson, 1987), p.29.

[19] Gisela Bock, 'Women's History and Gender History: Aspects of an International Debate', *Gender & History*, 1, no. 1 (1989), p.10.

[20] Joan Wallach Scott, *Gender and the Politics of History* (New York: Columbia University Press, 1988), pp. 25–6.

[21] Lyndal Roper, *The Holy Household: Women and Morals in Reformation Augsburg* (Oxford: Oxford University Press, 1989); 'Discipline and Respectability: Prostitution and the Reformation in Augsburg', *History Workshop*, 19 (1985), pp. 3–28; 'Will and Honor: Sex, Words and Power in Augsburg Criminal Trials', *Radical History Review*, 43 (1989), pp. 45–71.

[22] Alex Owen, *The Darkened Room: Women, Power and Spiritualism in Late Victorian England* (London: Virago. 1989).

[23] Poovey, *Uneven Developments*.

[24] Scott, 'Women in The Making of the English Working Class', in *Gender and the Politics of History*; Catherine Hall, 'The Tale of Samuel and Jemima: Gender and Working-Class Culture in Nineteenth-Century England', in Harvey J. Kaye and Keith C. McClelland (eds.), *E.P Thompson: Critical Perspectives* (Oxford: Polity Press, 1990); also relevant is the work of Anna Clark, *Women's Silence, Men's Violence: Sexual Assault in England 1770–1845* (London: Pandora, 1987), and 'Whores and Gossips: Sexual Reputation in London 1770–1825', in Arina Angerman et al. (eds.), *Current Issues in Women's History* (London and New York: Routledge, 1989); and John Gillis, *For Better, For Worse: British Marriages, 1600 to the Present* (New York: Oxford University Press, 1985).

[25] Denise Riley, *'Am I That Name?': Feminism and the Category of 'Women' in History* (Basingstoke: Macmillan, 1988)

[26] Judith Walkowitz, Myra Jehlen, and Bell Chevigny, 'Patrolling the Borders: Feminist Historiography and the New Historicism', *Radical History Review*, 43 (1989), pp. 23–44.

[27] This 'absence of a black British historiography' is charted in Ziggy Alexander, 'Let It Lie Upon the Table: The Status of Black Women's Biography in the UK', *Gender & History*, 2 no. 1 (1990), pp.22–33: the history of Asian communities in Britain is discussed in Rozina Visram, *Ayahs, Lascars and Princes: Indians in Britain 1700–1947* (London: Pluto Press, 1986). There is an important recent work on black women in the West Indies: Barbara Bush, *Slave Women in Caribbean Society 1650–1832* (Bloomington: Indiana University Press, 1989). Other approaches to the study of imperialism are discussed in: Catherine Hall, 'The Economy of Intellectual Prestige: Thomas Carlyle, John Stuart Mill and the Case of Governor Eyre', *Cultural Critique*, 12 (1989), pp. 167–96; Joanna de Groot, '"Sex" and "Race": The Construction of Language and Image in the Nineteenth Century', in Susan Mendus and Jane Rendall (eds.) *Sexuality and Subordination: Interdisciplinary Studies of Gender in the Nineteenth Century* (London: Routledge, 1989).

[28] T.C. Smout, *A Century of the Scottish People 1830–1950* (London: Collins, 1986), p. 292: this disgrace is just beginning to be remedied. See R.A. Houston, 'Women in the Economy and Society of Scotland, 1500–1800' in R.A. Houston and I.D. Whyte, (eds.), *Scottish Society 1500–1800* (Cambridge: Cambridge University Press, 1988); Linda Mahood, *The Magdalenes: Prostitution in the Nineteenth Century* (London: Routledge. 1990); Esther Breitenbach and Eleanor Gordon (eds.), *The World is Ill-Divided: Women's Work in Scotland in the 19th and Early 20th Centuries*, 2 vols. (Edinburgh: Edinburgh University Press, 1990). For the history of women in Wales, see Deidre Beddoe, 'Images of Welsh Women', in Tony Curtis (ed.), *Wales: the Imagined Nation – Essays in Cultural and National Identity* (Bridgend: Poetry Wales Press, 1986); Angela John (ed.), *Our Mothers' Land: Essays in Welsh Women's History, 1830–1930* (Cardiff: University of Wales Press, forthcoming 1991). *Llafur*, the journal of the Welsh Labour History Society, also carries important material on Welsh women's history.

[29] Marilyn Lake, 'Women, Gender and History', *Australian Feminist Studies*, 7–8 (1988), pp. 8–9.

(Karen Offen, Ruth Roach Pierson and Jane Rendall (eds.), *Writing Women's History: International Perspectives*, Macmillan, 1991)

2   JAMES JOLL, FROM *THE ORIGINS OF THE FIRST WORLD WAR*

The outbreak of the First World War in 1914 still seems to mark the end of an era and the beginning of a new one, even though we can see that many of the social, political, economic and cultural developments of the later twentieth century were only accelerated rather than produced by the war. The experiences of the war, and especially of the trench warfare on the western front, have entered deeply into the language and imagery of the countries of western Europe[1] and continue to haunt the imagination of writers and artists born years after the war ended. Its immediate consequences – the Russian revolution, the political and social upheavals of 1918–22 all over Europe, the redrawing of the maps with the emergence of new national states – have determined the course of history in the twentieth century. This alone would be enough to account for the continuing interest in the causes of war, but there are several other dimensions and perspectives to our views of the crisis of 1914.

The immediate origins of the war are better documented than almost any other question in recent history. This is largely because from the start the argument about the responsibility for the outbreak of war had great political importance; and with the signing of the Treaty of Versailles in June 1919, the question of war guilt – *Die Kriegsschuldfrage* – became one of intense political and emotional significance. The first reaction in the victorious countries after the end of the war was to put the blame for its outbreak on the Germans. Article 231 of the Treaty of Versailles – the 'War Guilt' clause – stated that 'Germany accepts the responsibility of Germany and her allies for causing all the loss and damage to the Allied governments and their nationals imposed on them by the aggression of Germany and her allies.' Elsewhere in the Peace Treaty the moral blame was made even more explicit and was attached particularly to the person of the German Emperor: 'The Allied and Associated Powers publicly arraign William II of Hohenzollern, former German Emperor, for a supreme offence against international morality and the sanctity of treaties.' The individual indictment of the Kaiser was the result partly of a blind instinct for revenge on the part of the public in Britain and France: 'Hang the Kaiser' had been a popular slogan in the British general election of November 1918. But the demand for a formal trial of William II was also the result of a more considered, though not necessarily more accurate, diagnosis of the role of the Emperor and the Prussian military caste in the origins of war. Already in 1914 Sir Edward Grey, the British Foreign Secretary, was obsessed with the evils of 'Prussian militarism'[2] while in the armistice negotiations at the end of war, President Wilson had stressed the necessity of getting rid of the Kaiser and doing away with what he called 'military masters' and monarchical autocrats'.[3]

During the latter part of 1919 and early 1920 there were vigorous attempts by the British and French governments to bring the Kaiser to trial and to persuade the government of the Netherlands, where William II had taken refuge, to hand him over. The British and French were extremely angry with the Dutch – and in the despatches of the British minister at the Hague one can see the accumulated bitterness at four years of Dutch neutrality. Lloyd George was particularly virulent against the Dutch and their refusal to see the Kaiser's personal responsibility in the same light as he did. In the Supreme War Council he ranted against the Kaiser, and his phrases were embodied in the note sent to the Netherlands government demanding his surrender. The Kaiser was, Lloyd George maintained, personally responsible for 'the cynical violation of the neutrality of Belgium and Luxembourg, the barbarous hostage system, the mass deportation of populations, the carrying away of the young women of Lille, torn from their families and thrown defenceless into the most promiscuous environment'.[4] The rhetoric was in vain, as were the threats to break off diplomatic relations with the Netherlands and even to impose economic sanctions. The Dutch government maintained its dignified refusal either to surrender William II or, on the analogy of Napoleon, to banish him to Curaçao in the Dutch West Indies.

The attitude of the Netherlands government made the idea of trying the Kaiser and of pinning responsibility for the war on him personally impossible to realize. The search for responsibility became less immediate and moved to another level. By the middle of the 1920s the idea was gaining acceptance that the war was a result of a faulty system of international relations. It was, on this view, the existence of a system of alliances dividing Europe into two camps which had made war inevitable, while the 'old diplomacy' was blamed for making sinister secret international agreements which committed countries to war without the knowledge of their citizens. As the *Manchester Guardian* had put it in 1914: 'By some hidden contract England has been technically committed behind her back to the ruinous madness of a share in the violent gamble of a war between two militarist leagues on the Continent.'[5] This view had been strengthened by the policies of the American administration after the Unites States had entered the war in April 1917. President Wilson was much influenced by the British radical tradition which throughout the nineteenth century had criticised secret diplomacy and called for a foreign policy based on morality rather than on expediency, on general ethical principles rather than on practical calculations about the balance of power. Thus when in January 1918, he enunciated his famous Fourteen Points which were to serve as the basis of a just peace, he stressed the need for 'Open covenants of peace openly arrived at, after which there shall be no private international understandings of any kind, but diplomacy shall proceed always frankly and in the public view.' The foundation of the League of Nations as an integral part of the peace settlement of 1919 encouraged the belief that a new system of international relations was about to come into being in which diplomatic bargains and secret military agreements would be abolished and international relations be conducted by consensus before the eyes of the public and under their control.

The search for an explanation for the outbreak of the war in terms of the nature of the international system – a view summed up in the title of an influential book published in 1926, *The International Anarchy 1904–1914* by the Cambridge classicist G. Lowes Dickinson – was aided by the publication by most of the governments in the war of numerous volumes of documents from their diplomatic archives. The first attack on secret diplomacy in which the publication of documents was used to discredit opponents was launched before the end of the war when Trotsky, the first Foreign Minister of the Bolshevik regime, ordered the publication of the secret treaties entered into by the Tsarist government, greatly to the embarrassment of Russia's allies France and Britain. Then after the German revolution of 1918, the republican government authorized the eminent socialist theoretician Karl Kautsky to prepare a volume of documents from the German archives on the events immediately preceding the outbreak of war. Subsequent German governments believed that one way to refute the allegations of Germany's war guilt was to show the detailed working of the old diplomacy and to demonstrate that the methods of all governments were much the same and that therefore no specific blame should be attached to the Germans. Accordingly, between 1922 and 1927 thirty-nine volumes of German diplomatic documents were published under the title *Die Grosse Politik der Europäischen Kabinette* (The High Policy of the European

Cabinets). This German initiative that aimed at countering the allegations of Germany's war guilt meant that other countries felt obliged to follow the example and show that they too had nothing to hide. Consequently the British Documents on the *Origins of War* appeared in eleven volumes between 1926 and 1938; the French Documents *Diplomatiques Français 1871–1914* began publication in 1930, though the last of the volumes did not appear until 1953. Eight volumes of Austro-Hungarian documents were published in 1930 by the government of the Austrian Republic, while the Italian documents were only published after the Second World War. Members of the Russian diplomatic service who remained abroad after the revolution published selections from their embassy archives, and the Soviet government printed a quantity of archive material in the 1920s and 1930s.[6]

This mass of published documentary material meant that, even though the government archives themselves in many cases remained closed until after the Second World War, historians had a great deal of evidence on which to base an examination of the diplomatic relations between the powers. The study of diplomatic history of the nineteenth century and of the background to the First World War became one of the most prestigious branches of historical investigation. A number of distinguished historians developed the idea of the autonomy of diplomatic history as a branch of historical study and so seemed to confirm the view of the great nineteenth-century German historian Ranke that it is the foreign policies of states which determine their internal development and decide their destiny. It is due to this generation of historians and the students trained by them that we know more in greater detail about the history of relations between states in the years before 1914 than in almost any other period. Many of these historians were still concerned with the allocation to the belligerent governments of responsibility in one form or another: Pierre Renouvin in France and Bernadotte Schmitt in the United States inclined to put the blame on Germany, another American, Sidney B. Fay, on Austria-Hungary, the German Alfred von Wegerer on Russia and Britain, to name only a few examples. The most monumental of these detailed studies, that by the Italian journalist and politician Luigi Albertini, only appeared after the Second World War had begun and it was some years before it achieved international recognition; and by then the focus of the discussion was changing.[7]

After the Second World War, for which the immediate responsibility was generally accepted to be that of Hitler and the National Socialist government of Germany, the discussion of the causes of the First World War tended to be linked to the discussion about the causes of the Second. How far did the Treaty of Versailles, and especially the War Guilt clause, contribute to the collapse of the Weimar Republic and the rise of Hitler? To what extent was there a continuity in foreign policy between the Kaiser's and Hitler's Germany. The notion of a continuity in German aims between 1914 and 1939 was familiar enough to Anglo-Saxon historians from their reactions to the Second World War, when for some of them, indeed, the tradition of Germany's inherent wickedness went back to Bismark or Frederick the Great or even Luther.[8] For many conservative German historians, although they were ready to accept German responsibility for the Second World War, it was extremely painful to face the fact that the notion of Germany's 'guilt' in the First World War was still flourishing outside Germany. This partly accounted for the violence of the controversy aroused in

Germany by the publication of the Hamburg historian Fritz Fischer's work *Griff nach der Weltmacht* in 1961[9] which showed not only the extent of German annexationist aims in the First World War but also suggested that the German government deliberately went to war in 1914 in order to attain them. Worse still from the point of view of many of Fischer's German colleagues, he suggested that there might be some continuity between Germany's aims in the First World War and those in the Second.

However, the aspect of Fritz Fischer's work which was most important for the discussion of the causes of the First World War has been the suggestion, made almost incidentally in *Griff nach der Weltmacht* but developed in his next book *Krieg der Illusionen*, and carried further by several of his students and followers, that it was domestic political and social pressures which determined German foreign policy before 1914.[10] This assertion of *the Primat der Innenpolitik* in reaction against the Rankean *Primat der Aussenpolitik* has made historians look again at the domestic political situation in Europe before 1914. The spread of this view was helped by the fact that in the 1960s many American historians and political scientists were analysing contemporary American foreign policy, including the origins of the Cold War and of the war in Vietnam, in terms of economic interests and pressure groups, so that it seemed natural to apply similar models to Europe before 1914 and to believe that, in Arno J. Mayer's words, 'the decision for war and the design for warfare were forged in what was a crisis in the politics and policy of Europe's ruling and governing classes'.[11] These ideas came close to the Marxist explanation that wars are inherent in the nature of capitalism and that the internal contradictions of capitalist society had by the beginning of the twentieth century reached a point where war was inevitable.

Such explanations can take us very far away from the immediate situation in 1914 and involve us in a consideration of the entire economic and social development of Europe for several centuries. And ideally, no doubt, an account of the causes of the First World War would lead to a moment of profound Hegelian insight in which everything in the world would be related to everything else and all the connections and patterns would become clear. However, this book has a more modest aim and will attempt to look at some of the reasons which have been suggested why this particular war occurred at this particular time.

Our explanations form a pattern of concentric circles, starting with the immediate decisions taken by the political and military leaders in the crisis of July 1914, decisions in which their characters and personal idiosyncrasies necessarily played a part. But these decisions were themselves limited both by previous choices and by the constitutional and political framework within which they were taken. They were influenced by recent international crises and by the diplomatic alignments contracted over the previous forty years. They were the result of an intricate relationship between the military and civilian leaders and of long-term strategic plans and armament programmes. They were subject to domestic political pressures, both short- and long-term, and to the conflicting influences of different economic groups. They depended on general conceptions of each nation's vital interests and of its national mission. Moreover the decision to go to war had to be acceptable and comprehensible to the public and to the soldiers who were going to fight; the reasons for going to war had to be expressed in language which would meet with an emotional response. And that response depended on long national traditions and the constant repetition of national myths.

The aim of this book is to look at the decisions of July 1914 which determined the outbreak of this particular war at that particular time and then to consider some of the factors which inspired those decisions and, perhaps more important, limited the options available. When we read an account of the crisis of July 1914, we often feel that the reasons which the politicians themselves were giving are somehow inadequate to explain what was happening and we are tempted to look for some deeper and more general cause to explain the catastrophe. We are often struck, as the Italian historian Luigi Albertini was, when he considered the decision-makers of 1914. By, as he put it, 'the disproportion between their intellectual and moral endowments and the gravity of the problems which faced them, between their acts and the results thereof'.[12] This is perhaps unfair in so far as they did not and could not know what the results would be or realize that the war they decided to fight would not be the war which actually followed, and that it would turn out to be longer and more destructive than any of them had ever imagined. It is pointless to speculate whether they would have chosen differently if they had known what the consequences of their choice would be. Their decisions must be examined within the context of what was open to them in 1914. As Isaiah Berlin has written, 'What can and cannot be done by particular agents in specific circumstances is an empirical question, properly settled, like all such questions, by an appeal to experience.'[13] The difficulty is, however, that the evidence which we have about the factors determining what could or could not be done in specific circumstances of July 1914 is vast, and it is not easy to decide which factor was dominant in a particular decision. All we can do is to look at the various kinds of explanation which have been suggested and try to see how far they account for the decisions actually taken. Accordingly, this book discusses some (but by no means all) of the suggested 'causes' of the war and tries to see how much each has contributed to the development of the crisis of 1914.

As we have seen, many people in the 1920s blamed the international system, the existence of rival alliances and the evil influence of the 'old diplomacy', and this indeed set the scene within which the crisis developed. Once it started, the freedom of action of the civilian ministers was limited, often more than they realized, by the strategic plans and decisions of the general staffs and admiralities, and these in turn were linked to the vast arms programmes which were a feature of the period immediately preceding the war. While some have seen the cause of the war in the international system or the plans of the military and naval authorities, others have blamed financiers and industrialists and the whole economic structure of international capitalism. What were the economic pressures for peace and for war? Then again, should we accept the idea of the *Primat der Innenpolitik* and look for the causes of war in the domestic social and political problems of the belligerent countries and the belief that war might provide a solution to them and avert the threat of revolution?

The war of 1914 has seemed to some the climax of an era of imperialism: and many have believed that it was imperial rivalries which led inevitably to war, so that we must also attempt to analyse what part these played in creating the situation in July 1914. Finally, we can try to see how far the mood of 1914 – the political, the intellectual and moral beliefs of the age – helped to make war possible and provided a scale of values to which governments could appeal once they had decided on war. In what follows, each chapter is devoted to a different type of explanation. The list is by no means exhaustive, but if we try to see how far each explanation fits what happened in July 1914, how far the different categories of historical phenomena relate to the decisions taken during the crisis, we may begin to form, not a complete picture of the causes of the First World War, but at least a sketch of the complex and multifarious factors which contributed to it.

Notes

[1] See, for example, Paul Fussell, *The Great War and Modern Memory* (London 1975).

[2] See Michael Ekstein, 'Sir Edward Grey and Imperial Germany in 1914', *Journal of Contemporary History*, **6**, No.3 (1971) pp. 121–31.

[3] *Foreign Relations of the United States, 1918* (Washington 1933) Supplement I, Vol I, p. 383.

[4] E. L. Woodward and Rohan Butler (eds) *Documents on British Foreign Policy 1919– 1939*, 1st series, Vol. 2 (London 1948) p. 913.

[5] *Manchester Guardian*, 31 July 1914, quoted in Lawrence Martin, *Peace without Victory* (New Haven 1958) p.47.

[6] For a discussion on these materials, see A. J. P. Taylor, *The Struggle for Mastery in Europe* (Oxford 1954) pp. 569–83.

[7] See e.g. Pierre Renouvin, *Les Origines immédiates de la Guerre* (Paris 1927); Bernadotte E. Schmitt, *The Coming of the War 1914*, 2 vols (New York 1928); Sidney B. Fay, *The Origins of the World War*, 2 vols (New York 1928); Alfred von Wegerer, *Der Ausbruch des Weltkrieges*, 2 vols (Hamburg 1939); Luigi Albertini, *Le Origini della Guerra del 1914*, 3 vols (Milan 1942–43).

[8] For example Rohan Butler, *The Roots of National Socialism* (London 1941).

[9] Fritz Fischer, *Griff nach der Weltmacht* (Düsseldorf 1961), Eng. Tr. *Germany's Aims in the First World War* (London 1972); *Krieg der Illusionen* (Düsseldorf 1969) Eng. Tr. *War of Illusions* (London 1974). For the controversy over Fischer's views, see e.g. John Moses, *The Politics of Illusion: The Fischer Controversy in German Historiography* (London 1975); H. W. Koch (ed.) *The Origins of the First World War* (London 1972); Wolfgang Schieder (ed.) *Erster Weltkrieg: Ursachen, Entstehung und Kriegsziele* (Cologne 1969).

[10] See the two volumes of essays celebrating Fischer's sixty-fifth and seventieth birthdays: Imanuel Geiss and Bernd Jürgen Wendt (eds) *Deutschland in der Weltpolitik des 19. und 20. Jahrhunderts* (Düsseldorf 1973); Dirk Stegmann and Peter-Christian Witt (eds) *Industrielle Gesellschaft und politisches System* (Bonn 1978), and especially the works of Hans-Ulrich Wehler, e.g. *Bismark und der Imperialismus* (Cologne 1969); *Das deutsche Kaiserreich 1871–1918* (Göttingen 1973).

[11] Arno J. Mayer, 'Internal crises and war since 1870' in Charles L. Bertrand (ed) *Revolutionary Situations in Europe* (Montreal 1977) p. 231. For a development of Mayer's view that the war was a last attempt by the old European aristocracy to preserve its position, see his *The Persistence of the Old Regime: Europe to the Great War* (New York 1981).

[12] Luigi Albertini, *The Origins of the War of 1914*, Vol. III (Eng. Tr. 1957) p. 178.

[13] Isaiah Berlin, *Historical Inevitability* (London 1954) p.33, fn. 1.

(James Joll, *The Origins of the First World War*, London, Longman, 1984)

3 FRITZ, FISCHER FROM 'THE FOREIGN POLICY OF IMPERIAL GERMANY AND THE OUTBREAK OF THE FIRST WORLD WAR'

Conclusions

Out of a continental war against France and Russia, envisaged in July–August 1914, there developed a world war. In place of the 'short war', it developed from November 1914 into a war of stopgaps, of exhaustion, an economic war, a war of resources, which was to last another four years, and a war for which Germany was not prepared. The German government had staked everything on one card (the civilians had subjected themselves to the military concept) and had lost first the battle of the Marne in September and then again the battle of Ypres and Langemark in November 1914 with dreadful losses of men. Falkenhayn, Moltke's successor, called the German army 'a broken tool'.[1] The Prusso-German Empire had passed the zenith of its power.

Was this a preventive war as Egmont Zechlin and Karl Dietrich Erdmann today maintain?[2] Or a preventive war, as Hillgruber maintains, in accordance with the German military doctrine which considered it as the right or even the duty of a statesman to prevent the threatened formation of a more powerful hostile coalition in two or three years' time, and this regardless of any political or diplomatic development that may have occurred during this period? Was there such a threat in the expansion of the Russian army (and fleet) to an enormous peacetime strength by the year 1917, together with the building of fortifications and railways? Was there a real danger that Russia and France together would attack Germany in 1917? Would Britain, the strongest partner in the Triple Entente, have given its approval and support to an offensive war by Russia and France against Germany?

But what is a defensive war? Who threatened or attacked Germany? It was at any rate clear to the German government under Bethmann Hollweg even before the war that France must be eliminated as a great power for the foreseeable future and should exist as an ally or vassal-state of Germany. The reasons for this were France's alliance with Russia and its continual clashes with Germany in Turkey and in the Balkans, mainly with the help of its 'arme financière'. No French territory was to be annexed (with the exception of Longwy-Briey and a few important military strongpoints). But France would have to disarm, to pay a high sum of war reparations and be integrated into 'Central Europe', an economic block dominated by Germany. Here all French resources would be put at the disposal of Germany, which lacked capital, and the whole of France would be a market for German goods, unrestricted by import duties.

As far as Russia was concerned, the German Chancellor, two days after his speech in the Reichstag on 4 August, already had a clear objective for the war on the eastern front. He described his aims as the liberation and securing of the races subjugated by Russia, the pushing back of the Russian frontier to Moscow and the establishment of a number of buffer states (Finland, Poland, Ukraine, Georgia) between Germany or Austria-Hungary and Russia.[3] This was over a month earlier than the much discussed 'September programme', which stated 'that Russia must be thrust back as far as possible from Germany's eastern frontier, and its domination over the non-Russian peoples broken'.[4]

Britain was expected to accept these changes on the continent and also to permit the acquisition of Portuguese, Belgian and French colonies for the creation of a defensible German Central Africa (this in an era when the idea of colonies was already disputed for economic as well as moral reasons). However one may judge these plans for the expansion of the German sphere of influence westwards and eastwards, disguised as it was by the Central European Economic Union (which was to be composed in the West of France and Belgium, the Netherlands and Denmark and eventually Norway and Italy; in the East of Austria-Hungary and Poland, but which should extend over Romania and Bulgaria as far as Turkey and the Hamburg-Baghdad line),[5] one thing is certain, namely, that this aim did not first originate in the war and that, intentionally or not, it amounted to a German hegemony on the continent.

Was it not the greatest of delusions that Germany believed it had to fight this war and that this was necessary for its own security? Bethmann Hollweg, the Russophobe, still claimed after the war in his memoirs that the war against Russsia was necessary to maintain the independence of the German Reich and of Austria-Hungary.[6] Yet Russia was still lagging far behind in its development and, furthermore, was threatened with internal revolution. Germany was rich, flourishing and industrially the most progressive country in Europe, having already overtaken France and even Britain in many sectors. This Germany, with its 67 million inhabitants, led the way in science, particularly in the natural sciences; it led the way with its technical universities and with its applied research. Germany had a rising share of world trade, flourishing shipping interests, a highly developed banking system which was dovetailed with industry, and at a time when industry and research were already of decisive importance for the standing of a country in the world.

The 'War-Guilt' Question

It is not legitimate to approach the issue of the origins of the First World War and the July crisis of 1914 in terms of the 'war-guilt' thesis of 1919 and the related reparations question. As the Swiss historian Adolf Gasser has observed, in 1914 war was still, from the standpoint of *international law*, a recognised means of policy, and so regarded by all the Great Powers of the era.[7] The British scholars Zara Steiner[8] and James Joll[9] share this judgement. Considered in *moral* terms, it is undeniable that all the Great Powers practised expansionist and power politics, even if some did so more with the intent of preserving rather than modifying the *status* quo. Viewed *politically,* however, the question arises as to whether in the case of Prussia-Germany it was clever, wise or practicable to aspire, in such a short time, with such impatience and vehemence, and by means of such a 'hothouse' naval and military armaments policy, to effect an alteration in the international political system; in short, to practise a policy which must more or less inevitably lead to war.

The Germans after 1914 and after 1919 – even among the educated classes – did not realise and did not recognise that the German government in 1914 bore a decisive part of the responsibility for unleashing the World War but instead fought a twenty-year apologia against the 'Kriegsschuldlüge' (the lie of German war-guilt). Neither did the Germans realise or recognise the defeat of 1918 (through the brave resistance of French and British soldiers and the aid of fresh American troops) but instead took refuge in the so-called 'stab-in-the-back-legend' (Dolchstoßlegende, that is, treachery by Jews, defeatists, pacifists, socialists, communists). And it was this twofold refusal by the German nation to see the truth that made it possible to lead this population to a new rearmament, to new expansionist policies and finally into a Second World War.

Notes

[1] F. Fischer, *War of Illusions*, p.545.

[2] Karl Dietrich Erdmann, 'Hat Deutschland auch den Ersten Weltkreig entfesselt? Kontroversen zur Politik der Mächte im Juli 1914'; Egmont Zechlin, 'Julikrise und Kriegsausbruch 1914' both in their *Politik und Geschichte. Europa 1914 – Krieg oder Frieden,* Kiel, 1985, pp.19–48, 51 and pp. 90 ff. respectively, for the German tradition of preventive war. For a refutation of Erdmann's and Zechlin's views, see H. Pogge von Strandmann, 'Germany and the coming of the War', pp.92–6, 107–14.

[3] Fritz Fischer, *Der Erste Weltkrieg und das deutsche Geschichtsbild*, Düsseldorf, 1977, esp. pp.151–206: 'Deutsche Kriegsziele, Revolutionierung und Separatfrieden im Osten 1914–1918', cit. p.158.

[4] 'Septemberprogramm' in F. Fischer, *Germany's Aims*, pp. 103 ff.

[5] 'Central European Economic Union' in ibid., p 104, Program No. 4.

[6] Theobald von Bethmann Hollweg, *Betrachtungen zum Weltkriege,* vol. I: *Vor dem Kriege,* Berlin, 1919, and vol II: *Während des Krieges,* Berlin, 1921, ed F. Bethmann Hollweg; See vol.1, pp 188, 189; vol. II, pp. 65 f., 67 f.

[7] Adolf Gasser, 'Der deutsche Hegemonialkrieg von 1914' in *Deutschland in der Weltpolitik des 19. und 20. Jahrunderts. Festschrift für Fritz Fischer zum 65. Geburtstag,* ed. Imanuel Geiss and Bernd Jürgen Wendt, Düsseldorf, 1973, pp. 307–39, esp. p. 338; reprinted in Adolf Gasser, *Ausgewählte historische Schriften*, Basel, Frankfurt a. M., 1983, pp.47–82.

[8] Zara S. Steiner, *Britain and the Origins of the First World War,* London, 1977, pp. 213–41.

[9] James Joll, *The Origins of the First World War,* London, New York, 1984; German ed: *Die Ursprünge des Ersten Weltkrieges,* Munich, 1988, *passim.*

(Gregor Schöllgen (ed.), *Escape into War? The Foreign Policy of Imperial Germany,* German Historical Perspectives no. VI, Oxford, Berg, 1990)

4   MICHAEL R. GORDON, 'DOMESTIC CONFLICT AND THE ORIGINS OF THE FIRST WORLD WAR: THE BRITISH AND THE GERMAN CASES'

For those interested in the First World War, two recent debates loom especially large. The first inspired by Fritz Fischer, concerns the degree of German responsibility for the war's outbreak and course. The second, which has in part been thrashed out in [the *Journal of Modern History*] between Arno Mayer and Peter Loewenberg, concerns the proper way to study international conflict –

wars in particular. The present paper joins both debates and tries to show how they interrelate.

I

More than thirteen years have gone by since Fritz Fischer first startled the German historical profession with *Griff nach der Weltmacht*, and just about five since his follow-up work, *Krieg der Illusionen*.[1] Of his numerous challenges to orthodoxy, not the least provocative lies in the books' methodology. Both, but especially the second, have broken cleanly with the traditional explanatory model (or logic) of diplomatic history.

Briefly, the key assumption underlying this model is about the 'primacy of foreign policy'. From it three or four postulates follow. The model distinguishes rigorously between domestic and foreign politics; it tends to treat the state as a unified, monolithic actor operating within an external environment of competition and imperatives, and it lays down that these actors are primarily motivated by rational power considerations – by the cold rules of statecraft. The controlling concepts for describing these rules are national interest and national security, power, prestige and perhaps reasons of state. The explanatory power of the model derives from a pattern of inferences about the relationship between specific situations and the state's adherence to these rules: the state – as a rational, unitary decision-maker uninfluenced by domestic politics – will presumably choose the one alternative in the situation that best promises to maximize its security, its power, its prestige, and other interests. The state may turn out to have miscalculated, of course; nevertheless, the grounds for its actions are largely reducible to these considerations. It follows that the crucial evidence for a foreign-policy move will be located in the 'minutes of bilateral or multilateral negotiations or the texts of foreign office dispatches'; and for the scholarly investigator, the problem is then to reconstruct the motives and other causes behind the move through careful textual analysis.[2]

In the renewed debate over the origins of the First World War, this traditional model has proved diminishingly fruitful. Even some of Fischer's most hostile critics have come to scrap it.[3] Its main drawback is its inability to explain why the same foreign office document can serve to underpin two totally opposed interpretations.[4] Such ambiguity can be overcome, or at any rate delimited, only if the traditional postulates are dropped or relaxed in favor of a wider perspective. On the Fischer side of the debate, for instance, he and his sypathizers have tried to uncover the degree to which German foreign policy was prompted by the logic of domestic bargaining maneuvers – by concern for the social status quo, for the prestige of the imperial regime, for the needs of the economic elites. In Fischer's second book, this domestic impact even becomes decisive. Its argument – stripped to the bone – amounts to a thesis of aggressive war, launched by the principal German policy-makers in 1914 to preserve an expansionary future in the belief that expansion alone could preserve the threatened status quo at home. Not for nothing has a younger generation of German historians come to turn Ranke on his head and to speak of the 'primacy of domestic policy'.[5]

All this is extremely thoughtful and stimulating, a major scholarly accomplishment. None the less, two important problems remain.

First, for all his clearing away of old and unfruitful assumptions. Fischer has not been so explicit about the methods and assumptions that he has put in their place. As things stand now, he has clearly effected a productive shift in perspective: whether this perspective adds up to a consistent and realistic pattern of explanatory logic is, however, not too clear. His second book, for instance, uses a mixture of categories and concepts from Marxist theories of imperialism, from elitist theorists like Robert Michels, from standard liberal critiques of German militarism and equally standard conservative critiques of mass society; and therefore, although the resulting argument is massively documented and his findings possibly sound, the criteria governing his choice of materials remain ambiguous – and so does the logical status of his inferences. It is hard to be categorical here, and I wish to stress my uncertainty. But that is also precisely the problem; a greater degree of explicitness seems desirable.[6] And second, as well as being insufficiently explicit, Fischer's work is also inadequately comparative. As a result, he has left himself exposed to the charge that he and his sypathizers have unfairly singled out Germany as the culprit in the war controversy.

It is at this point that the second debate between Mayer and Loewenberg joins the first. Like Fischer, both have broken with the traditional model and argued for an alternative framework of analysis. Mayer, in a series of theoretically bold writings, has developed a completely explicit and comparative model of domestic violence, counter-revolutionary reaction, and precautionary or diversionary war.[7] To Loewenberg, Mayer's model is too structural and macroscopic; he believes that a more psychological approach – especially depth-psychological – would be better.[8] But for reasons that will emerge later, I take exception to both alternatives – Loewenberg seems wrong in regarding psychological and structural explanations as incompatible: handled properly, the two are complementary to one another, not contradictory. As for Mayer, his model – theoretically provocative though it is – strikes me as one-sided and to apply, at most, to one of the two nations under study here.

The model used here is taken from theories of economic development and political modernization. Intended to uncover more of the 'why' of things in the Fischer debate, it compares the domestic impact on foreign policy in Britain as well as Germany before and during the July crisis, 1914. [...]

II

The first task is briefly to describe British and German foreign policies before 1914.

As far as German policy is concerned, its readiness to risk war for its own ends – either a local Balkan war fought by its ally in Vienna or a larger, continental-sized war in which it, France and Russia participated – now seems unshakably established.[9] Albertini, Schmitt, Renouvin and Taylor had already argued this point persuasively before 1961, and the debate sparked by Fischer has underpinned it with different sources of evidence and methods of argument. By either one of these two wars the German government thought its interests would be served: at a minimum. a successful localized war – kept limited by Russia's backing off in fear – would in the German view probably break up the Franco-Russian alliance, shore up the tottering Austro-Hungarian empire, and clear the way in Central Europe for an eventual German breakthrough to successful *Weltpolitik*. On a more ambitious level, the German government was convinced it could also secure these aims even more emphatically in a triumphant continental war. As for the world war that happened, German leaders did not consciously aim at it, not at any rate in 1914, and for that matter not even Fischer has claimed this. What they hoped was that Britain would remain neutral or at least a nonbelligerent at the outset. None the less, the possibility of British intervention was appreciated at the very outset, even by Bethmann himself: and by risking its occurrence, the German government bore the responsibility for the ensuing worldwide struggle in at least the sense of conditional intent.[10] To this extent the work of Fischer and his sympathizers see to be unchallengeable. Fischer himself is probably justified, therefore, when he claims that the debate has now moved irretrievably away from any thesis of coequal responsibility or international anarchy, let alone of German innocence, and toward convergence on a thesis of 'preventive war'.[11]

What remains controversial is the precise meaning of a 'preventive German war policy' and especially the motives behind it. Fischer started out in his first book with an argument that the motives were coolheaded, deliberate instances of outright expansionist goals. Some of his pupils, however, came to lay less emphasis on such goals and more on 'the German mood of 1914, that strange mixture of ideological despair, political bankruptcy and overwhelming economic and military power' as the propellant behind the plunge into war.[12] Most scholars of the subject, it is fair to say, hew closer to the latter interpretation – without, however, necessarily buying the argument that the motives were therefore 'defensive'. Fischer himself, though willing in his latest book to allow for an explosive bundle of German ambitions and complexes, has persisted in imparting to the motives as 'aggressive' a cast as possible. This article will itself have something to say later on about these motives.

As for British foreign policy, it was something quite different in the period before and right through the July crisis. Except for prevailing opinion in inter-war Germany and some revisionist historians elsewhere, nobody has made a charge of bellicosity stick. On the contrary, if any charge can be levelled at Sir Edward Grey, the foreign secretary, it is that he did not pursue as effective and energetic a policy as he might have during the crisis – that, instead, he wavered between two inconsistent courses, backing France and, to a lesser extent, Russia in order to deter Germany on the one hand, and on the other hand playing the role of the disinterested mediator; that, in addition, he never clarified his policy one way or another until the very end, by which point German policy-makers had already decided to risk even a world war; and that, consequently, British influence during the crisis fell far short of what British power in the international system warranted at the time.[13]

Judged strictly in terms of the traditional model – that is, from the, viewpoint of external pressures and national interests – the ineffectuality of British policy remains an impenetrable puzzle. After all, neither Grey nor Asquith, the prime minister, had overlooked the multitudinous danger signs hinting at German aims over the years. Just the reverse; the major premise of Grey's diplomacy ever since coming to office, in 1906, had been to avoid a situation in which Britain might face a German menace without any allies.[14] Hence the ententes with France, and Russia; hence, too, the reinforcement of ties, especially to France, including recurring staff talks since late 1905 and the important naval arrangements of 1912.[15] These were weighty moves, which nudged Britain away from isolation and toward alliance relationships. Why, accordingly, did the Liberal government not pursue more rigorously the logic behind the effort to reorient British policy? Why settle for a dangerous half-way adjustment, which went far enough to entail uncertain commitments and so a limitation on British freedom, but which stopped short of a full-fledged alliance that might have created both an effective control over French policy and an effective deterrent to German belligerence?[16]

The answer is to be found, of course, in places outside the scope of the traditional model – in domestic politics, especially the resistance to a reoriented policy on the part of the radical wing within the Liberal party and Cabinet. A courageous campaign of re-education might have reduced the ranks of the resisters; the Foreign Office, for one, had long thought so and advised accordingly.[17] Yet Grey and Asquith, far from undertaking to lead such a campaign, shied away from spelling out the implications of their new policy to even the Cabinet. It was largely for this reason that British diplomacy remained stuck, when the July crisis erupted, with an 'unsatisfactory compromise' as a guide – with a 'policy of partisan and unforeseen commitment'.[18] The result was widespread confusion on the Cabinet level, and also no little self-delusion.[19]

As this last line of argument suggests, British policy cannot be fully accounted for in terms of the traditional model.[20] The same can be said (and will be argued) about German policy. Those scholars who work with the traditional explanatory logic balk at recognizing this: they persist in trying to explain German and British behavior by reference to unified decision-makers, objective and perceived threats, and the rules of statecraft.[21] The fact is, however, that the international situations of the two countries did not differ enough to justify such contradictory responses to the July crisis – British policy hesitant and wavering, German policy rash and aggressive. If anything, Germany's future prospects in the international system looked brighter by far than Britain's. In industrial productivity, economic growth, and foreign commerce – in literate population, technology and military weight – Germany had a decisive advantage not only over Britain but over all its European rivals.[22] It is true that Germany's ability to achieve a breakthrough in *Weltpolitik* seemed temporarily hemmed in by several factors in 1914. But it is equally true that Britain's pre-eminent position was under assault, both from within and from without, at almost every point on the globe.[23] Moreover, these strains soon colored British psychology in several quarters. A spiral of apprehension shook British life in repeated waves after 1900: invasion scares, scares about imperial disintegration, scares even about the quality if the British 'race', abounded.[24] Nor were fears about encirclement a German monopoly. Recurringly, after 1880, British policy-makers were haunted by the specter of a hostile coalition.[25]

Given these trends, might not the traditional logic of statecraft point to a reversal of policies? Should it not have been British policy-makers who were rash and desperate, determined to stave off decline in a bold showdown struggle, and German policy-makers who were increasingly buoyant, increasingly confident that their nation was riding a glorious wave of history?

III

If, then, the gap between British and German foreign policy is too great to be explained fully by their international situations, the next task is to inquire whether their domestic situations differed enough to account for it.

At first glance this does not seem a promising undertaking. What immediately strikes one is the apparent parallel between the domestic scenes before 1914. Each nation experienced an alarming wave of unsettling events, resulting in social strife, economic dislocation, and left–right polarization. In both a constitutional crisis was emerging and with it the prospect of large-scale violence.

In Germany, the situation heated up in proportion as the enemies of the existing system (*Reichsfeinde* [enemies of the state] as Bismark had branded them) advanced in numbers and organizational strength. At one time the Catholic center figured among these enemies; by the turn of the century the term referred almost exclusively to Social Democrats (SPD) and the trade unions. Their advance seemed irresistible. In fact, the more the nation industrialized and modernized, the more the social structure that underpinned the Reich at its founding, in 1871, inevitably altered in their favor. The SPD's revisionism did little to assuage the fears of the *staatserhaltende Kraefte* - the forces of order. On the contrary, the most moderate proposals for electoral and fiscal reforms were denounced as though tantamount to revolution. And, indeed, in a sense they were: for the Bismarckian system, fabricated for a traditional social order, could hardly accommodate strong bourgeois participation – let alone that of the working class.[26] Following the SPD advances in the 1912 Reichstag elections, a precarious situation, latent for years, was thus pushing to the surface. The more the forces of change pressed for reforms, the more the forces of order took fright. Hence the alarming wave of fanatical chauvinism, mass demagogy, and crude racism that enveloped the nation from the right in the years before the war.[27] Hence, too, the revised interest in *coup d'état* schemes.[28] The whole interrelated but untenable system of power and privilege was moving toward crisis and probably breakdown.[29]

As for Britain, classic home of political stability, it too was undergoing a cycle of internal unrest and tensions. Class conflict was spiraling, unions were growing militant, women suffragettes resorted to violence. Worse, with segments of the army dabbling in mutiny and the Conservative-Unionist party toying with sedition, the prospect of civil war loomed ever likelier in Ireland.[30] Culturally, a jittery mood of unease and dislocation pervaded much of Edwardian England; 'decay, decline, fall, and decadence were the language of the time and not of party'.[31] Neither inherited political habits nor tested mechanisms of adjustment could readily cope with the sudden upsurge in strife. The English Constitution was based largely on tacit gentlemanly agreements – implicit rules of the game. On the Tory side, however, these rules were no longer being observed. In fact they were being openly flouted, as the ancient props of patrician Britain (land, paternalism, the House of Lords, the Church) came under repeated blows.[32] Even Liberals suffered from the distempers of the time. Divided between Whigs and Radicals over domestic affairs, and between Imperialists and Internationalists over foreign policy – faced also with an emerging Labour party on its left – the Liberal party could not spawn a coherent vision of a new society to replace the one currently under attack. Amidst these circumstances, the Cabinet itself tended more and more to postpone and to wobble – Asquith, indeed, was something of a master at inaction. By July 1914 a sense of national disaster lurked in the air.

In many respects, then, the German and the British situations over-lapped. But the parallel between them goes only so far. Dig deeper, and certain crucial differences are found that still separated the two nations – not least, in the strength (or really lack thereof) of the British extreme right as compared with its German counterpart. The fact is that the social base for powerful reactionary or counter-revolutionary mass movements was built into the very structures of Imperial Germany; in Britain, by contrast, it was almost wholly lacking. Again, a strong state but a weak regime reinforced the prospects for such extremist activity in Germany; in Britain no such state apparatus existed. The importance of this contrast cannot be overestimated. Because of it, the quality of politics in the two nations diverged in essential ways.

For decades, and not just after 1912, the elites in Wilhelmine Germany lived in an ambivalent and anxiety-ridden condition regarding modernism. On the one hand the inexorable industrial advance was welcomed by them as a means to national aggrandizement, a step toward successful *Weltpolitik.* On the other hand, few were optimistic about the future of an industrial society, and the social and political changes it created.[33] At the same time the existing ruling groups lacked a political system with built-in mechanisms of political adjustment – indeed they steadfastly opposed changes that might create such mechanisms; even a moderate like Bethmann Hollweg was no major exception.[34] Finally, Germany was still, for all its advanced industry, predominately pre-industrial in social structure; this meant that millions of threatened peasants in the countryside and more millions of old *Mittelstaende* [middle class] within the cities were available for political mobilization from extremists on the right against the working class or the pitifully small progressive middle class.[35] Edwardian England, by contrast, was simply not fertile ground for right-wing extremism of a mass sort, any more than was depression-laden England in the 1930s. By then there were no peasants to mobilize, and no militaristic aristocrats to lead them.[36] By then, too, the commercial and industrial middle classes were numerous, articulate, and independent minded, putting a liberal stamp on British politics. As for the lower-middle classes, they were, it is true, growing in number, but unlike those caught up in turmoil of Germany's rapid industrialization, they had long been assimilated to modern life and took it for granted.[37] Moreover, there was no standing army, no powerful state bureaucracy, no large state role in the economy – in fact, despite recent changes, hardly a state in any modern sense at all.[38] Least of all was there, for all the jitters of the time, a potent antimodernist tradition on which an embattled right could draw in order to rally mass support. The contrary was the case: thus, whereas Bethmann was a fatalist and full of forebodings for the future, Asquith remained certain that something good would turn up even over Ireland.[39] For all these reasons, accordingly, even to speak of an extreme right-wing movement is to speak at best of what might have happened and not what did in fact happen, as a noted left-wing historian concedes.[40] Indeed, Unionist flirtation with extraconstitutional methods, far from mobilizing mass enthusiasm, did not even command widespread support within the Unionist party itself.[41]

The reasons for these contrasting situations remain to be set forth. What is important to note here, before leaving this section, is the hook-up with foreign policy. Owing to the divergent political conditions, not only were the domestic crises in the two nations approached in contrary ways by the British and the German governments, but so, too, were the problems of foreign policy that faced each. German political elties (as will be seen) had an overwhelming incentive to use foreign policy as a method of domestic control: in fact, they had been doing so for years. No similar temptation offered itself to British elites, nor is there evidence that they ever used foreign policy to that end. It follows that any effort to explain British and German decisions to wage war is equivalent terms, as comparable cases of diversionary war seems misplaced.[42]

[...]

V

If the various strings of the argument are now drawn together, the following conclusion emerges.

Domestic conflict had a contrary impact in the two nations. In Britain, for all the turmoil that erupted before 1914 foreign policy remained moderate and largely defensive; and this was so even though the nation's world position was itself on the decline and under challenge at almost every point on the globe. None the less, internal conflict did take its toll. It added to the defensiveness of Britain's posture, indeed increasing reactiveness, by inhibiting Grey's efforts to reorient foreign policy and leaving the nation stuck, therefore, at a dangerous point halfway between isolation and full-fledged alliances. The result was the ambivalent policy 'of partial and unforeseen commitment' with which the Liberal Cabinet approached the July Crisis, uncertain whether it should try to act as mediator in the old 'free hand' sense of Salisbury's days or to act as an ally of France and Russia so as to deter Berlin. In the event, Grey's cautious zigzagging as the crisis unfolded only 'reinforced the German hope that England would stand aside'.[43]

Grey's advisers at the Foreign Office saw that his policy revisions added up to an unsatisfactory compromise, with consequent confusion both at home and abroad. Again and again, accordingly, they pressed him to clarify his actions and carry his campaign for reorientation through to its logical end; yet again and again Grey balked, well knowing that the Liberal party, and hence the Cabinet itself, was too divided to permit such clarification. 'I do not know', Arthur Nicolson, the permanent under-secretary, wrote in April 1914, 'how much longer we shall be able to follow our present policy of dancing on a high rope and not be compelled to take up some definite line or other'.[44] But the high-rope act went on; what else could Grey do in view of the political situation? Mayer argues that he and Asquith could move toward the right, toward the hawkish Unionist party – that, in fact, they did precisely this during the July Crisis, overcoming the waverers and the non-interventionists in the Cabinet with a threat to create a Liberal-Unionist coalition.[45] There are some scattered indications that Asquith toyed with such a threat.[46] Yet it does not appear to have had nearly the effect that Mayer maintains it did.[47] On the contrary, Asquith himself thoroughly feared the reactionary consequences that would follow from such a coalition.[48] In short, as before 1914, so throughout the July

Crisis itself: partisan conflict and internal Liberal discord continued to obstruct a clarification of foreign policy one way or another.[49]

In Germany, even though domestic conflict appeared to be more latent than in Britain, it was in fact even more politically far-reaching, and its repercussions on foreign policy were pronounced of an aggressive sort. Three such repercussions have been distinguished here. First of all, quite apart from deliberate foreign-policy decisions, there was a set of spillovers that arose from the very national situation of the Reich in 1871 and after. Among the most prominent of these were the unsolved problem of national identity, doubts about the viability of the Reich's borders, and the unforeseen consequences of tariff policies that arose out of the bargains struck between the industrialists and Junkers. There was a second set of spillovers, on the other hand, that did derive directly from calculated political maneuvers. These maneuvers aimed at trying to control an increasingly impossible domestic situation by ever-greater efforts of social imperialism, mass propaganda, *Weltpolitik*, armaments programs, and diversionary quests for prestige of the quickest and cheapest sorts – in short, the whole complex of foreign adventures and aggressive diplomacy that embittered relations with other great powers and created diplomatic isolation. Finally, somewhere in between there was a third pattern of repercussions, a psychological pattern by which the fears and grudges that German elites nurtured in domestic politics were turned outward and led them to detect international specters all over Europe. Bismarck, who had unified the nation, had spoken ominously of his 'nightmare of hostile coalitions'. By 1914 the whole nation, at any rate to the right of the Social Democrats, was tormented by such nightmares, even if they were overwhelmingly self-induced. The upshot of all three kinds of repercussion was the calculated gamble in favor of war that was taken in July 1914. With one sudden desperate charge, the Reich's leadership hoped to achieve that ultimate breakthrough in *Weltpolitik* that would safeguard the nation's expansionist future and its conservative order at home. By 1917, to take a date that was uppermost in German thinking at the time, it would be too late. By then, Russian and French military reforms would be completed and the chances of a successful breakthrough, therefore, that much less.

Bethmann Hollweg himself, it has been argued, had doubts that a war would actually strengthen the conservative order.[50] He seemed in fact to fear that it might hasten its decline and lead through mass mobilization to democratic concessions or worse. But one should not make too much of these qualms. For one thing, as Fischer notes, Bethmann's warnings in this respect 'only confirm how widespread the contrary view was'.[51] For another thing, he clearly embraced the 'curious blend of contradictory beliefs – social Darwinism, misunderstood romanticism, and cultural pessimism – all pointing to German expansion as the only alternative to stagnation'.[52] In this respect, as Stern also hastens to add, there was really no fundamental divergence of political aims between Bethmann and the other leaders of Imperial Germany; 'the general consensus about Germany's national destiny was too broad and the Kaiser's tolerance for dissent too narrow' to permit anyone who dissented too much from continuing in office.[53] For a third thing, finally – as Riezler's diary makes clear – he unequivocally hoped that 'if war comes and the veils fall, the whole nation will follow, driven by necessity and peril'.[54]

Notes

[1] Fritz Fischer, *Graff nach der Weltmacht: Die Kriegszielpolitik des kaiserlichen Deutschland 1914/1948*, Dusseldorf, 1961; *Krieg der Illusionen: Die deutsche Polltik von 1911 bis 1914*, Dusseldorf, 1969.

[2] Arno J. Mayer, 'Internal causes and purposes of war in Europe, 1870–1956: a research assignment', *Journal of Modern History*, 41, September 1969, 302. Admittedly, owing to the brevity of formulation, a pretty sharp and simplified picture of the traditional model has been sketched in. None the less, I do not think that it is a caricature. On the contrary, even though many diplomatic historians had come to modify the key postulates long before Fischer was heard of, most have probably continued to use a variant of the traditional model until quite recently.

[3] For instance, Egmont Zechlin, 'Bethmann Hollweg. Kriegsrisiko und SPD' and 'Motive und Taktik der Reichsleitung 1914', in *Erster Weltkrieg: Ursachen, Enstehung und Kriegsziele*, Wolfgang Schieder (ed.) Cologne and Berlin, 1969, pp.165–204.

[4] James Joll, *1914: The Unspoken Assumptions*, London, 1968, p.7.

[5] See Hans-Ulrich Wehler. 'Einleitung', in Eckart Kehr, *Der Primat der Innenpolitik*, Hans-Ulrich Wehler. 'Einleitung', in Eckart Kehr, *Der Primat der Innenpolitik*, Hans-Ulrich Wehler (ed.) Berlin, 1970, pp.1–30; Michael Stuermer (ed.) *Das kaiserliche Deutschland: Politik und Gesellschaft 1870–1918*, Dusseldorf, 1970.

[6] In other words, to paraphrase a general argument of Richard Hofstadter: Fischer's analysis does a better job of accounting for 'what' happened and 'how' it happened than 'why' it did so: yet until the 'why' of things emerges more clearly, one cannot be fully confident about the 'what' and the 'how' (see 'History and Sociology in the United States', in *Sociology and History: Methods*, Seymour Martin Lipset and Richard Hofstadter (eds) New York, 1968, pp.8–18).

[7] In addition to the article in no.2 above, see Arno J. Mayer. 'Domestic causes of the First World War' in *The Responsibility of Power: Historical Essays in Honour of Hajo Holborn*, Leonard Krieger and Fritz Stern (eds), New York, 1967, pp.286–300; *Dynamics of Counterrevolution in Europe, 1870–1956: An Analytic Framework*, New York, 1971.

[8] Peter Loewenberg, 'Arno Mayer's "Internal Causes and Purposes of War in Europe, 1870–1956" – an inadequate model of human behavior, national conflict and historical changes', *Journal of Modern History*, 42, December 1970: 628–36.

[9] Fischer, *Krieg der Illusionen*, pp.663–82; Konrad H. Jarausch, 'The illusion of limited war. Chancellor Bethmann Hollweg's calculated risk, July 1914'. *Central European History* 2 March 1969, 48–77; Fritz Stern, 'Bethmann Hollweg and the war: the limits of responsibility" in *The Responsibility of Power*, p.268.

[10] See Hermann Kantorowicz (ed.) *Gutachten zur Kriegsschuldfrage 1914: Aus dem Nachlass*, Frankfurt, 1967, Imanuel Geiss, for the meaning of the term.

[11] Fischer, *Kreig der Illusionen*, pp.663–4.

[12] Imanuel Geiss (ed.) *July 1914: The Outbreak of the First World War: Selected Documents*, New York, 1967, pp.367–8.

[13] Herbert Butterfield, 'Sir Edward Grey in July 1914'. *Historical Studies*, 5, 1965, 20.

[14] George Monger, *The End of Isolation: British Foreign Policy 1900–1907*, London, 1963, pp. 329–31.

[15] Samuel R. Williamson, Jr., *The Politics of Grand Strategy: Britain and France Prepare for War, 1900–1914*, Cambridge, Mass., 1969, especially pp.284–5.

[16] Pierre Renouvin, 'Britain and the Continent: the lessons of history', *Foreign Affairs*, 17, October, 1938, pp.111–27.

[17] A. J. P. Taylor, The Struggle for Mastery in Europe, 1848–1918, London, 1954. pp.525–6; Zara S. Steiner, The Foreign Office and Foreign Policy 1898–1914, Cambridge, 1969, pp.131–9.

[18] J. A. S. Grenville, *Lord Salisbury and Foreign Policy; The Close of the Nineteenth Century*, London, 1964, p.436.

[19] Monger, p.330.

[20] Cameron Hazelhurst, *Politicians at War: July 1914–May 1915*, New York, 1971, pp.88–91.

[21] See, for instance, Joachim Remak, '1914 – the Third Balkan War: origins reconsidered', *Journal of Modern History*, 43, September 1971, 353–66.

[22] Derek H. Aldcroft and Harry W. Richardson, *The British Economy 1870–1939* London, 1969, pp.101–68; David Landes, *The Unbound Prometheus*, London, 1969, pp.326–58. More generally, Ross Hoffman, *Great Britain and the German Trade Rivalry*, New York, 1964.

[23] Ronald Robinson and John Gallagher, *Africa and the Victorians: The Climax of Imperialism*, New York, 1968, pp.287–9: Max Beloff, *Imperial Sunset*, London, 1969, pp.5–24.

[24] Samuel Hynes, *The Edwardian Turn of Mind*, Princeton, NJ, 1968, pp.15–54.

[25] Lord William Strang, *Britain in World Affairs*, New York, 1961, p.222.

[26] Guenther Roth, The Social Democrats in Imperial Germany: A Study in Working-Class Isolation and National Integration, Totowa, 1963, p.59.

[27] Fischer, *Kreig der Illusionen*, pp.117–45; Dirk Stegmann, *Die Erben Bismarcks: Pateien und Verbaende in der Spaetphase des Wilhelminischen Deutschlands: Sammlungspolitik 1897–1918*, Cologne and Berlin, 1970, pp.262–3; Klaus Wernecke, *Der Wille zur Weltgeltung: Aussenpolitik und Oeffentlichkeit in Kaiserreich am Vorabend des Ersten Weltkriegs*, Dusseldorf, 1970, pp.288–314.

[28] Hartmut Pogge-v. Strandmann, 'Staatsstreichplaene, Alldeutsche und Bethmann Hollweg', in *Die Erforderlichkeit des Unmoeglichen*, Hartmut Pogge- v. Strandmann and Imanuel Geiss (eds), Frankfurt, 1965, pp.11–45.

[29] Hans-Juergen Puhle, 'Parlament, Parteien und Interessenverbaende 1890–1914' in *Das Kaiserliche Deutschland*, pp.361–4.

[30] The classic study is George Dangerfield, *The Strange Death of Liberal England*, New York, 1961.

[31] Hynes, *The Edwardian Turn of Mind*, p.45.

[32] Robert Blake, *The Conservative Party from Peel to Churchill*, New York, 1970, p.190.

[33] Kenneth D. Barkin, *The Controversy over German Industrialization 1890–1902*, Chicago, 1970, pp.1–15, 131–2; Ralf Dahrendorf, *Society and Democracy in Germany*, New York, 1967, pp.9–10; Fritz Stern, *The Politics of Cultural Despair: A Study in the Rise of German Ideology*, Berkeley, Calif., 1961.

[34] See Klaus Hildebrand, *Bethmann Hollweg, der Kanzler ohne Eigenschaften? Urteile der Geschichtsschreibung: Eine kritische Bibliographie*, Dusseldorf, 1970, pp.50–64.

[35] As late as 1895, more than half of the German work-force was still employed in preindustrial occupations – 36 per cent in agriculture alone (see Juergen Kocka, 'Vorindustrielle Faktoren in der deutschen Industrialisierung. Industriebuerokratie und 'neuer Mittelstand', in *Das kaiserliche Deutschland*, pp.279–280).

[36] In 1911 only 8.6 per cent of the British work-force was still on the land, and only an additional 6.0 per cent still in other preindustrial occupations (see Aldcroft and

Richardson, *The British Economy*, p.14; also F. M. L. Thompson *English Landed Society in the Nineteenth Century*, London 1963, pp.9–24, 269–70).

[37] S. G. Checkland, *The Rise of Industrial Society in England 1815–1885*, London, 1964, pp.301–14.

[38] A. J. P. Taylor, *English History 1914–1945*, New York, 1965, p.1.

[39] Stern, 'Bethmann Hollweg and the War?' p.262; R. C. K. Ensor, *England 1870–1914*, London, 1960, p.452.

[40] E. J. Hobsbawm, *Industry and Empire*, New York, 1968, p.163.

[41] Alfred Gollin, *Proconsul in Politics: A Study of Lord Milner in Opposition and in Power*, London, 1964, pp.200–1; Blake, *The Conservative Party*, p.192.

[42] It is precisely for this reason that Mayer's thesis of counterrevolution – diversionary war – illuminating though it is in the German case, goes astray in the British.

[43] Williamson, *Politics of Grand Strategy*, p.345.

[44] Quoted in Steiner, *The Foreign Office and Foreign Policy*, p.138.

[45] Mayer, 'Domestic causes of the First World War', pp.288–9, 298–300.

[46] Hazelhurst, *Politicians at War*, pp.103, 112–113.

[47] Williamson, *Politics of Grand Strategy*, pp.345–60; Steiner, *Foreign Office and Foreign Policy*, pp.153–64.

[48] Hazelhurst, *Politicians at War*, p.136.

[49] Taylor, *Struggle for Mastery in Europe*, p.525.

[50] Jarausch, 'The illusion of a limited war', p.58; Stern, 'Bethmann Hollweg and the war', p.263.

[51] Fischer, *Krieg der Illusionen*, pp.13, 693.

[52] Stern, 'Bethmann Hollweg and the War', p.257.

[53] Ibid., pp.259–60; see, too, Fischer, *Krieg der Illusionen*, p.158; Imanuel Geiss, *July 1914*, p.47.

[54] Quoted in Jarausch, 'Illusion of Limited War', p.58.

(*Journal of Modern History*, no. 46, June, pp.191–226, 1974)

5   WOLFGANG MOMMSEN, 'DOMESTIC FACTORS IN GERMAN FOREIGN POLICY BEFORE 1914'

The argumentation of Fritz Fischer appears to me to be much more important, and without doubt much more to the point. Whatever may be said about his opinions, he definitely deserves to be honoured for having once more opened up the discussion of a vital issue which German historians had erroneously believed to be definitely settled. However, it remains to be seen whether his findings can also be considered the last word on German policy before 1914.

Fischer maintains that in the last analysis German foreign policy was the necessary outcome of an aggressive nationalism which pervaded almost all sections of German society and which, of course, was particularly strong among the ruling classes. In 1961 Fischer argued that Germany had been deliberately heading for a European war during the July crisis in 1914, in order to become a world power. Thereafter, step by step, he radicalized his position even more, eventually arriving at the thesis that Germany had decided upon going to war as early as 1911, or at any rate by December 8, 1912, in order to break out of the deadlock to which her previous attempts to acquire colonial territories and greater political influences overseas had led. He also maintained that the war aims Germany pursued after 1914, could be traced long before the war. He argued that this was particularly the case with regard to the acquisition of Longwy-Briey, but was also true with regard to the plan of establishing economic predominance on the European continent, possibly including the Balkans as well, by means of a German-led European Economic Association. In his most recent book, *Der Krieg der Illusionen*, Fischer assembled enormous source material, partially derived from Wernecke's study on German public opinion before 1914, in order to substantiate the thesis.

It is not possible to present here a detailed critical analysis of Fischer's presentation of German politics between 1911 and 1915. Yet it seems obvious that he has been driven too far regarding his main thesis: Germany's "will to power." It may be said, for instance, that Fischer is not all that clear as to the question of which sections and groups of German society really advocated a policy of war in order to cut at one stroke the Gordian knot of German imperialism. Was it the government, the emperor, the military establishment, the Conservatives, the industrialists, or the nation at large, any one of them, or all of them? Actually Fischer's arguments constantly shift, charging at times one group, at times another with warlike tendencies; but they are never consistent in this respect. And he does not claim that the various groups and persons with which he is dealing were all, and at all times, committed to going to war. Although at many points we gain important new insights into what was going on, his overall thesis is far from clear.[1] To mention just one point, Fischer attributes the greatest importance to the informal war council which William II held on December 8, 1912, in a sudden outburst of war panic; Fischer contends that the German Empire was henceforth resolved to take up arms as soon as a convenient opportunity turned up, and that the German public was systematically prepared for war. This interpretation has been supported recently by J. C. G. Röhl in a somewhat qualified way; Röhl also is inclined to take literally Tirpitz's words in the so-called "War Council" of December 8, 1912, that the German Fleet would be ready for war by June 1914.[2] It is questionable, however, whether the decisions arrived at on this occasion were as crucial as Fischer, Röhl, and Geiss would have it. There is not the slightest evidence to support the argument that William II's excited order to prepare the country for war by means of an official press campaign was followed up by deeds. Neither can it be said that the German government henceforth was deliberately heading for war. The chancellor was informed of the conference of December 8 only eight days later, and even then only through semi-official channels.[3] If the so-called "War Council" had indeed arrived at the decision that Germany should go to war in eighteen months, and that adequate support for this policy should be secured in the country by a systematic press campaign, it would have been very strange indeed to leave the responsible statesman as well as the *Wilhemstrasse* completely in the dark about it for more than a week! Two things can be gathered from the discourse at the conference on December 8, namely, that the military establishment seriously considered solving the problems of German "world policy" by a preventive war, and that Moltke was in favor of going to war as soon as possible, on the grounds that the German military position was deteriorating rapidly. The conference also resulted in accelerating the preparation of the new armaments bill, which had already been under way. Otherwise, the direct effects of the conference were negligible. The plan to introduce another navy bill was effectively checked by Bethmann Hollweg. He also prevented the implementation of the emperor's order "ordentlich in die Presse zu gehen," to the extent to which it had been taken seriously at all, quietly and effectively.[4] There is little doubt that warlike tendencies were ascending both inside and outside official circles, but it is quite a different matter to say that the German government was bent on war from 1912 on.

It is also open to some doubt whether German imperialism had really come to a dead end by 1914, as is gloomily argued over and over again by Fischer. Germany's economic position in the Ottoman Empire had been consolidated, although this had necessitated some concessions both to French and British interests in this sphere. But it had *not* been diminished, even given the chronic problem of the relative scarcity of capital for "political" investments overseas.[5]

It would appear that the very nature of Fischer's approach makes it difficult for him to give proper consideration to the forces of moderation. He draws his conclusions rather from what people said than from what they actually did. Thus, the aggressive nationalist outbursts of the politicians concerned are often taken as the whole story. On the other hand, it must be admitted that Fischer makes a serious attempt to get beyond an interpretation dealing mainly with ideological aspects, at least in his "second" book, although not always with the same degree of success. None the less, it seems warranted to conclude that he arrives at all too radical conclusions, mainly because he tends to isolate quotations of a nationalist or imperialist nature from the context, and bases his conclusions on those quotations rather than on a coherent analysis of the political and social structures.

There is still another point worth mentioning. The premise of Fischer's interpretation of Wilhelmine politics, that an aggressive nationalism lay at the bottom of all that happened, induces him to describe the actions of other powers as mere reactions prompted by German diplomacy itself. Yet neither French nationalism nor the growing militarist tendencies in Russia can be properly explained in such a way. A comparative study of European nationalism would reveal that the gradually growing participation of the masses of the population in the political process was everywhere accompanied by an intensified nationalism.

Notes

[1] For a more detailed assessment of Fritz Fischer's views, as well as of their development, see Mommsen, "The Debate on German War Aims," and idem, "Die Deutsche 'Weltpolitik' and der Erste Weltkrieg," *Neue Politische Literatur, XVI* (1971), 482ff.

[2] Cf. Fritz Fischer, *Krieg der Illusionen*, pp. 2311f. The account given by John C. G. Röhl, "Admiral von Muller and the Approach to War 1911-1914," *Historical Journal*, XII (1966), demonstrates that Walter Gorlitz, the editor of the diaries of Admiral von Muller (cf. *Der Kaiser, Aufzeichnungen des Chefs des Marinekabinetts Admiral Georg Alexander v. Muller uber die Ara Wilhelms 11.* [Göttingem, 1965], pp. 124ff.), on which almost all our knowledge on this conference depends, omitted vital passages from the text, in particular the second half of the following passage, beginning with the words "aber er." This passage clearly shows Moltke in favor of a preventive war: "Der Chef des Grossen Generalstabs sagt: Krieg je eher, desto besser, aber er zieht nicht die Konsequenz daraus, welche ware: Russland oder Frankreich oder beide vor ein Ultimatum zu stellen, das den Krieg mit dem Recht auf unserer Seite entfesselte. Nachmittags an den Reichskanzler wegen der Pressebeeinflussung geschrieben." It is difficult to escape the conclusion that the whole conference was dominated by the assumption that war might break out at any moment (as, indeed, it might have, for Europe was at the very height of a serious Balkan crisis), and that one vital issue was how to justify in the eyes of the German public a European war on behalf of Austria-Hungary's desire to create a semi-independent Albania. Hence the suggestion of William II: "Nun gehen Sie ordentlich in die Presse," according to Bethmann Hollweg's message for Kiderlen-Wachter of December 17, 1912. *Die grosse Politik der europaischen Kabinette* (Berlin, 1922-27), xxxix, No. 15553. Cited as GP.

[3] As follows from the last document cited in n. 17, the chancellor learned not before December 16 that there had been a sort of "War Council". Admiral von Müller apparently did not refer to the "conference" at all when he wrote on the afternoon of December 8 to the chancellor pointing out that something should be done to influence the press in order to bolster up public opinion in respect to the possibility of a European war on behalf of Austria-Hungary at that juncture. This would seem to indicate that von Müller was indeed of the opinion that the result of the conference had been "gleich null"! It is, by the way, not likely that von Müller would have led Bethmann Hollweg astray on purpose in this instance, as he usually acted as the chancellor's ally against Tirpitz.

[4] Bethmann Hollweg succeeded in calming the emperor down by explaining that Grey's message was, after all, not all that disastrous, at least as long as Germany avoided all provocative steps (cf. Memorandum of Bethmann Hollweg of December 18, 1912, *GP*, xxxix, No. 15560,pp. 9f.). He had already suggested to Tirpitz and Heeringen that they not launch an official propaganda campaign for new armaments; cf. Memorandum of December 14, 1912, *ibid.*, No. 15623. It makes rather amusing reading to see that on this occasion the chancellor pointed out to both men: "Ich müsse aber mit allem Nachdruck verlangen, dass sie sich hinter meinem Rücken auch seiner Majestät gegenüber nicht bänden, dass von Vorarbeiten, die sie innerhalb ihrer Ressorts etwa vornähmen, auch nicht das geringste in die Öffentlichkeit dringen dürfe, und dass ich irgenwelche Pressetreiberei zugunsten der Projekte unter keinen Umständen dulden könne" (ibid., pp. 147f.). None of these gentlemen would seem to have dared taking recourse to the arguments put forward by William II a few days earlier at the so-called "War Council" of December 8, 1912!

[5] Fischer's interpretation rests upon the unspoken assumption that Germany had a position of predominant economic influence in the Ottoman Empire to start with, and that it was confronted with increasing competition by other industrial nations only in the last few years before 1914. In fact, all German enterprises in this area had been substantially dependent on assistance from the "Caisse de la Dette Publique," which was dominated by the French, and had been intimately associated with foreign, primarily French banking houses, in particular the Banque Ottomane. The earlier sections of the Bagdad Railway could not have been built without the substantial support of these groups. Cf. Donald C. Blaidell, European Financial Control in the Ottoman Empire (New York, 1966), pp. 124ff. It may be further pointed out that the Germans succeeded in increasing their proportion of shares in the "Dette Publique" from an initial share of 8% to about 30% by 1914, and consequently their influence was substantially enhanced, although the French continued to be the strongest group of shareholders. Cf. Raymond Poidevin, Les Relations Economiques et Financieres entre la France et L'Allemagne de

1898 ? 1914 (Paris, 1969), p. 697. The separation of the respective economic activities of the western powers which took place in the Ottoman Empire after 1909 did not necessarily imply an infringement on the German position. The treaty between a German and a French group on February 15, 1914, regarding their respective spheres of interest and economic engagement in the Ottoman Empire, as well as the agreement reached in March 1914 between the d'Arcy Group and the Deutsche Bank on the joint exploitation of the Mesopotamian and Anatolian oil fields, could have been more favorable to the German side, but the Deutsche Bank was thoroughly pleased with it. See, for instance, GP, XXXVII/ 1, No. 14888, p. 435. Fischer's presentation in Der Krieg der Illusione, pp. 424ff., is rather misleading.

(*Central European History*, vol. 6, no. 1, pp.11–15, 1973)

6 JOHN C.G. RÖHL, FROM *THE KAISER AND HIS COURT: WILHELM II AND THE GOVERNMENT OF GERMANY*

Dress Rehearsal in December: military decision-making in Germany on the eve of the First World War

For Fritz Fischer

Few documents on the history of imperial Germany have caused as much of a stir – but also as much racking of brains – amongst historians[1] as the entry for 8 December 1912 in the diary of the Chief of the Kaiser's Naval Cabinet, Admiral Georg Alexander von Müller.[2] It reads:

> Sunday. Ordered to see His Maj. at the Schloss at 11 a.m. with Tirpitz, Heeringen (Vice Admiral) and General von Moltke. H.M. speaks to a telegraphic report from the Ambassador in London, Prince Lichnowsky, concerning the political situation. Haldane, speaking for Grey, has told Lichnowsky that England, if we attacked France, would unconditionally spring to France's aid, for England could not allow the balance of power in Europe to be disturbed. H.M. greeted this information as a desirable clarification of the situation for the benefit of those who had felt sure of England as a result of the recent friendliness of the press.
>
> H.M. envisaged the following:
>
> Austria must deal energetically with the foreign Slavs (the Serbs), otherwise she will lose control of the Slavs in the Austro-Hungarian monarchy. If Russia supports the Serbs, which she evidently does (Sasonoff's declaration that Russia will immediately move into Galicia if Austria moves into Serbia) then war would be unavoidable for us too. We could hope, however, to have Bulgaria and Rumania and also Albania, and perhaps also Turkey in our side. An offer of alliance by Bulgaria has already been sent to Turkey. We have exerted great pressure on the Turks. Recently H.M. has also pressed the Crown Prince of Rumania, who was passing through on his way back from Brussels, to come to an understanding with Bulgaria. If these powers join Austria then we shall be free to fight the war with full fury against France. The

fleet must naturally prepare itself for the war against England. The possibility mentioned by the Chief of the Admiralty Staff in his last audience of a war with Russia alone cannot now, after Haldane's statement, be taken into account. Therefore immediate submarine warfare against English troop transports in the Scheldt or by Dunkirk, mine warfare in the Thames. To Tirpitz: speedy build-up of U-boats, etc. Recommendation of a conference of all naval authorities concerned.

General von Moltke: 'I believe a war is unavoidable and the sooner the better.[3] But we ought to do more through the press to prepare the popularity of a war against Russia, as suggested in the Kaiser's discussion.'

H.M. supported this and told the State Secretary [Tirpitz] to use his press contacts, too, to work in this direction. [Tirpitz] made the observation that the navy would prefer to see the postponement of the great fight for one and a half years. Moltke says the navy would not be ready even then and the army would get into an increasingly unfavourable position, for the enemies were arming more strongly than we, as we were very short of money.

That was the end of the conference. The result amounted to almost 0.

The Chief of the General Staff says: War the sooner the better, but he does not draw the logical conclusion from this, which is to present Russia or France or both with an ultimatum which would unleash the war with right on our side.

In the afternoon I wrote to the Reich Chancellor about the influencing of the press.

There are certainly profound and complicated reasons for the confusion surrounding this document. A major cause of the trouble was that the Müller diaries were originally published in a deliberately distorted and mutilated form, in which the last sentences of the entry for 8 December 1912 were simply omitted.[4] The impression was thereby created that Müller himself was withdrawing half of the message of his diary record by dismissing the result of the conference in an apparent conclusion as 'almost zero'. Müller's disappointment that the Chief of the General Staff, Helmuth von Moltke, had not insisted on presenting an ultimatum to Russia or France (or both) which would have 'unleashed war with right on our side', therefore remained unknown, as did the fact that Reich Chancellor von Bethmann Hollweg was personally informed by Müller on the same day of the 'discussion of the military-political situation' that had taken place and received from him the 'All-Highest command to enlighten the people by means of the press what great national interests were at stake for Germany, too, in a war arising from the Austro-Serbian conflict'.[5] Years elapsed before the confusion produced by the falsified publication of the diary could be cleared up. However, an accurate version of the complete diary entry has been publicly available from 1977 at the latest, and as the handwritten original of the diary is stored in the Bundesarchiv-Militärarchiv in Freiburg and can be examined there by scholars, there is now no room for doubt about the authenticity of this key document.

In the meantime, further reports on the 'military-political conference' of 8 December 1912 have come to light which – even if at second hand – fully confirm what the Chief of the Naval Cabinet had written in his diary and in certain respects even amplify it. Thus the Saxon Military Plenipotentiary in

Berlin, Major-General Freiherr Leuckart von Weissdorf, wrote to the Saxon Minister of War Freiherr von Hausen on 12 December 1912:

> I have heard in the *strictest confidence* from a reliable source that last Sunday H.M. the Kaiser had a frank discussion in Potsdam [*sic*] with the Chief of the General Staff of the Army and the State Secretary of the Reich Navy Office. His Excellency von Moltke wants war, because he believes that it would not now be welcome to France, as is shown by the fact of her intervention in support of a peaceful solution to the situation. His Excellency von Tippitz on the other hand would prefer it if it came in one year's time, when the Canal and the harbour for submarines in Heligoland would be ready. On this occasion H.M. the Kaiser is said to have declared on the basis of secret information that England, if war should break out in Europe, would stick unconditionally to the Entente and stand on France's and Russia's side. And this despite the continuing friendly assurances of England and the declaration of intimate relations between Germany and England made by the Reich Chancellor![6]

Three days later the Bavarian Military Plenipotentiary in Berlin, General von Wenninger, reported to his superior, the Bavarian Minister of War, Freiherr Kress von Kressenstein:

> In my last report I held out the prospect of an oral briefing for Your Excellency. But as His Excellency von Lerchenfeld has just informed me that he has made a report on the same matter today to His Excellency von Hertling, I think it is necessary that I also submit a brief report to Your Excellency. Whereas the Reich Chancellor, in his official statements and through his press, expresses his confident hope in peace, the Kaiser himself is in an openly war-like mood.
>
> A week ago today H.M. summoned Moltke, Tirpitz and Müller (Bethmann, Heeringen and Kiderlen were not invited!) and informed them in a most agitated state that he had heard from Lichnowsky that Haldane had come to tell him, probably on Grey's orders, that England would stand on the side of Germany's enemies, whether Germany attacked or was herself attacked. (Echo of the Chancellor's speech!) England could not look on while France was thrown completely to the ground and a power arose on the Continent which possessed absolute hegemony in Europe.
>
> Moltke wanted to launch an immediate attack; there had not been a more favourable opportunity since the formation of the Triple Alliance. Tirpitz demanded a postponement for one year, until the Canal and U-boat harbour on Heligoland were finished. The Kaiser agreed to a postponement only reluctantly. He told the War Minister the following day only that he should prepare a new large Army Bill immediately. Tirpitz received the same order for the Fleet. The War Minister likewise demanded the postponement of the introduction of the Bill until the autumn because the entire structure of the Army, instructors, barracks etc., could not digest yet more big increases; all troop exercising areas were overfilled, the armaments industry could not keep pace. The War Minister told me this himself and he authorised me to tell Your Excellency that he would request first and foremost a repeated and substantial rise in the numbers comprising companies, squadrons and battalions so that they would never again face the situation they do now, with 47 men to a company with the immediate prospect of war.

The Kaiser instructed the General Staff and the Admiralty Staff to work out an invasion of England in grand style.

Meanwhile his diplomats are to seek allies everywhere, Rumania (already partly secured), Bulgaria, Turkey, etc.

Your Excellency will see that the picture behind the scenes is very different from that on the official stage.[7]

Finally, a diary entry by the then Naval Captain Albert Hopman, a close confidant of Admiral von Tirpitz, has also been published. It confirms everything which appears in Müller's record but contains the further interesting claim that besides Moltke, Tirpitz, Müller and the Chief of the Admiralty Staff, Vice-Admiral August von Heeringen, the latter's brother, the Prussian Minister of War General Josias von Heeringen, and the Chief of the Military Cabinet, Moritz Freiherr von Lyncker, were present at the conference in the Berlin Schloss. On 9 December Hopman noted:

Schultz has told me that a conference took place yesterday morning at H.M.'s, at which the State Secretary of the R[eich] N[avy] O[ffice], the War Minister, the Chief of the Admiralty Staff, The Chief of the General Staff and the two Cabinet Chiefs took part. Afterwards Tirpitz told me that the matter under discussion had been the following. Lichnowsky had reported that Haldane had come to see him and indicated all sorts of rhetorical embellishments etc. that if it were to come to a general European war, England would stand on France's side, since it could not tolerate that any particular power should have a distinct superiority on the Continent. H.M. therefore regards the situation as being very serious, particularly as Sassonow is supposed to have said that Russia would let loose if Austria should attack Serbia. H.M. sees in Austria's demands the vital interests of the Habsburg Monarchy which it can under no circumstances give up and which we must support. Doesn't believe that Serbia will eat humble pie. The Chief of the General Staff sees war as unavoidable and says the sooner the better. Tirpitz contradicted him and said that it was in the interests of the Navy to postpone war if possible for another 1–2 years. The Army, too, could do much before then to improve the exploitation of our population surplus. Rumania stands firm by Austria, and Bulgaria too is leaning towards the Triple Alliance. I myself do not *yet* believe in the inevitability of war, and believe, on the contrary, that it will not come to that. Haldane's declaration is a counter-move against the Chancellor's speech and is a bluff, a method used constantly by all governments these days.

The English City is doing everything possible to avoid war, in which it can only lose, at least for the next few years; the same is true of High Finance in all the other countries. The whole story has lasted too long already for it to develop into a general world conflagration. But who knows. 8 o'clock in the evening, went to dinner at Tirpitz's house, at which the Kaiser had said that he would be present. Those invited were Admirals von Müller, von Heeringen. The Admirals of the R[eich] N[avy] O[ffice] and 4 gentlemen from the Central Department. H.M. was in a very good mood. I heard nothing of any significance of his conversation.[8]

The evidence on the secret 'military-political conference' of 8 December 1912 must therefore be described as unusually abundant. If historians nevertheless encounter difficulties in interpreting this meeting, that is primarily because the 'war council' – as Bethmann Hollweg angrily described it on 20 December 1912[9] – cannot be separated from the emotive controversy on the immediate causes of the First World War which overshadows it. With few exceptions, even those historians who see German policy in the July crisis of 1914 as the main cause of the outbreak of the world war are reluctant to accept that this policy was formulated a year and a half earlier by the Kaiser and 'his faithful followers in the army and navy' meeting in a hastily convened 'war council'. Historians of all shades of opinion have thus placed themselves in the unusual position of arguing to a certain extent against the sources. For them, the evidence on the 'war council' of 8 December 1912 is too sharp, too exact, 'too good to be true'. One almost has the feeling that the evidence would be easier to accept if the timing and the method envisaged for the unleashing of war – by means of an Austrian-Serbian conflict after the completion of the widening and deepening of the Kiel canal in July 1914, exactly one and a half years after the conference of December 1912 – had conformed less precisely to the actual course of events!

The wider question of the historical significance of the 'war council', and in particular of the relationship between the deliberations of 8 December 1912 and German policy in the July crisis of 1914, must therefore remain open until further new sources, such as for instance the missing pre-war diaries of Bethmann's confidant Kurt Riezler (which were allegedly destroyed in Munich as late as the mid-1960s[10]), permit a less ambiguous conclusion. If we nevertheless regard an assessment of the pre-history and history of the 'war council' as worthwhile, this is because no other event is capable of illuminating so clearly the military-political decision-making process in the Kaiserreich on the eve of the First World War. Even if there was no direct causal connection between 8 December 1912 and German policy in the July crisis of 1914, the men who in December 1912 stood on the threshold of a world war were (with the exception of the Heeringen brothers and Foreign Secretary Alfred von Kiderlen-Wächter, who died suddenly at the end of December 1912) the same as those who, after the assassination in Sarajevo, were prepared to risk the 'leap into the dark'. Such an investigation reveals in frightening clarity their political relationships with one another, the extent of their influence in the confused power-structure of the Bismarckian Kaiserreich in its final phase, their mentality following the domestic and foreign catastrophes of the Bülow years, the second Morocco crisis of 1911 and the disastrous Reichstag elections of January 1912. It reveals how Kaiser Wilhlem II remained the focus of the military-political decision-making process even if now, more unstable and lacking the counter-balance of Eulenburg and his Liebenberg circle, he was more vulnerable than ever to manipulation by the generals and his military entourage; how Reich Chancellor von Bethmann Hollweg and the Foreign Office under Kiderlen, though they had from the outset adopted a forceful stance on the first Balkan war which had broken out in October 1912, were nevertheless excluded from the 'war-council' because, as mere civilians, they were responsible only for 'purely political' questions and not 'military-political' matters even though the issue under discussion was whether (or rather when to start a war! Above all, our investigation demonstrates how mistaken it would be to seek to understand the mechanism of decision-making in the final phase of the Wilhelmine Reich – and therefore in the July crisis of 1914 itself – without acknowledging that the decisive power in such matters had long ago slipped away from the Reich Chancellor and the Foreign Office and was exercised instead largely by the Supreme War Lord in conjunction 'with his faithful followers in the army and navy'. [...]

When, early on 8 December 1912, Kaiser Wilhelm II read Lichnowsky's Report on his conversation with Haldane, he covered it with the most violent marginal comments. In a characteristic attack of anger, he declared the English principle of the 'balance of power' to be an 'idiocy' which would make England 'eternally into our enemy'. The principle of the balance of power was nothing more than an attempt by that 'nation of shopkeepers' to prevent other Powers from defending their interests with the sword. Above all the Kaiser was disappointed that in the unavoidable 'final struggle [*Endkampf*]' between the Slavs and the Teutons', the 'Anglo-Saxons will be on the side of the Slavs and Gauls'.[11] Wilhelm II had already threatened at the end of September 1912 that if England refused to comply with Germany's wishes, then 'we shall be able to take our mobilisation plans out of the drawer, for then everything will be clear'.[12] Now, on 8 December, he greeted Haldane's statement to Lichnowsky on Britain's position in the event of a European war as 'a desirable clarification, which from now on must form the basis of our policy'; all 'veils of uncertainty' had been torn asunder. In the coming 'struggle for existence [*Existenzkamf*]' between the 'Teutons' and the 'Slavs supported by the Latins (Gauls)', the Kaiser thundered, England – motivated by 'envy and hatred of Germany' and by her 'fear that we are becoming too strong' – would stand on the side of the Slavs and Gauls.[13]

On that Sunday morning, as we have seen, Kaiser Wilhlem II summoned his Chief of General Staff von Moltke and the three Admirals von Tirpitz, von Heeringen and von Müller (and possibly also the Chief of the Military Cabinet Moritz von Lyncker) to the Schloss and informed them that in a future war of the Triple Alliance against France and Russia, England would stand at the side of her Entente partners. This news, which had just arrived from Lichnowsky, was, he declared, a 'desirable clarification of the situation'. Austria should now deal energetically with the Serbs, since she would otherwise lose control of the Slavs within the Danube Monarchy. Should Russia support the Serbs, 'which she evidently does', then 'war would be unavoidable for us too'. But Austria could count on the military support of Bulgaria, Rumania, Albania and perhaps Turkey as well, and Germany would then be free to 'fight the war with full fury against France'. The fleet would have to prepare for a war against England, since 'the possibility ... of a war with Russia alone' must now be discounted. 'Therefore immediate submarine warfare against English troop transports in the Scheldt or by Dunkirk' and mine warfare in the Thames'. These statements by the Kaiser were enthusiastically supported by the Chief of the Great General Staff. He too considered 'that war was unavoidable, and the sooner the better', though he did argue that first 'we ought to do more through the press to prepare the popularity of a war against Russia'. Grand Admiral von Tirpitz, on the other hand, objected that 'the navy would like to see the postponement of the great fight for one and a half years' – until the completion of the widening of Kiel Canal in the summer of 1914![14]

The Kaiser's excitement over the declarations of Haldane and Grey persisted for at least a week. On 9 December he wrote to the heir to the Austrian throne, Archduke Franz Ferdinand, that Haldane's statement had been 'typically English'. 'Full of poison and hatred and envy of the good development of our mutual alliance and our two countries.' Britain's 'balance of power' policy had been revealed 'in all its naked shamelessness' as the playing off of the Great Powers against each other to England's advantage'. 'This has come as no surprise to me', the monarch added, 'and the necessary precautions will be taken.'[15]   Three days later, Wilhelm wrote to his brother Heinrich that Haldane's statement to the effect that England 'could *not tolerate* our becoming the strongest Power on the Continent and that the latter should be united under our leadership!!!' amounted to a moral declaration of war on Germany. At least the clarification of the situation had made Germany's 'preparatory measures' easier to undertake.[16]   The Kaiser also wrote to the Prussian Envoy in Karlsruhe, von Eisendecher, on 12 December that Haldane had declared 'in unscrupulous, raw and typically English terms ... that if Germany were to become involved in a war with Russia-France – in support of Austria – England would not only not remain neutral, but would immediately come to France's aid'; according to Haldane, England could 'not tolerate Germany's becoming the predominant Power on the Continent and that the latter should unite under its leadership!!' In terms of military preparations, England would from now on count as Germany's enemy. Marschall's mission, like that of Lichnowsky, had been 'to secure England's neutrality towards us, at all events in the case of a conflict with Russia-France', but that had now finally failed.[17]

On the following day, Kaiser Wilhelm II visited the Bavarian envoy in Berlin, Count Lerchenfeld, and told him too that Haldane had explained to Lichnowsky that England 'could not permit Germany to subjugate France, after which there would be only one Power on the Continent which would then exercise an absolute hegemony'. The 'Germanic English', the outraged Kaiser exclaimed, would therefore 'fight with the French and Russians against their own racial comrades'. To the long-serving representative of Bavaria, the 'salient point' in his detailed and agitated conversation with the Kaiser was the realisation that 'soon everything might be at stake for Germany'.[18]   When on 14 December Theodor Schiemann spoke to the Kaiser in Potsdam, he also observed that Wilhelm saw in Haldane's statement – 'that in the event of a general war, England would be compelled to stand on France's side in order to prevent Germany from becoming all-powerful' – a threat to which he must respond with a new Navy Bill.[19]

The veteran Swiss ambassador in Berlin, Alfred de Claparède, was not a little surprised when, after having lunch with the Kaiser on 10 December, Wilhelm launched into a 'grave and agitated' tirade on the situation in the Balkans and in Europe as a whole. The war of the Balkan states against Turkey was, the monarch exclaimed, 'not a religious war but purely a racial war, the war of Slavdom against Germandom'. Russia clearly intended 'to unite all Slavs, not merely those in the Balkans, but the Slavs of other States, in particular of Austria-Hungary, so weakening Austria militarily through the loss of so-and-so many million Slavs'. Austria was fully aware of the danger, however, 'as are we in Germany too, and we will not leave Austria in the lurch: if diplomacy fails, we shall have to fight this racial war'. Only a few days earlier, the Kaiser told Claparède, he had learnt that Lord Haldane had announced to Lichnowsky 'that England would never tolerate Germany's taking a predominant position over her neighbours in Central Europe. Is this not an impertinent statement which should really have been answered by a breaking of diplomatic relations?', the Kaiser demanded indignantly. 'Is it not incredible ... that these Anglo-Saxons with whom we are related by common ancestry, religion and civilisatory striving, now wish to allow themselves to be used as the tools of the Slavs', Wilhelm demanded. The Kaiser then declared that Austria and Germany would have to prevent the creation of a strong Serbian state. The vital interests of both empires required that they must not be 'encircled by a Slav ring'. Again he stated emphatically: 'If this question ... cannot be solved by diplomacy, then it will have to be decided by armed force. The solution can be postponed', declared the Kaiser, echoing the discussion in the 'war council' of two days earlier. 'But the question will arise again in 1 or 2 years'. The Kaiser then repeated: 'The racial struggle cannot be avoided, – perhaps it will not take place now, but it will probably take place in one or two years.'[20] On 15 December the Kaiser told Albert Ballin in undiminished excitement that a '*racial struggle* [*Rassenkampf*]' between the 'Teutons [*Germanen*]' and the 'insolent Slavs' could not be avoided because at stake was the future of the Habsburg Monarchy and 'the very *existence* of our Fatherland'. But Haldane had now declared that England could not tolerate 'a subjugation of France by ourselves'. It could not allow 'us to achieve a predominant position on the Continent under which the Continent could then be united'.[21]

Is it possible that we are mistaken in assuming that these agitated exclamations of the Kaiser in the period 8–15 December 1912 reveal his innermost intentions of making the German Reich 'the strongest Power' with 'absolute hegemony' over the European Continent? It seems to have been axiomatic for him that such a breakthrough to predominance in Europe could only be achieved by means of a war against France and Russia. Instead of being warned off this course of action by Haldane's 'honest and well-meaning attempt ... to urge caution upon us',[22] however, the Kaiser's determination not to wait too much longer but to unleash a world war before Austria-Hungary became worthless as an ally because it had been 'under-mined by the Slavs' appears only to have hardened. Indeed, at the 'war council' of 8 December 1912, he together with the Chief of General Staff von Moltke argued for an 'immediate attack' and accepted the 'postponement of the great fight for one and a half years' demanded by Tirpitz only 'reluctantly'. Müller too recorded his disappointment at the postponement of the war in his diary, as we saw at the beginning. He wrote: 'That was the end of the conference. The result amounted to almost 0. The Chief of the Great General Staff says: War the sooner the better, but he does not draw the logical conclusion from this, which is to present Russia or France or both with an ultimatum which would unleash the war with right on our side.'[23]

These discussions as to the merits of triggering a war at once or alternatively after the completion of the widening of the Kiel Canal in the summer of 1914, remained anything but secret. Captain Hopman learned all the salient details of the 'secret' conference as early as the following morning – through Schultz, his masseur! The numerous letters Wilhelm II sent, the agitated discussions he held with German and foreign diplomats, in themselves ensured a wider audience. As Bethmann Hollweg complained to Eisendecher on 20 December, the Kaiser had 'told God and the whole world about Haldane's conversation, fantastically embellished'.[24] Soon the Military Plenipotentiaries of Bavaria and Saxony, who were in daily contact with the Prussian War Minister von Heeringen (whose brother had taken part in the 'war council'), were able to report that Moltke had argued for an immediate war, while Tirpitz 'would prefer it if it came in one year's time, when the Canal and the harbour for submarines in Heligoland would be ready'.[25] The Bavarian General von Wenninger reported more fully still on the 'war council' after he learned that Count Lerchenfeld had already written to the Bavarian Minister-President Count Hertling on the subject. The Kaiser, Wenninger stated in his report of 15 December , was 'in an openly war-like mood'. At a conference held a week before, Moltke had spoken out in favour of an 'immediate attack', as 'there had not been a more favourable opportunity since the formation of the Triple Alliance'. Tirpitz on the other hand had 'demanded a postponement for one year, until the (Kiel) Canal and the U-boat harbour on Heligoland were finished'. The Kaiser, Wenninger continued, 'agreed to a postponement only reluctantly'. He ordered new Army and Navy Bills to be introduced immediately, a plan for the 'invasion of England in grand style' to be worked out', and new alliance partners to be sought.[26] After Lerchenfeld's and Wenninger's Reports, it is not surprising that the new Prince Regent of Bavaria, the future King Ludwig III, should ask Bethmann in consternation what lay behind the news that the Kaiser was pressing for war and planning an invasion of England.[27]

Within the officer corps, too, the conviction was widespread that a great war would soon begin. On 14 December Admiral von Müller had to inform the Kaiser of the 'numerous withdrawals from bank accounts and the deposition in gold in the safety-vaults of the banks of the sums thus withdrawn, as well as the sending of bank deposits abroad (Zürich)'. Wilhelm II was already aware of this and observed that 'many high-ranking officers were also involved.[28]

How did the so-called 'responsible government' react to the decisions taken by the Kaiser and his 'faithful followers in the army and navy' at the so-called 'war council'? Does the fact advanced by Mommsen, Turner and Baumgart that neither Bethmann Hollweg nor Kiderlen-Wächter took part in the deliberations of 8 December suffice to deny that 'military-political conference' the status of a decision-making meeting? Is it, as Hölzle maintains, a 'misunderstanding of the political leadership of the Kaiserreich' to believe that the basic direction of the foreign and armaments policy of the Prusso-German military monarchy was in the final analysis laid down not in the Wilhelmstrasse 76 or 77, but by the Kaiser in the Berlin Schloss or in the New Palace in Potsdam, following discussion with his top-ranking generals and admirals? After the catastrophic collapse of the authority of the 'responsible government' in favour of the monarch and his court in the decade after Bismarck's fall, and after the fiasco of Bülow's tentative efforts to reassert the Reich Chancellor's authority in the years 1906–9, did Theobald von Bethmann Hollweg really possess the power (assuming for the moment that he had the will) to 'put the Kaiser in his place' and to 'nullify' the decisions taken at the 'war council'?[29] These are all questions which now urgently require clarification through further research. A detailed examination of Bethmann's reaction to the 'war council' suggests, however, that he was far better and much sooner informed than some historians have assumed, and that with the single exception of the new Navy Bill demanded by the Kaiser, Bethmann accepted and carried out (either personally or through the appropriate administrative department) every decision made at that military-political meeting.

It is simply not correct, as Wolfgang J. Mommsen has claimed, that the Chancellor was only informed a week later of the 'war council', and even then semi-officially; it is also not correct, as Mommsen again asserts, that 'there is not the slightest evidence to support the argument that William II's excited order to prepare the country for war by means of an official press campaign was followed up by deeds'.[30] Immediately after the 'war council', Admiral von Müller officially informed the Chancellor in writing that 'a conference on the military-political situation [took place] today in the Royal Schloss', in accordance with which the Kaiser was now ordering Bethmann Hollweg 'to enlighten the people through the press of the great national interests, which would be at stake also for Germany, if a war were to break out over the Austro-Serbian conflict. The people must not be in a position of asking themselves only at the outbreak of a great European war, what are the interests that Germany would be fighting for.' The Chief of the Naval Cabinet hinted that further decisions had been taken in the course of the meeting: he was, he said, only informing the Reich Chancellor of the command regarding the new press policy because this was 'a purely political measure'.[31] It was obviously the admiral's view that the 'military-political' discussions and decisions of the 'war-council' were not the business of the civilian Reich leadership.

Bethmann Hollweg and Kiderlen-Wächter carried out the Kaiser's instruction without further ado and to the latter's complete satisfaction. Kurt Riezler himself wrote an article with the title *For the sake of Durazzo?* which was published as early as 9 December in the *Deutsche Tageszeitung* and which the monarch, still in his agitated state, approved as 'very good'.[32] On 10 December the Reich Chancellor sent this 'article on Germany's interest in the event of an Austro-Russian war' to the Kaiser, stating expressly that it had been 'prepared at this end in accordance with Your Majesty's Most Gracious instruction conveyed to me by Admiral von Müller'.[33] On Wednesday, 11 December 1912, Foreign Secretary Alfred von Kiderlen-Wächter had an audience with the Kaiser on the subject of the new press policy, following which he informed Müller that 'the matter ... would be pursued further in the press'.[34] In the light of such clear evidence it is surely impossible to continue to maintain that 'the responsible statesmen as well as the Wihelmstrasse' were left 'completely in the dark' about the new orientation of official press policy.[35] [...]

Within the German army, too, steps were taken in December 1912 which might point to the conclusion that the unleashing of a great war had been decided on, not immediately but in the foreseeable future. As early as 12 December the Reich Chancellor and the War Minister jointly decided to allow Christmas leave for officers and men to go ahead and for the usual duration.[36] At the same time the army command arrived at the decision that while the current war academy courses 'should not be terminated prematurely, for the new ones a shorter length was to be laid down from the beginning'.[37] This shortening of the war academy courses from nine to seven months was admittedly, as the Prussian War Minister stated, 'not intended as a preparation for war', but it did amount, in Wenninger's words, to 'a kind of Krümper system' with the aim 'of filling up more quickly the many posts which are at present vacant.[38] In the Military Cabinet on 14 December, Wenninger asked what was behind the rumour that the army was 'holding back retirements because of the danger of war'. This was 'most emphatically denied', he reported, and 'on the contrary it was stated that the opportunity offered by the current war mood would be used on a large scale to persuade the "weak links" – i.e. those higher officers who would not be capable of matching up to their positions of leadership in war, – to retire *beforehand*.[39]

Some of these measures, and most especially the gigantic Army Bill of 1913, bore the character of a time bomb, as Dieter Groh has shown.[40] The massive army increases of 1913, which 'overstretched the entire framework of the army', admittedly made it impossible to unleash war while the reorganisation was taking place, but they made the implementation of the Schlieffen Plan within a certain timescale almost a necessity. (It is highly significant that the 'Great Eastern Campaign Plan' for a war against Russia alone was abandoned by the General Staff in April 1913.[41]) For on the one hand it could be foreseen that both Russia and France would follow Germany by introducing their own army increases and that then, after transitional difficulties had been overcome, the Entente Powers would achieve a military superiority which would again negate the Schlieffen Plan's chances of succeeding. On the other hand yet another strengthening of the German army was impossible because, as Groh argues and as is shown by the most recent research, 'the Wilhelmine Reich was not in a position, for reasons of domestic politics, to arm any further'.[42] It is true that Groh and some other historians still speak of a 'defensive readiness for preventive war' on Germany's part which, they claim, was transformed into a concrete readiness to go to war only after the assassination at Sarajevo – even if as a 'systematic and logical consequence' of the decisions of December 1912.[43] Against this we must ask whether, in the light of the thought patterns and decision-making processes which we have reconstructed here for the last three months of 1912, it is not more credible to assume that the men who ruled in Berlin – not just the Chief of General Staff von Moltke and his generals, for whom this can hardly be disputed, but also Kaiser Wilhelm II and Reich Chancellor von Bethmann Hollweg – acted in full awareness of the very serious longer-term consequences which the decisions they took in December 1912 were bound to have.

At the very time when Kaiser Wilhelm II was holding his now so controversial 'war council' with his 'faithful followers in the army and navy', the Reich Chancellor had a meeting with Field Marshal Colmar von der Goltz on the latter's return from Turkey. Their conversation ran as follows:

BETHMANN: We can get any military demand we make approved [by the Reichstag].

GOLTZ: Well in that case let us make our demands.

BETHMANN: Yes, but if we make such large demands, we must have the firm intention of striking soon.

GOLTZ: Yes of course, then we would be pursuing a proper policy!

BETHMANN: But even Bismarck avoided a preventive war in the year [18]75.

GOLTZ: That's right! He could do that after fighting three preventive wars for the benefit of the Fatherland[44]

Notes

[1] On the controversy on the so-called 'war-council' of 8 December 1912, see: Fritz Fischer, *Krieg der Illusionen* (Düsseldorf 1969), pp. 231ff; Adolf Gasser, 'Der deutsche Hegemonialkrieg von 1914' in Immanuel Geiss and Bernd-Jürgen Wendt (eds.),

Deutschland in der Weltpolitik des 19. und 20. Jahrhunderts. Festschrift für Fritz fischer (Düsseldorf 1973), pp. 307ff; Adolf Gasser, 'Erster Weltkrieg und "Friedensforschung"', *Allgemeine Schweizerische Militärzeitschrift* 140 (1974) pp.235ff; Adolf asser, *Preussischer Militärgeist und Kriegentfesselung 1914. Drei Studien zum Ausbruch des Ersten Weltkrieges* (Basel and Frankfurt 1985); Imanuel Geiss, *German Foreign Policy 1871– 1914* (London 1976), pp. 142ff; John C.G. Röhl, *1914:Delusion or Design? The Testimony of Two German Diplomats* (London 1973), pp. 28ff; John C. G. Röhl, 'Admiral von Müller and the Approach of War, 1911–1914' *The Historical Journal* 12 (1969) pp. 651ff; John C. G. Röhl, 'An der Schwelle zum Weltkrieg: Eine Dokumentation über den "Kriegsrat" vom 8. Dezember 1912' *Militärgeschichtliche Mitteilungen* (1977), pp. 77–134; John C. G. Röhl, 'Die Generalprobe. Zur Geschichte und Bedeutung des "Kriegsrates" vom 8. Dezember 1912' in D. Stegmann, B. –J. Wendt and P.-C. Witt (eds.), *Industrielle Gesellschaft und politisches System* (Bonn 1978), pp. 357–73; L.C.F. Turner, 'The Edge of the Precipice. A comparison between November 1912 and July 1914' *Royal Military College Historical Journal 3* (1974), p. 18; L.C.F. Turner, in *The Australian Journal of Politics and History,* 20 (1974), pp. 121ff; L.C.F. Turner, *Origins of the First World War* (London, 1970), p. 49; Klaus Hilderbrand, in *Historische Zeitschrift* 223 (1976), p. 478; see also Klaus Hilderbrand, 'Imperialismus, Wettrüsten und Kriegsausbruch 1914', *Neue Politische Literatur* 20 (1975), pp.160ff; Winfried Baumgart, in *Historisches Jahrbuch der Görres-Gesellschaft* 93 (1973), pp. 471ff; Wolfgang J. Mommsen, 'Domestic Factors in German Foreign Policy before 1914', *Central European History* 6 (1973), pp. 12f; Wolfgang J. Mommsen, 'Die latente Krise des Deutschen Reiches 1909–1914' in *Handbuch zur Deutschen Geschichte, Deutsche Geschichte der neuesten Zeit von Bismarks Entlassung bis zur Gegenwart,* part I. *Von 1890–1933.* Section Ia (Frnakfurt 1973), pp. 56f; Wolfgang J. Mommsen, 'The Topos of Inevitable War in Germany in the Decade before 1914' in Volker R. Berghahn and Martin Kitchen (eds.), *Germany in the Age of Total War. Essays in Honour of Francis Carsten* (London 1981) Wolfgang J. Mommsen, 'Kaiser Wilhelm II and German Politics', *Journal of Contemporary History* 25, nos. 2–3 (May–June 1990), pp. 307f.; Egmont Zechlin, 'Die Adriakrise und der "Kriegsrat" vom 8. Dezember 1912' in *Krieg und Kriegsrisiko. Zur deutschen Politik im Ersten Weltkrieg* (Düsseldorf 1979), pp. 115–59; Erwin Hölzle, *Die Selbstentmachtung Europas. Das Experiment des Friedens vor und im Ersten Weltkrieg* (Göttingen 1975), pp. 180ff; Willibald Gutsche, Probleme des Verhältnisses zwischen Monopolkapital und Staat in Deutschland vom Ende des 19. Jahrhunderts bis zum Vorabend des Ersten Weltkrieges' in Fritz Klein (ed.), *Studien zum deutschen Imperialismus vor 1914* (Berlin 1976), p.66; Volker R. Berghahn, *Germany and the Approach of War in 1914* (London 1973), pp. 165ff; Bernd-Felix Schulte, *Die Deutsche Armee 1900–1914. Zwischen Beharren und Verändern* (Düsseldorf 1977); Bernd-Felix Schulte, *Vor dem Kriegsausbruch 1914. Deutschland, die Türkei und der Balkan* (Düsseldorf 1980), pp. 8ff, pp. 75–122; Bernd-Felix Schulte, *Europäische Krise und Erster Weltkrieg. Beiträge zur Militärpolitik des Kaiserreichs, 1871–1914* (Frankfurt and Bern 1983), *passim,* Bernd-Felix Schulte, 'Zu der Krisenkonferenz vom 8. Dezember 1912', *Historisches Jahrbuch* 102 (1982), pp. 183–97; Isabel V. Hull, *The entourage of Kaiser Wilhelm II, 1888–1918* (Cambridge 1982), pp. 248–53; Ivo Nikolai Lambi, *The Navy and German Power Politics 1862–1914* (Boston 1984), pp. 382ff; Stig Förster, *Der Doppelte Militarismus. Die Deutsche Heeresrüstungspolitik zwischen Status-quo-Sicherung und Aggression 1890–1913* (Stuttgart 1985), pp. 252–7; Wilhelm Deist, 'Kaiser Wilhelm II. als Oberster Kriegsherr' in John C. G. Röhl, *Der Ort Kaiser Wilhelms II. in der deutschen Geschichte* (Munich 1991), pp. 34ff; Terence F. Cole, 'German Decision-Making on the Eve of the First World War: The Records of the Swiss Embassy in Berlin' in Röhl, *Der Ort Kaiser Wilhelms II.,* pp. 62ff; R.J.W. Evans and Harmut Pogge von Strandmann (eds.), *The Coming of the First World War* (Oxford 1998), pp. 6, 112f *et passim.*

[2] Müller, diary entry for 8 December 1912, BA-MA Freiburg. Printed in Röhl, 'An der Schwelle', document no. 4. Cf. the previously published version in Walter Görlitz (ed.), *Der Kaiser ... Aufzeichmungen des Chefs des Marinekabinetts Admiral Georg Alexander von Müller über die Ära Wilhelms II.* (Göttingen 1965), pp. 124f.

[3] The words 'the sooner the better' were inserted by Müller in his own hand between the original lines. It is not clear from the manuscript when this insertion was made.

[4] Görlitz, *Der Kaiser*, pp. 124f. For a critical assessment of the Görlitz edition of the Müller diary in general, see John C.G. Röhl, 'Admiral von Müller and the Approach of War, 1911–1914', *The Historical Journal* 12 (1969), pp. 651–73.

[5] Müller to Bethmann, 8 December 1912, Röhl, 'An der Schwelle', document no. 5.

[6] Röhl, 'An der Schwelle', document no. 14. Leuckart's report was first discovered by Volker R. Berghahn in the Staatsarchiv, Dresden, and was first published in Röhl, 'Admiral von Müller', p. 662.

[7] Röhl, 'An der Schwelle', document no. 22.

[8] Albert Hopman, diary entry for 9 December 1912, BA-MA Freiburg, Hopman papers, N326/12. Printed in Schulte, 'Zu der Krisenkonferenz vom 8. Dezember 1912 in Berlin', *Historisches Jahrbuch der Görres-Gesellschaft* 102 (1982), p. 196. It is quite probable that the Chief of the Military Cabinet von Lyncker was present at the meeting. In Wenninger's Report of 15 December 1915, on the other hand, it is expressly stated that the Prussian War Minister Josias von Heeringen was *not* invited.

[9] Bethmann to Eisendecher, 29 December 1912, Röhl, 'An der Schwelle', document no. 36.

[10] See Karl Dietrich Erdmann (ed.), *Kurt Riezler, Tagebücher, Aufsätze, Dokumente* (Göttingen 1972), pp. 7ff. Cf. Bernd Sösemann, 'Die Tagebücher Kurt Riezlers. Untersuchungen zu ihrer Echtheit und Edition', *Historische Zeitschrift* 236 (1983), pp. 327–369; Erdmann's reply in ibid., pp. 371–402; Fritz Fischer, *Juli 1914: Wir sind nicht hineingeschlittert. Das Staatsgeheimnis um die Riezler-Tagebücher* (Frankfurt 1983); Bernd-Felix Schulte, *Die Verfälschung der Riezler-Tagebücher. Ein Beitrag zur Wissensschaftsgeschichte der 50er und 60er Jahre* (Frankfurt, Bern and New York 1985).

[11] Kaiser Wilhelm II, marginal comments on Lichnowsky's report of 3 December 1912, *Grosse Politik*, xxxix, no. 15612.

[12] Kaiser Wilhelm II to Bethmann Hollweg, 30 September 1912, ZStA Merseburg, Rep. 53J, Lit. B, no. 7, quoted in Röhl, *1914 – Delusion or Design?*, p. 42.

[13] Kaiser Wilhelm II to Kiderlen-Wächter, 8 December 1912, *Grosse Politik*, xxxix, no. 15613.

[14] See the four documents on the 'war council' of 8 December 1912 quoted at the beginning of this chapter, above pp. 162–5.

[15] Kaiser Wilhelm II to Archduke Franz Ferdinand, 9 December 1912, printed in Röhl, 'An der Schwelle', document no. 8. See R. A. Kann, 'Emperor William II and Archduke Francis Ferdinand their Correspondence', *American Historical Review* 57 (1952), pp. 344f. See also R. A. Kann, *Erzherzog Franz Ferdinand. Studien* (Munich 1967), pp. 74f.

[16] Kaiser Wilhelm II to Prince Heinrich of Prussia, 12 December 1912, printed in Röhl, 'An der Schwelle', document no. 12.

[17] Kaiser Wilhelm II to Karl von Eisendecher, 12 December 1912, ibid., document no. 13. See also Fischer, *Krieg der Illusionen*, pp. 236f.

[18] Count Hugo von Lerchenfeld to Count Georg von Hertling, 14 December 1912, in Ernst Deuerlein (ed.), *Briefwechsel Hertling-Lerchenfeld. Dienstliche Privatkorrespondenz zwischen dem bayerischen Ministerpräsidenten Georg Graf von Hertling und dem bayerischen Gesandten in Berlin Hugo Graf von und zu Lerchenfeld* (Boppard-am-Rhein 1973), part I, pp. 189ff. See also Karl Alexander von Müller in *Süddeutsche Monatshefte* (July 1921), pp. 294f.

[19] Klaus Meyer, *Theodore Schiemann als politischer Publizist* (Frankfurt 1956), p. 181, note 537.

[20] Alfred de Claparède, report of 10 December 1912, printed in Terence F. Cole, 'German Decision-Making on the Eve of the First World War. The Records of the Swiss Embassy in Berlin' in John C. G. Röhl (ed.), *Der Ort Kaiser Wilhelms II. in der deutschen Geschichte* (Munich 1991), pp. 62f.

[21] Bernhard Huldermann, *Albert Ballin* (Oldenburg 1922), pp. 273f.

[22] Alfred von Kiderlen-Wächter to Karl von Eisendecher, 19 December 1912, printed in Röhl, 'An der Schwelle', document no. 35.

[23] Müller, diary entry for 8 December 1912, see above pp. 162f.

[24] Bethmann Hollweg to Eisendecher, 20 December 1912, Röhl, 'An der Schwelle', document no. 36.

[25] Ibid., document no. 14. See above, pp. 163f.

[26] Ibid., document nos. 15, 20, 21 and 22. See above, p. 164.

[27] Bethmann Hollweg, memorandum of 20 December 1912, ibid., Document no. 34; *Grosse Politik*, XXXIII, no. 12496.

[28] Müller, diary entry for 14 December 1912, BA-MA Freiburg.

[29] Erwin Hölzle, *Die Selbstentmachtung Europas*, pp. 180ff.

[30] Mommsen, 'Domestic Factors in German Foreign Policy', pp. 12f.

[31] Müller to Bethmann Hollweg, 8 Decemeber 1912, printed in Röhl, 'An der Schwelle', document no. 5. See Imanuel Geiss, *Julikrise und Kriegsausbruch 1914*, 2 vols. (Hanover 1963/4), I, p. 45.

[32] Röhl, 'An der Schwelle', document no. 9, appendix, with the Kaiser's marginal comment.

[33] Bethmann Hollweg to Kaiser Wilhelm II, 10 December 1912, ibid., document no. 9.

[34] Kiderlen-Wächter to Müller, 11 Decemeber 1912, ibid., document no. 10.

[35] Mommsen, 'Domestic Factors in German Foreign Policy', pp. 12f.

[36] Röhl, 'An der Schwelle', documents nos. 14, 15 and 21.

[37] Leuckart's Report, 12 December 1912, ibid., document no. 14.

[38] The Krümper system was adopted by Prussia in the years 1808 to 1812 as a means of quickly increasing the size of the army with partially trained reservists.

[39] My italics. Wenninger's Report, 14 December 1912, ibid., document no. 21.

[40] Dieter Groh, 'Je eher, desto besser', pp. 501ff.

[41] See Adolf Gasser, 'Deutschlands Entschluss zum Präventivkrieg 1913/14' in *Discordia Concors. Festschrift für Edgar Bonjour* (Basel 1968), p. 173; Dieter Groh, *Negative Integration und revolutionärer Attentismus. Die deutsche Sozialdemokratie am Vorabend des I. Weltkrieges, 1909–1914* (Berlin 1973), pp. 406–14.

[42] Groh, 'Je eher, desto besser', p. 506. See the important new study by Stig Förster, *Der Doppelte Militarismus*, pp. 247ff.

[43] Groh, 'Je eher, desto besser', p. 503.

[44] Memorandum on a conversation between Reich Chancellor von Bethmann Hollweg and Field Marshal Baron von der Goltz, in the Mudra Papers, BA-MA Frieburg, printed in Bernd-Felix Schulte, *Vor dem Kriegsausbruch 1914*, p. 156. The memorandum carries the note by Mudra: 'Goltz said more or less this to me on 10.12[19]12.'

(John C. G. Röhl, *The Kaiser and his Court: Wilhelm II and the Government of Germany*, Cambridge, Cambridge University Press, 1994)

7   DEREK ALDCROFT, *FROM VERSAILLES TO WALL STREET 1919–1929*

It is difficult to say exactly what would have happened to economic and social life had the First World War never occurred, though no doubt one day this counterfactual proposition will be put to the econometric test. There are reasons for assuming that the international economy would have continued developing much in the same way as it had in the half century or so before the outbreak of hostilities, though certainly there would have been ever-increasing symptoms of strain. But the type of development, the growth structure and spread of incomes etc. would not have departed radically from the secular trends which had been going on for some time.

growing   If this assumption is correct we are justified in treating the war as a large exogenous shock which so upset the pattern of development and its underlying equilibrium that it eventually resulted in the breakdown of the type of integrated international framework which characterized the nineteenth century, especially the latter half. Alternatively, if this assumption is incorrect, the war may be seen as an initial shock which for a time disturbed both the cyclical and secular processes of economic development, but that after a short adjustment stage economies reverted to their previous trends without marked effects. In this case the impact of the war had little bearing on the 1929 downturn in economic activity and the subsequent disintegration of the international economy.

Objections can be raised to both these extreme lines of reasoning. To take the second hypothesis first: it is possible to argue that the war produced a fairly severe initial impact, upsetting both cyclical and secular forces, but that the readjustment was soon made and by the middle of the 1920s pre-war patterns of development were re-emerging as the economic process adapted itself. Recovery was strong in the latter half of the decade, and all that happened was a delay to the growth process, an occurrence not without precedent as an examination of past history will show. Moreover, if we ignore the small oscillations in economic activity during the 1920s the pattern of fluctuations was not all that different from that before the war, apart from the somewhat steeper amplitude. On the other hand, if one probes a little more deeply there appear all sorts of distortions and maladjustments in the international economy at large and within individual countries; and there is the dramatic and prolonged downturn of 1929, longer and more severe than most of the cyclical upsets of the nineteenth century. The question which then arises is whether these things would have occurred had there been no war. It seems that the repercussions of war were so profound and long-lasting that it is not possible to write the war off as a once-and-for-all short term disturbance.

Unfortunately the first line of reasoning is also open to debate. The war did shock in the traumatic sense, it did release new forces, forces which exerted almost 'evil' influences on the international economic mechanism, and it did leave behind a legacy of partly insoluble problems. Yet to associate the economic downturn of 1929, or the 1931 financial crisis which more or less completed the dissolution of the old economic order, directly with the war would perhaps stretch things too far. Though the war did create new forces and new problems it also aggravated or accentuated tendencies which were already present before 1914. And again, the smooth operation of the international economic mechanism before 1914 was perhaps more apparent than real. It *worked* in a sense partly because of a fortuitous set of favourable circumstances, a convergence process, and partly because the costs, especially the social ones, of its operation were either ignored or not accepted as important at the time. In a different situation, when the convergence of favourable factors ceased to operate and when the consequences of human actions counted for more, the system worked miserably. Whether the change in circumstances can be ascribed solely to the war is another matter. On this line of argument we are probably forced to rule out endogenous cyclical forces as causes of the slump of 1929–32.

Thus neither explanation squares with the facts neatly and we are left, as so often in economic matters, floundering in the dirty grey area where 'this, that and the other' all have some bearing on the situation, but unable to attach quantitative measurements to the factors involved. Yet we cannot say that the 1929–32 depression was caused by the war and nothing but the war, nor can we dismiss the war as having no impact on the crisis of capitalism of the inter-war period.

As a way of escape for the moment from this 'awkward corner' (the phrase is Joan Robinson's) let us see what contemporaries thought about the matter. They had few doubts. They felt that the pre-war machinery had worked well and that there was every reason to expect it to do so in the future. The pre-war direction had been all right , and little guidance or management had been required to steer development along the desired root. Hence it was simply a question of getting things quickly back to normal, and to all intents and purposes normal meant the way things were before 1914. Nor was there any doubt that it would be possible to skip merrily back into a bygone age. Such attitudes were reflected in the almost indecent haste with which war-time controls were abandoned and governments reduced their economic commitments, in the desire of America to withdraw from western Europe and not participate in the League of Nations, and in the almost fanatical belief that monetary and exchange stability must be restored at all costs. The latter desire was embodied in the frantic attempt to restore the gold standard; so great was the faith in the virtue of the former 'golden age' that statesmen and administrators were prepared to devote much of their energy during the 1920s towards the resurrection of the system. How different the position was to be after the Second World War. Then there was no question of looking back to old ideals; it was a matter of 'facing the future' with a new set of ideas and tools to guide development in a different direction.

This belief or faith in the old order may well have been genuine, though with hindsight it often appears more like a blind act of faith in the virtues of the known as opposed to the unknown. The businessmen, politicians and others who regarded the normal as the world of 1913 'failed to appreciate that modern war is a revolution, and that the economic world of 1913 had already passed into history as much as had the Habsburg and Romanoff Empires'.[1] This judgement may be harsh . It is possible that the system could have been made to work again had some of the major economic powers been prepared to make greater sacrifices. Failure was not due to any defects in the system itself; it was partly because national powers failed to recognize that circumstances had so changed as to make the system less easy to work, and partly because the powers no longer accepted the costs of operating it. And from this it follows that they were no longer ready to pursue policies which would have assisted its survival. Furthermore, this failure to appreciate that conditions had changed and a keen desire to restore the well-tried monetary system meant that little attention was paid to adapting the system to changed circumstances.

Such motives and attitudes were reflected in national economic policies throughout the 1920s. The restoration of currency stability and with it the gold standard came to be regarded as a prestige symbol or as a sign of national economic virility. But no coordinated plan of restoration was ever attempted: countries fixed their exchange rates on an *ad hoc* basis almost without reference to one another and regardless of whether the rates accorded properly with relevant costs and prices. Currency stabilization was a long drawn out affair which occupied virtually the whole decade; in the event many countries emerged with the wrong parties, the most notable cases being those of France and the United Kingdom. Having restored the pre-war system with great effort, or what amounted to an image of it, most countries were not prepared to behave in the way which had ensured its success before. The pre-1914 international monetary mechanism was essentially an exchange system in that its primary purpose was to safeguard external stability even if this meant, which it often did, sacrificing domestic stability. After the war counting the domestic cost of policy actions became much more common so that national policies were often geared towards domestic needs. This was particularly true of debtor countries anxious to foster their own industrial development but it was also true of some creditor nations, for example France, the U.S.A. and even the U.K. at times. Economic policy became more self-centred or nationalistic: in effect it was more concerned than previously with safeguarding domestic interests and less concerned with ensuring that the international economic mechanism worked smoothly. In other words, the domestic situation was no longer sacrificed completely to external needs and hence external equilibrium had to be secured by more restrictive policies. This was manifest in increasing restrictions of trade, capital and labour flows, the freedom of movement of which had been the sheet-anchor of the pre-war system. Such measures however only served to weaken the system and assist its collapse.

It is easy, however, to get the events of the 1920s out of perspective since one's views are readily influenced by the experience of the 1930s. The shift in policy emphasis was only partial in the 1920s: such restrictions and policies as were imposed to protect external equilibrium were nothing compared to the extremes of the following decade. In any case it would be difficult to argue, given the variety of factors which complicated the situation, that policy shifts were of crucial importance in reducing the viability of the international economic system. The war left behind a legacy of problems which upset the process of readjustment and made the restoration of 'normal' conditions almost impossible. For example, war debts and reparations were on a scale so vast that the problem of their solution and means of payment occupies the entire decade; this caused much international friction and intensified the difficulties of operating the international monetary system. The war also aggravated the problem of debtor countries, especially those in eastern Europe which suffered from military activity and later from currency depreciation. Supply and structural problems also featured prominently. Some of the more mature industrial economies faced excess capacity and structural problems as a result of lopsided war-time expansion, while certain primary producing countries were confronted with an over-supply situation, a factor which led to falling incomes and a decline in their imports of industrial products in the later 1920s. A consequence was increasing resort to restrictive action to maintain prices which, together with increasing tariffs and other restrictions, only made adjustment more difficult.

Yet apart from war debts and reparations, the war alone did not create all these difficulties. The origins of many can be traced back to the late nineteenth and early twentieth centuries. Increasing industrialization and competition in Europe, in Japan and even in some of the primary producing territories on the periphery of the international system gave rise to adjustments in tariff barriers and started off the drive towards economic nationalism, which became such a powerful force in the inter-war years. Problems of over-supply in primary products were not endemic in this period but the rate at which new territories were being made productive, Canada and the Argentine for example, together with the speed of technological advance, brought forward an enormous surge in the supply of certain basic products, notably coffee, wheat, and rubber, which spelled difficulties for the future. Control of prices and production of both primary commodities and manufactured goods was still in its infancy but becoming more common. And similarly, though excess capacity in industrial economies was still fairly rare, visible signs of it, especially in Britain, were certainly present. Even the international financial mechanism was not working so smoothly in 1914 as it appeared to have done some ten to fifteen years earlier.[2]

Though many post-war problems can be traced back to the period before 1914 there can be no denying that the war greatly aggravated or accentuated them. It intensified the drive towards industrialization in the as yet underdeveloped or semi-industrial areas, India, south-east Asia, Japan, Australia and parts of Latin America, and at the same time fostered the nationalistic sentiments which were burgeoning prior to the war. The war distorted the normal demand and supply relationships so that some sectors were greatly expanded in relation to normal peacetime needs. Perhaps the most striking examples were the vast expansion in shipbuilding capacity and the increase in cereals production in the regions of recent settlement. On top of these long-run problems the war also gave birth to new difficulties; it caused much physical destruction and loss of human life; it created a number of new nation states and left a legacy of political debts and currency problems.

It is clear therefore that the 1920s faced difficult economic problems of a type of severity never before experienced. Many remained partly unsolved at the end of the decade. It is equally clear that but for the war the magnitude of many would have been very much less. At this point we turn back to the question raised earlier: would the 1929–32 crisis have occurred without the war? Did the war produce so many fundamental maladjustments that the international economy could never regain its former equilibrium and the only way out was in the Great Crash?[3] Or can the crash simply be attributed to factors which are not connected with the war in any specific way? Here I am thinking of an explanation of the downturn purely in terms of internally generated causes in which policy factors dominate. The crucial role accorded to U.S. monetary policy by some writers fits the bill in this case.[4] This certainly proves very much simpler since it relieves one of the task of assigning weight to a series of war-induced causes, though it does not solve the problem completely.

We should also consider at this stage whether the 1929 downturn needs explaining in any special way. Was it not simply part of the business cycle history, that the 1929–32 depression was not unexpected and that it was no more spectacular than some previous crises except possibly in terms of duration and world-wide pervasiveness.[5] The war did nor break the pre-war pattern of business cycles.[6] In 1914 most industrial countries were about to move into a depression phase but the outbreak of war postponed this and produced a distorted continuation of the major upswing which eventually peaked in 1919–1920. The reaction came in the sharp slump of 1920–21 which was then followed, with minor interruptions, by another major upswing to a peak in 1928–29. Thus the Juglar pattern was preserved and a depression was due in about 1929. Moreover, the 1929–32 depression was no greater in amplitude in some cases than the immediate post-war slump, while its duration had been matched in crises of the nineteenth century though not simultaneously with the same intensity. Even the world-wide scope of the depression was not entirely without precedent; the post-war slump fell not far short in this respect,[7] while international recessions were not unknown in the nineteenth century. The question is therefore whether we should simply regard it as another contraction of the business cycle sequence, or whether it was unique in itself and needs to be explained by special circumstances, in particular by the maladjustments in the economic system associated with the wartime shock.[8] Obviously we shall have cause to consider this question.

Turning to a different matter we may ask whether the 1920s are an unusual decade, a special or transitional decade. Most authors cannot resist the temptation to describe their particular period as special or different from the periods immediately preceding or following. It is difficult not to succumb when so many unusual features and dramatic events dominate the period. As against the decade or so before the war it certainly seems spectacular, and even compared with the 1930s, a period fraught with the problems of recovery and the social consequences of massive unemployment, the 1920s appear eventful and lively. Beyen has described the 1920s as 'years of hope and vigour' which 'ended in despair', whereas the 1930s were simply 'years of frustration'.[9] The decade is bounded by the aftermath of the Great War and all it entailed in reconstruction and adjustment, and by the beginnings of a severe economic crisis. Economic problems not only dominated the period but were of international scope: they involved continents as well as nations. And some issues were of such magnitude that they exercised the minds of statesmen for the entire period.

Since other volumes in this series cover the war period and the 1930s[10] the present study will stick fairly closely to the confines of the 1920s. This does not mean that reference will not be made to other periods, but for the most part study begins with the aftermath of war and ends on the point of depression in 1929. No attempt will be made to discuss the depression in detail[11] but an appraisal of its causes forms the basis of one later chapter. Because of its attempted world-wide coverage it is impossible to deal with all aspects of economic development in detail. Attention is therefore focused on some of the main issues and problems which appear to be important in this period. The chapter sequence may be outlined briefly as follows.

Chapter 2 discusses the main consequences of war and the problems of adjustment while Chapter 3 examines in some detail the relief of Europe and then goes on to look at the boom and slump of 1919–21. The chronological sequence is then broken in order to deal with war debts and reparations which form the basis of Chapter 4. Chapter 5 takes up the story of recovery and reconstruction down to the middle of the 1920s. Two chapters are then devoted to monetary matters: Chapter 6 covers the stabilization problem and Chapter 7 looks more closely at the operation of the international monetary mechanism and its weaknesses. The boom of the later 1920s forms the subject of Chapter 8, which is then followed by Chapters 9 and 10 dealing with the problems of primary producers, debtor countries and the whole question of international lending. Chapter 11 reviews some explanations of the turning point of 1929 and suggests a possible sequence of events based on the analysis of the previous chapters. The final Chapter 12 then shifts ground and analyses the overall performance of the 1920s against the longer-term perspective.

Notes

[1] D. Thompson, *Europe Since Napoleon* (1966), p.601

[2] Hints to this effect are given in W. A. Brown, Jnr, *The International Gold Standard Reinterpreted, 1914–1934* (1940, 2 vols.). It should be noted, however, that recent research has shown that the international monetary system never worked as smoothly or as automatically as many contemporaries imagined. See A. I. Bloomfield, *Monetary Policy under the International Gold Standard, 1880–1914* (1959), and 'Rules of the Game of International Adjustment', in C. R. Whittlesey and J. S. G. Wilson (eds), *Essays in Money and Banking in Honour of R. S. Sayers* (1968).

[3] Briggs has suggested that it can be shown generally, using Frisch's pendulum analogy, that the dislocation casued by war produced such a shock to the economic system that great swings followed, the greatest in 1929–32, and continued throughout the entire inter-war period. But Frisch believed that the economic system was disposed to produce damped fluctuations which were only prevented from dying away by periodic shocks of one sort or another. On this basis therefore the war shock would produce its most violent reaction in 1919–21, and in the absence of a further shock the 1929–32 downswing should have been damped. The fact that it was not and that there was no additional shock of comparable magnitude suggests that we must look to other causes. See A. Briggs, 'The World Economy: Interdependence and Planning', Chapter 37, C. L. Mowat (ed.), *The Shifting Balance of World Forces, 1898–1945* (1968, vol. xii of the New Cambridge Modern History), p. 54.

[4] See M. Friedman and A. J. Schwartz, *A Monetary History of the United States, 1867–1960* (1963), and J. Pedersen, 'Some Notes on the Economic Policy of the United States during the Period 1919–1932', in H. Hegeland (ed.), *Money, Growth and Methodology: Essays in honour if Johan Akerman* (1961).

[5] Though even this requires some modification.

[6] D. H. Aldcroft and P. Fearon (eds), *British Economic Fluctuations, 1790–1939* (1972), p. 13. For what seems to be a similar view see R. A. Gordon, 'Cyclical Experience in the Interwar Period: The Investment Boom of the "Twenties"', *in National Bureau of Economic Research, Conference on Business Cycles* (1951) p. 164.

[7] Given the severity of the post-war downturn it is surprising how much less attention has been paid to it compared with the one of 1929–32.

[8] The 1929–32 crisis may be regarded as unique in that it can be said to represent the grand climax to trade cycle history (ignoring the minor dip of 1937–38) after which the

growth cycle took its place. See M. Bronfenbrenner (ed.), *Is the Business Cycle Obsolete?* (1968).

[9] J. W. Beyen, *Money in Maelstrom* (1951), p. 3.

[10] Gerd Hardach, *The First World War, 1914–1918* (1977), and C. .P. Kindleberger, *The World in Depression, 1929–1939* (1973).

[11] For which see C. P. Kindleberger, *The World Depression, 1929–1939*.

(Derek Aldcroft, *From Versailles to Wall Street 1919–1929*, Harmondsworth, Penguin, 1987, pp.2–10)

8   KARIN HAUSEN, 'THE GERMAN NATION'S OBLIGATIONS TO THE HEROES' WIDOWS OF WORLD WAR I'

Writing the social and economic history of the Weimar Republic "from below" has usually meant digging no deeper than the normal situation of the lower classes. But beneath that level there was yet another social group whose history has been forgotten – the victims of World War I, among them millions of women and children, the families of soldiers who died in the war.[1] Their story requires two narrative tracks: one tracing how they were discovered and dealt with as a "problem group" in society, and another showing how, under conditions of public support and social control, they faced crises in their private lives.

German war widows, especially those with children, paid the costs of World War I in installments of their daily lives. They were "war victims," along with disabled veterans and their wives and the mothers and fathers of fallen sons.

The war victims' pensions secured only a bare subsistence for most. Inflation, initiated by the war and increasing until late 1923, hit those dependent upon pensions particularly hard. If they wanted to earn a much-needed supplementary income, they faced as a group meager chances in a labor market already stretched by high unemployment.

When the publications of wartime and postwar social agencies are combed, they yield up testimony of these women and their sufferings, such as the following, written by a forty-six-year-old German woman in 1930:

In August, 1914, after five years of happy marriage, my husband was called up for military service. He left me behind with three children, aged one, two and three years. In September, 1916, he was wounded and in December sent back home to work for three months. On March 17, 1917, he died from his war injuries. At that time I was 10 weeks pregnant ... The oldest boy started school in Easter. I had to go on poor relief for six months because [my husband's] war injury was being investigated. I received sixteen marks support weekly and the rent money. The money was already greatly devalued and covered only the bare necessities. Clothing or other purchases were out of the question ... On September 24 my last boy was born, a child who never knew his father. On September 26, my second day in childbed, I was informed that the pension had been approved ... Thus I could ... support my children and myself and do home work on the side ... I stayed up working many nights while others slept and when morning came returned exhausted to my household duties.

The widow goes on to recount the fates of her three sons, who, lacking the funds for university education, had learned trades and then faced long periods of unemployment with only minimal relief. The youngest son, then thirteen, was still in school.

Because of the war I had to work to the point of exhaustion in order to supplement my meager pension. Thus, in 1923, after long sacrifice and much work, I had to drop everything and take care of myself. After a five-week illness at home [complete nervous breakdown, the effects of cold, undernourishment, and severe anemia], I had to go into the hospital for complete rest and then to a sanitarium.

When the children were small I always hoped things would get better when they were older and were earning money ... For the last two years I have not been able to earn anything because my household makes demands on me different from those it made when the children were younger. Besides, I am forty-six years old and I do not have much strength left after a life of so much worry and labor.[2]

Sixteen years of wartime and postwar history as it was lived by one woman: she finally lost hope that her situation might improve when her children grew up. The world economic crisis left only the grim prospect of continuing poverty and loneliness in old age. Other widows surveyed in 1930 echoed her lament: "The great inflation was the most terrible time for the dependents of the war dead. The state can never redress what we and our children had to suffer through the total devaluation of our pensions." Another recalls, "I remember that my pension for two weeks once only bought four pounds of bread. I was forced to send my youngest out begging in the neighbourhood so that the others could take some bread to work." And a third: "Many times we went to bed hungry. I still remember how the widows and orphans thronged the local war relief office."[3] For these women and their families, wartime conditions did not end with the armistice but persisted for decades afterward.

According to the first published figures of 1922, of the 13.25 million German men called up for military service, 1.69 million had died. Later estimates placed the number of people who had died in or as a result of the war at 2.4 million.[4] Of these men, nearly half were twenty-five or younger when they met "a hero's death," and nearly a third were married. In 1924 the government recognized the right to support of approximately 1.6 million financial dependents of the men killed in the war. These included 371,795 widows, 1,031,409 orphans and half-orphans, 113,607 widowed mothers, 17,580 widowed fathers, and 62,734 parents as couples.[5] The total number of women widowed by the war must have been about 600,000, but by 1924 approximately one third of them had apparently remarried and become ineligible for widows' pensions. In the period that followed, the number of widows eligible for pensions scarcely changed, remaining at around 362,190 in 1930. Of the 364,950 widows still receiving pensions in 1924, 88.9 percent were between thirty and fifty years old. Some 286,624 of them supported 594,843 children under eighteen who were still eligible for dependents' allowances. Nearly one third of the widows had one child, 24.9 percent had two children, 13.8 percent had three, and 9.3 percent had four or more children to support.[6]

In order to assess the magnitude of these figures, it should be added that the German Empire in 1925 had a total population of 62.4 million, and that 2.8 million widows and 182,536 divorced women lived alongside 12.7 million married women. There were thus two widows for every nine married women, as opposed to only two widowers for every twenty-nine married men.[7] Among the nation's widows, the 400,000 war widows stood out because they were younger and had smaller children and better pensions than the others.

In the prewar society of the German Empire, families without "breadwinners," children without the "strong hand" of a father, and women without the "moral support" of a husband would have been seen as anomalies when measured and judged against the norm of an orderly family life. But this society would have paid less attention to the poor but honest widow or abandoned wife supported and supervised by a poor relief fund than to the unwed mother whose baby, not least out of pronatalist considerations, was to be given better physical and moral chances of survival. World War I, with its mass slaughter of husbands and fathers, blurred the previously clear border between socially marginal groups and an established, norm-setting majority with "orderly" family circumstances. To remedy this perceived threat to German family life, social leaders proposed war welfare for all soldiers' families.

War widows and orphans became a new client group in this welfare program on April 16, 1915, when a conference on "Social Welfare for War Widows and Orphans" opened at the Reichstag in Berlin with these words: "Every day the German soldier faces his enemy and looks death in the eye, but today it is our duty to remove his heaviest care, that for his wife and child. In this conference we are to suggest the ways and means to absolve the German people's debt of gratitude and to do justice to those left behind by our fallen soldiers."[8]

The "soldier cares" and the "debt of gratitude," not the hard living conditions of widows' children, served as the rationale for a conference whose first task was to grapple with the fact that the misery of those left behind by the war had been little considered during the mobilization of the homefront. Initiated by the German Federation for Poor Relief and Charity (Deutscher Verien Für Armenpflege and Wohltätigkeit), the central organization of private, communal, and regional poor relief associations, the conference attracted over thirteen hundred representatives of all levels of government, the churches, old age insurance institutions, federations and societies, as well as individuals from all over Germany and Austria. All parties, denominations, classes, and interest groups, men and women, were represented. Only the war widows themselves were nowhere to be seen. No shrill or discordant notes disturbed the display of harmonious national unity that characterized the two-day conference.

In the papers and discussions, war widows appear as a social problem first of all because the prewar law on allowances for military casualties' dependents regulated pensions solely on the basis of military service grades, without differentiating accordingly to the social position of the fallen. This problem was intensified because the war widows' plight assigned them contradictory sets of responsibilities: those of mother and breadwinner. It was considered especially important to protect the now fatherless children from neglect. Providing for children in homes for war orphans was suggested but rejected. According to one of the conferees, "[i]t is true that when the father dies, the family loses its head, the strong hand of the educator, and the breadwinner, but, on the other hand, the child needs the love, care and work of its mother if she can somehow fulfill the duties of feeding and education."[9] So the question of waged work for widows with several small children became central to the discussion.

Was it true that "the problem of employment and motherhood, of employment and housework, could not be solved,"[10] even by emergency action, or did the war open opportunities for far-reaching innovations? All the conferees agreed that children must remain with their mothers, but it was the feminists who, as an extension of their prewar discussions, came forward with a provocative solution. They did not fall back on home work as the best way to combine family and workplace. Instead they maintained that paid employment must no longer be measured solely against male work patterns. It would be necessary to find "time arrangements and workloads which would not interfere with the maternal role."[11] Gertrud Hanna, the secretary for women workers in the socialist labor unions, argued even more decisively: "[a]s long as housework is still based upon the individual households, and as long as there are no major changes in child care, the household economy and children, especially the smaller children, must remain in the hands of the housewife and mother." She considered it appropriate to guarantee the economic situation of mothers with small children because "the higher compensation for such mothers is nothing more than their compensation for the work they perform for the public good in caring for and educating their children. This work deserves compensation as much as any occupation."[12]

Kaethe Gaebel, known for her activities in home work reform, argued that paying "capable" mothers for raising their own children, just as foster mothers were paid, would create an "inner recognition that the occupation of mother is a public service performed in the national interest."[13] Finally, Helene Simon, who later organized welfare offices for dependents of fallen soldiers, carried the radical wages-for-housework argument a step further to include unwed mothers.

In their discussion the conferees covered all the central issues and problems of widows' paid employment: that women would be divided between their work as mothers and as wage-earners, that they could fail to advance professionally, that widows because of drawing an additional income from pensions could dangerously depress wages, and that the jobs suitable for widows in the civil and municipal service might later be needed for long-service noncommissioned officers or disabled veterans.

This discussion on widows as mothers and motherhood as a profession deserving compensation reveals the gender ambiguities of wartime society. The conferees were aware that, because men's patriotic engagement at the front rendered precarious public and private male dominance at home, they had to tread carefully on men's vested interests. In the discourse of the conference, the concern over male prerogatives was reflected in the contrast between a vigorous emphasis on the desirability of the presence of the father and breadwinner, and the simultaneous consideration of ways to organize the social replacement of these fathers, whose absence was now both real and, in the case of the war widows, permanent. In this context Helene Simon skillfully combined both sides of the contemporary understanding of war widows and orphans. She couched her remarks on the pathos of the patriotic front:

> War widows must not be forced to take outside employment. It is our most sacred duty to the fallen soldier, so proud of his home and of being able to free his wife from the burden of wage work, to allow her to devote herself completely to maintaining his home and children. ... We are not asking for alms or supplementary pensions, but rather for payment for worked performed, sufficient to redeem all the moral and economic, national and individual value of the mother's professional achievement.[14]

Essential elements of future family policy were foreshadowed in these discussions. The children's allowance came after 1933, with the significant revision that it was not paid as part of the mother's income but rather as a supplement to the breadwinner's.

Until the Reichstag conference, relief for dependents of men killed in or dead as a result of the war had been regulated by the 1907 Military Casualties' Dependents' Law (*Militärhinterbliebenengesetz*), which proved insufficient to handle the results of the mass mobilization practiced for the first time in World War I.[15] The law determined the size of pensions solely on the basis of military rank, allowing for no consideration of social situations or local differences. Widows of enlisted men, who made up 98 percent of the casualties, received a monthly pension of 33.33 marks plus 14 marks for each child. It was already apparent in 1914 that the pension payments were inadequate, even for minimum subsistence, for a widow with one to three children in a large city or industrial region. Despite repeated intervention, a thorough legal revision of relief for families of fallen soldiers was rejected during the war, prompting charitable organizations to call for the conference as a means of drawing attention to the dire situation of these dependents.

In the period that followed, some temporary – and insufficient – measures were taken under the direction of the Ministry of War in an attempt to prevent downward mobility. A decree of August 14, 1915, authorized payment of a hardship compensation based upon the prewar wages of the deceased. The total income of fatherless families was not to exceed 75 percent of the dead man's prewar income, with a ceiling of 3,000 marks a year. Because it was intended to maintain status rather than to aid the impoverished, however, the decree *excluded* families whose prewar income was less than 1,500 marks for enlisted men and 1,700 marks from noncommissioned officers.

With the accelerating inflation rate the financial situation of those drawing pensions worsened even in comparison to that of military families. Out of consideration for the mood at the front, relief to families of living soldiers was raised twice during 1916, but pensions for dependents of fallen soldiers remained the same, and demands for an inflation supplement for them were also rejected. Welfare agencies protested repeatedly against this ruling, arguing that "discontent" and "bitterness" would surely result if a woman were confronted with not only the report of her husband's death but also a significant loss of income. Women living in Berlin who received 67.50 marks a month as a soldier's wife collected only 47.33 marks as a widow. Even if some widows received an additional orphan's allowance under the Imperial Insurance Law of

1911, their financial situation nevertheless declined because upon their husband's death they lost both their municipal rent allowance and the support frequently offered by former employers of soldiers.[16]

Not until April, 1917, were needy soldiers' widows and children eligible for a rent supplement. The decree of November 26, 1917, stipulated that the additional allowances could be paid as continuous support without an upper limit, in order to equalize the incomes of families of living and dead soldiers. A few cities had already undertaken such an adjustment out of their own funds. In 1916, for example, Cologne began paying widows 42 marks in addition to their widow's pensions, plus 16.50 marks per child.[17] Even though by the end of 1917 the purchasing power of the mark had sunk to half its prewar strength, the policy remained "to approve revocable allowances and equalization benefits only in case where the present family income was below 75 percent or in some cases 100 percent of the prewar level."[18]

A general increase in dependents' allowances did not come until June, 1918. War widows received an additional 8 marks, and each child under sixteen received 3 marks, without having to demonstrate need. In light of rapidly rising prices, a one-time inflation supplement of 50 percent of dependents' monthly payments was approved on January 22, 1919. Not until June 1, 1919, were dependents with a right to claim relief awarded a continuous inflation supplement of 40 percent of their monthly pensions. This regulation followed large national demonstrations by disabled veterans and dependent families in April, 1919. Further inflation supplements followed until May 12, 1920, when, as a long-overdue amendment to the Military Casualties' Dependents' Law, the National Relief Law (*Reichsversorgungsgesetz*) was passed. This bill took account of all grievances voiced during the war and, for the first time in German social legislation, considered child maintenance in calculating widow's pensions. Even this recalculation of pensions had to be constantly revised under conditions of galloping inflation.

During the entire period of the war and the immediate postwar years, the pensions of fallen soldiers' families were insufficient for even the most urgent necessities.[19] Families with children in particular remained dependent upon donations of clothing and shoes. Worst placed of all were those who were ineligible for relief for one of several reasons: the cause of death was not considered a result of military service, the man was missing, or he had committed suicide on the front.

The Germans' enthusiasm for the war stimulated the development of numerous charitable activities alongside the state's dependents' relief programs. The Mutual Insurance Funds for the 1914 War, founded in 1914 to provide a kind of reinsurance for men whose patriotism had led to irresponsibility toward their families, were quickly frustrated by lack of financing. Some professional organizations and businesses started to sponsor the education of members' or employees' war orphans. Public old age disability insurance institutions made honorary, one-time payments (called *Ehrenbeihilfen* or *Dankes-und-Ehrengaben*) to the widows and orphans of insurance policy holders.[20] On December 18, 1916, the National League for the Sponsorship of War Orphans (Reichsverband fur Kriegspatenschaften) was founded with much pomp at the Reichstag. Under the patronage of the Prussian Ministry of War, it served propaganda purposes rather than effectively aiding dependents. In the opinion of its initiators, "the undertaking of sponsorship of war orphans is to express our feelings of gratitude to the soldiers who have given their lives for the fatherland. The sponsors will fulfill the testament of the fallen men by seeing that their children are raised to be capable people, sound in mind and body. Any German man or woman who possesses the appropriate personality and character traits can sponsor a war orphan."[21]

Only the National Foundation for Dependents of Fallen Soldiers (Nationalstiftung für die Hinterbliebenen der im Kriege Gefallenen), founded in 1914 under the chairmanship of the Prussian minister of the interior, achieved nationwide significance.[22] Its purpose was to organize a broad-based relief system for the families of soldiers that would supplement the legal pension program through individualized support and thus prevent the downward social mobility of dependents. The foundation's capital was drawn from donations. The main support came from organizations such as The War Contribution of Grateful German Women (*Kriegesspende Deutscher Frauendank 1915*), a collection campaign run jointly by all the larger women's organizations, and from industry. In 1916 the Krupp Foundation joined the National Foundation with 20 million marks. From 1916 to the end of 1918, the foundation spent a total of 20.25 million marks on dependents' relief. It also began to provide more than merely financial aid – its state, provincial, and local offices became points of departure for institutionalized social welfare programs for dependents of military casualties.

To return to the development which had its beginning in the Reichstag conference of April, 1915: this conference strove to institutionalize a unified approach to social relief for dependents of military casualties on a municipal and local level, and to develop a central organization to coordinate local interests on a national level. To this end, a Central Committee for War Widows' and Orphans' Welfare was formed at the conference, with fifty-six men and fifteen women as members. In June, 1915, a working committee was formed by a smaller group of men and women well known for their involvement in various charity, social welfare, and social reform organizations.[23] In an effort to promote the installation of an efficient, uniform national system of welfare, they publicized the problems and attempted solutions of individual communities and made important suggestions for uniform procedures and organization. In 1918 the Central Committee merged with the National Foundation.[24]

As welfare provisions and regulations became more elaborate, more complex bureaucratic machinery was needed to put them into effect. For example, applications for the "revocable supplements" paid in addition to dependents' pensions requires individual investigation and approval. At first the police performed this task, but by 1916 the Prussian government was beginning to turn it over to welfare agencies with official connections, and eventually communal agencies were established for this purpose.[25] By the end of 1917 there were at least five thousand official dependents' welfare offices in the Reich, including those organized by government authorities, committees of the National Foundation, and other relief agencies.[26] The insitutionalization of dependents' welfare was intended to be permanent. A regulation of February 8, 1919, finally organized social welfare for disabled veterans and dependents of military casualties on a uniform basis.

During the war, the progressive interconnection of all dependents' relief activities and the centralization of all relevant information in one local office was considered advantageous because it allowed an overview of support activities and thus ensured "the most just and efficient distribution of relief possible."[27] The integration of various communal, church, and private relief agencies into a more centralized local welfare system under state control may have opened the way for more efficient aid, but at the same time it installed the preconditions of greater social control. To be sure, bureaucratic procedures varied from one agency to another. In some places war widows had files at the local dependents' welfare office even before they sought help. In others, files were not requested until the widow came to seek aid. But all offices wanted to have as much information as possible about "their" clients.

At times, the welfare offices' detailed investigation of the circumstances of those seeking advice and aid imitated the style of the police. In 1916, when the director of the welfare agency for war widows and orphans in Gleiwitz found that few clients were visiting the office, he determined to summon several widows at a time for appearances. Female assistants interviewed the clients and also had "the task of visiting the women at home, checking the circumstances they found there against the application, and making an extensive report on the questionnaire."[28] This extreme example illustrates not only the process of social control but also the division of labor by gender that pervaded welfare offices. Agencies also sought to influence their clients' behaviour. A report from the city of Recklinghausen noted: "The 'dutiful' housewives were rewarded with special donations, clothing collections, and so on. As a result even the negligent ones began to place more importance on their households and made efforts to keep their homes clean."[29]

As in prewar time, social control and social relief went together, even for war widows, whose legal claim to pensions did not guarantee them an existence. But the practical aid offered by the welfare offices might have been quite essential for their clients. They assisted widows in applying for pension supplements or establishing their eligibility for public social insurance funds. If a widow needed help to arrange rent payment, pay off debts on furniture, or procure moving allowances, a temporary advisor could be appointed. Indigent families received food, clothing, and fuel grants as well as health care, sanitarium care, medical treatment allowances, and medication. Occupational counseling and employment were also provided. For widows with small children who had to earn money, agencies proposed childcare arrangements with relatives, provided home work, and in some cases arranged for education grants to help unite motherhood and wage work.

The efficient but probably also very costly welfare bureaucracy undertook investigations into welfare cases and maintained documents with the same enthusiasm that it brought to individual problems. In general the welfare agencies seem to have offered effective aid in the period immediately following the husband's death. At the same time, they clearly invaded their clients' privacy, claiming the right to unlimited observation of their living conditions, and freely engaging in surveillance, manipulation, and control.

It is difficult, but not impossible, to go beyond the intentions and actions of relief bureaucrats and get to the widows and orphans themselves. One can find descriptions of particularly striking cases, such as the story of Mrs B. from

Berlin, who was accustomed to her husband's monthly income of 400–500 marks and had to survive after his death on a pension of 69 marks along with her children, two and three years old. There is also the case of a sickly forty-three-year old woman with a fifteen-year-old daughter, whose monthly income slid from 300–400 marks in peacetime to 51 marks during her husband's military service and then to 47.33 marks after his death. We can see the dramatic effects of the economic emergency in the case of a family with three children whose father was discharged from the military service in September, 1914 with tuberculosis. He could not work and received only unemployment relief of 5 marks a month until his death in May, 1915. From then until October, 1916, the welfare office helped his wife in her eventually successful fight for a war widow's pension.[30]

The welfare offices also attempted to gather statistics to describe the war widows under their care. The figures suggest that in general widows seeking help at the local welfare offices were almost all (95 percent) younger than forty, half of them under thirty. All but 12 percent had children to support; 31 percent had one child, 27 percent had two, 15 percent had three and 15 percent had four or more. Over half the children were six or under. During the war, the number of widows who performed wage work varied from place to place and from year to year. A report on 1,900 widows in Hamburg for the end of 1917, a time of labor shortage, revealed that before marriage 78 percent of the women had been employed, but only 5 percent continued working for wages after marriage. As widows, 52 percent of them were again earning money – as unskilled workers (20.8 percent), house servants (19 percent), skilled workers (18.6 percent), white-collar workers (13 percent), civil service employees (12 percent), by running businesses (7.4 percent) and renting rooms (4.6 percent), and through other occupations (4.6 percent). In Mönchen-Gladbach only 41 percent of 220 widows had taken up paid employment by mid-1916, although 89 percent had worked for wages before marriage. In Hagen, 77.5 percent of the widows had held jobs before marriage, 64 percent of them as servants, but in mid-1916 only 46 percent were working for wages. The percentage of employed widows in Berlin-Schöneberg, 88.8 in mid-1915, was very high in comparison. Some 95 percent had had work experience before marrying, 57.4 percent as servants. As widows, 29 percent were daily cleaners in the households of others and 29 percent did home work, that is, work on the lowest end of the pay scale.[31]

Information on the widows' husbands reveals just how much their incomes plummeted during the war. Ninety-eight percent of them had died as enlisted men or at most noncommissioned officers. One-third had been unskilled workers in civilian life. Skilled workers and master craftsmen, at 45 percent, represented the largest group. Before the war more than 80 percent had earned a monthly income of more than 100 marks; with entrance into military service, this had shrunk to a minimum. In Berlin, 174 households consisting of war widows with children were surveyed by the relief office in mid–1915.[32] Their incomes, composed of war relief, communal supplement, rent supplement, and in some cases support from the husband's employer, followed a sharp downward course (see table).

Monthly Income of Prewar, Soldiers', and War Widows' Households

	Prewar	Soldiers'	Widows' (mid-1915)
0–100 marks	6.3%	78.7%	78.1%
101–150 marks	65.5	15.5	17.8
151–200 marks	21.3	3.4	2.3
201–300 marks	6.3	2.3	1.7
301+ marks	0.6	–	–

The longer the war continued, the more difficult it became for women to cope with radical reductions of the household budget. Wartime conditions, inflation that halved the value of the mark, shortages – above all of clothing and shoes – and the constant need to pay black-market prices for essential foods destroyed families' living standards. As early as mid-1915, the Berlin Center for Private Relief noted that, of the 500 war widows who had applied to them, 252 were ill. Alongside internal and lung ailments (63.5 percent of illnesses), 92 women were found to be suffering from nervous and physical exhaustion (36.5 percent of illnesses). Eleven women were pregnant.[33] The widows' health must have worsened rapidly with the immiserization of war.

When it became clear that upon her husband's death the old standard of living was gone forever, impossible economic problems accumulated for the widow. Her apartment was often too expensive, and it became increasingly difficult to find lodgers. The rent allowances provided to soldiers' wives by the municipal authorities were unavailable to widows. Back rent mounted while the woman looked for a smaller, affordable apartment. Many families were still burdened with installment payments on items purchased before the war, especially furniture, and furniture dealers used all possible means to retrieve the outstanding payments. The situation was even more critical if the husband had borrowed money to set himself up in a trade or small shop and the widow was not in a position to carry on the business. Selling the business was difficult and often entailed heavy losses.

According to all reports the transition period was particularly crucial. The despondent widow, often ill and weakened, found her life encircled by debts, her choices restricted by small children, and her possibilities for returning to wage work limited. In this situation she might get help from relatives or neighbours or find her way to the welfare office, which could solve or at least alleviate some of her overwhelming problems with donations or personal advice and aid. Given the magnitude of their problems and the relative dearth of resources, it is astonishing that so many women and their families were able to survive the descent into extreme poverty and eventually learn to cope with their new condition.

The silence surrounding the hard, gray, everyday realities of wartime and postwar life is part of the pathos of hero worship. The innumerable war monuments in the city squares block our view of the realities of war for these women. Instead, women are portrayed as pietas, suffering the glory of their heroic sons. The president of the German Reichstag expressed this mode of commemoration at the opening of the third wartime session on December 2, 1918:

Heavy, too, the losses of human life demanded by the war. Many a woman's heart is consumed by grief at the death of her fallen husband and brother, many a father's and mother's heart aches for the sons torn from them. We honor their pain and mourn with them, but the fatherland thanks them and is proud of so many heroic sons who have spilt their blood and laid down their lives in the World War we are fighting for our own existence.[34]

Such lofty words provided little comfort for the hungry, homeless, and insecure widows whose anxieties about their own welfare and that of their children would linger for years to come. But the discourse of public commemoration could not simultaneously maintain the mythos of male heroism and also acknowledge women's real, if mundane, hardships. Instead, the widows were silenced, their testimony locked away in bureaucratic files.

Notes

[1] Only recently has this situation been changed by the new book of Robert Weldon Whalen, *Bitter Wounds: German Victims of the Great War, 1914–1939* (Ithaca: Cornell University Press, 1984); and Michael Geyer's important article, "Ein Vorbote des Wohlfahrsstaates, die Kriegsopferversorgung im Frankreich nach dem ersten Weltkrieg," *Geschichte und Gesellschaft 9* (1983), 230–77, which concentrates on the disabled soldiers. But the subject of war widows is omitted, for example, in such studies as J. Kocka, *Klassengesellschaft im Krieg: Deutsche Sozialgeschichte 1914–1918*, Göttingen, 1973, repr. 1978); and G. Mai, *Kriegswirtschaft und Arbeiterbewegung in Württemburg, 1914–1918* (Stuttgart, 1983); as well as more detailed case studies such as K.-D. Schwartz, *Weltkrieg und Revolution in Nürnberg* (Stuttgart, 1971); and V. Ullrich, *Die Hamburger Arbeiterbewegubg vom Vorabend des Ersten Weltkriegs bis zur Revolution 1918/19* (Hamburg, 1976). Literature on women and war, such as U. V. Gersdorff, *Frauen im Kriegsdienst, 1914–1918* (Stuttgart, 1969); and C. Boyd, "*Nationaler Frauendienst*: German Middle-Class Women in Service to the Fatherland, 1914–1918" (Ph.D. diss., University of Georgia, 1979), does not take account of daily life problems. See the forthcoming Ph.D. dissertation by U. Daniel (University of Bielefeld) on the social history of the German homefront.

[2] H. Hurwitz-Stranz, *Kriegerwitwen gestalten ihr Schicksal: Lebenskämpfe deutsche Kriegerwitwen nach eigenee Darstellungen* (Berlin, 19131), 85–88.

[3] Ibid., 58, 78–79, 86.

[4] Figures may be found in *Wirtschaft und Statistik 2*, (1922), 385–87, 487; E. Kirsten, E. W. Buchholz, and W. Köllmann, *Raum und Bevölkerung in der Weltgeschichte*, pt.3 (Würzburg, 1955) 296. The 1.69 million mortalities break down as follows: 241, 343 soldiers in 1914; 434,034 in 1915; 340,468 in 1916; 281,905 in 1917; 379,777 in 1918; and 14,314 in 1919.

[5] *Wirtschaft und Statistik 5* (1925) 28–30; *Reichsarbeitsblatt* (1925), no. 4. Unofficial part. pp. 64–73; ibid (1926), no. 24, unofficial part, pp. 424–29; and *Deutschlands Kriegsbeschädigte, Kriegshinterbliebene und sonstige Versorgungsberechtige. Stand Oktober von 1924. Bearbeitet im Reichsarbeitsministerium nach Zahlung der Statistischen Reichamts* (n.p., n.d).

[6] Hurwitz-Stranz, Kriegerwitwen gestalten ihr Schicksal, 133–34.

[7] *Statistik des Deutschen Reichs* 401(Berlin, 1930), 174–75.

[8] See *Soziale Fürsorge für Kriegerwitwen und Kriegerwaisen, Allgemeine Deutsche Tagung einberufen vom Deutschen Verien fur Armenpflege und Wohltätigkeit am 16. Und 17. April 1915, im Plenarsitzungssaal des Reichstags in Berlin: Stenographische Berichte uber die Verhandlungen* (Munchen, 1915), 2.
The sources for my essay are primarily printed publications of the Soziale

Kriegshinterbliebeneinfürsorge. For the larger context of social policy and welfare in Germany, see R. Landwehr and R. Baron, *Geschichte der Sozialarbeit: Hauptlinien iherer Entwicklung im 19. Und 20. Jahrhundert* (weinheim, 1983); L. Preller, *Sozialpolitik in der Wiemarer Republik* (1949, repr. Kronberg/Th., 1978); G. A. Ritter, *Sozialversicherung in Deutschland und England: Entstehung und Grundzüge im Vergleich* (München, 1983); and F. Tennstedt, *Sozialgeschichte der Sozialpolitik in Deutschland* (Göttingen).

[9] *Soziale Fürsorge*, 15.

[10] Ibid., 53.

[11] Ibid., 56

[12] Ibid., 61.

[13] Ibid., 125.

[14] Ibid., 29–30. For the prewar discussion, see B. Greven-Ashoff, *Die bürgerliche Frauenbewegung in Deutschland, 1894–1933* (Göttingen, 1981), 62–69; I. Stoehr, "'Organisierte Mütterlichkeit': Zur Politik der deutschen Frauenbewegung um 1900," in K. Hausen, ed., *Frauen suchen ihre Geschichte* (München, 1982), 221–49.

[15] Critical comments in *Soziale Praxis* 25 (1916), 346–50; *Soziale Kriegbinterbliebenenfürsorge* (cited hereafter as *SKHF*) (1917), 118–20. The following statements are based on *Denkschrift des Reicharbeitsministeriums betr. Die bisherigen Aufwendungen für Kriegshinterbliebene vom 16. Oktober 1916*, in *Stenographische Berichte der Verhandlungen des Deutschen Reichstags*, vol. 339, Aktenstück 1281, 1276–80. It should be added that, in spite of the famous Bismarckian social insurance programs in place in prewar Germany, most working-class widows had no claim to a pension.

[16] *SKHF* (1917), 21, 38, 57, 76; *SKHF* (1918), 34.

[17] See *Zur Theorie und Praxis der Kriegshinterbliebenenfürsorge (Schriften des Arbeitsausschusses der Kriegerwitwen- und Waisenfürsorge, ed. Im Auftrage des Hauptausschusses, n. 3)* (Berlin, 1916), 32 (cited hereafter as *Theorie und Praxis*).

[18] *SKHF* (1917), 143; estimates of inflation rates in Kocka, *Klassengesellschaft*, 17, SKHF (1919), 40–41 noted critically that the well-organized disabled veterans received a one-time inflation supplement of 100 percent on December 31, 1918, while the widows got only 50 percent on January 22, 1919.

[19] For the development of pensions and allowances and the total amount paid by the Reich, see *Reichstag*, vol. 339, 1277–78.

[20] Information in *Soziale Praxis* 23 (1913–14), 1325, 1353; *SKHF* (1918), 4; *Soziale Praxis* 24 (1914–15), 202.

[21] Speech at the foundation, quoted in *Soziale Praxis* 26 (1916), 258.

[22] For the following see *SKHF* (1916), 4; *SKHF* (1917), 19, 76–77, 92; *Reichstag*, vol. 339, 1279.

[23] *Theorie und Praxis*, 6–29.

[24] *SKHF* (1918), 15–20, 29.

[25] *Theorie und Praxis*, 41.

[26] *SKHF* (1918)

[27] *SKHF* (1917)

[28] *Theorie und Praxis*, 41.

[29] IBid., 58.

[30] Ibid., 10, and *Die Frau* 24 (December 1916), 137–38.

[31] Information on Charlottenburg, Schöneberg, Berlin, and Worms in *Aus der Praxis der Kriegshinterbliebenenfürsorge* (*Schriften des Arbeitsausschusses*, n. 2) (Berlin, 1916); on Bochum, Hagen, Frankfurt, and Mönchen-Gladbach in *Theorie und Praxis;* on Hamburg in *SKHF* (1918), 100; on Landkreis Recklinghausen in *SKFH* (1919), 8.

[32] *Hinterbliebenenfürsorge: Mitteilungen aus der Zentrale für Privatfürsorge e.V. in Berlin, August, 1915* (Berlin, 1915), 44–46.

[33] Ibid., 41.

[34] *Reichstag*, vol. 306, 14.

M. R. Higgonet *et al.*, *Behind the Lines: Gender and the Two World Wars*, New Haven, Yale University Press, 1987, pp.126–40)

9   IAN KERSHAW, FROM *HITLER 1889–1936: HUBRIS*

The mass of German people had no part in, or knowledge of, the intrigues of high politics in the second half of 1932. They were by now largely powerless to affect the political dramas which would determine their future. As autumn turned to winter, they were entering upon the fourth year of deepening misery in the apparently unending Depression.

Statistics provide only an abstract glimmer of the human suffering. Industrial production had fallen by 42 per cent since 1929. The stocks and shares index had dropped by more than two-thirds. In the hard-hit agrarian sector, which had felt crisis long before the general Depression had caught hold, compulsory farm-sales had more than doubled. Falling demand, prices, and income had brought mounting indebtedness. Above all, the dark shadow of mass unemployment on an unprecedented scale hung over the country. The Employment Offices recorded 5,772,984 persons without work at the end of 1932; in January 1933 the figure was 6,013,612. Taking into account short-time workers and hidden unemployment, it was reckoned that the real total already in October 1932 had reached 8,754,000. This meant that close on half of the work-force was either fully or partially unemployed. Towns offered free meals at soup kitchens, cheap or free warm baths for the unemployed, and warming-houses where they could shelter in winter.

The politically radicalized among the unemployed had fed mainly the ranks of the KPD [Communist Party of Germany] – *par excellence* the party of the young, unemployed males – the overwhelming proportion of whose 320–360,000 members by late 1932 had no work. Not a few also found their way to the Nazi stormtroopers. Both the Communists and the Nazis offered an organizational framework of support, forms of political activism, and the vision of a better society to the young unemployed. But alongside the unemployed who became radicalized, a great number were simply resigned and apathetic, imagining that all governments had failed and none was capable of mastering the problems which had brought about their fate. A few days before Hitler's appointment to the Chancellorship, in conditions of freezing cold, the people of the small town of Ettlingen in Baden could not engender the slightest interest in an SA parade.

There had been no shortage of demonstrations, they said. 'If only we had as much bread and work.'

Nor could a younger generation whose 'working lives' had been entirely without work find much enthusiasm for a self-professed working-class party, the SPD, which had – however necessary it had objectively been – kept Brüning in office and voted Hindenburg back to power. Not a few would shrug their shoulders several years later and say that at least Hitler had brought them work, which the working class parties before 1933 had failed to do. It was abbreviated logic. But it was how many felt.

Mass unemployment split and atomized the working class not just at the party-political and ideological level, but at its social roots. For those still fortunate enough to have work, self-confidence was eaten away by fear of losing their jobs, by the loss of the power of the unions, exposure to employer aggressiveness, and – so far as they were sympathizers of the Social Democrats [the SPD] – by the SPD's perceived failure to look after working-class interests. The disorientation and disillusionment of so many former SPD supporters after 1933, however little they were won over by the Nazi regime, stemmed from what they saw as its unmitigated failure in the crisis of the state of which it was the main pillar.

In the countryside, too, there was a widespread feeling of hopelessness. Apathy sprang from the sense that there was no sign of improvement, whoever was in government. The mood of deep resignation had spread in areas of bedrock Nazi support in autumn 1932 after Hitler had turned down a chance of entering government and the NSDAP's [Nazi Party] promises were no nearer realization. From one district of Franconia, where the NSDAP had built up a high level of support, it was reported in the first days of January 1933 that 'the mood of the rural population is calm but extraordinarily depressed on account of the continued fall in prices of all agricultural products. A certain despondency has taken over. One gains the impression that many of those who had previously put their hopes in Hitler have become sceptical and have lost hope in any improvement.' The sentiments, the report claimed, were general ones, not confined to that district.

The disconsolate mood intermingled with enormous bitterness and political radicalization. From Lower Bavaria in January 1933 it was reported that 'all attacks on the government find a lively echo among the peasants; the more caustic the language, the more pleasant it sounds in their ears'. The anger was further fired up by news that 'Eastern Aid' (*Osthilfe*), intended for restoring agricultural prosperity on impoverished properties in eastern Germany, was lining the pockets of big landowners and being used for luxury expenditure. Bitterness towards all Weimar governments and parties, each of which was seen to have failed the people, was a hallmark of popular feeling in the countryside as it was in the towns. 'No one wants to know anything of parliamentary government, since all large parties had failed' was the reported mood in one Bavarian region in December 1932 – a feeling certainly not confined to that part of the country. The Nazi Party was not excluded from such criticism. 'The party leaders are blamed for being led in their decisions less by considerations of people and Fatherland than by those of the party and themselves. It is especially held against the NSDAP that it has recently shunned responsibility and does not follow its wide-ranging promises with action.' No expectations were placed in

Hitler in this region. 'Apart from National Socialists,' the report went on, at this point reflecting the weighting of a heavily Catholic region, 'more or less all the remaining sections are negatively disposed towards a Hitler dictatorship.' It concluded: 'Under the impact of economic distress and the disunity of other parties, the KPD is flourishing.' At the same time, the despair was such that *any* political leader outside the ranks of the dreaded Marxists who could bring about economic improvement was guaranteed – at least in the short term – to attract support. This was to Hitler's advantage once he became Chancellor. The feeling that Hitler should at least be given the chance to see what he could do coexisted with initial scepticism.

For other social groups, too, the expectations placed in Hitler's movement and the motivations that underpinned their subsequent support or antipathy were strongly influenced by experiences in the Depression years. The way society and government had fallen apart in those years brought to the boil the welling resentment at the democratic system and sense of national humiliation that had been simmering throughout the Weimar era. The depth of anger towards those held responsible was one side of the response. The desire for social harmony and unity – to be imposed by the elimination of those seen to threaten it – was the other, and intrinsically related side.

The report from one locality in Franconia in December 1932 brought out how sectionalized grievances combined to create generalized disaffection. Businessmen were complaining about poor turnover, ran the report, farmers about low produce prices, teachers and civil servants about their salaries, workers about unemployment, the unemployed about levels of support, and war-cripples and war-widows about drops in their pensions. All in all, there was 'general discontent, the best preparation (*Wegbereiter*) for Communism'.

Middle-class disaffection was, naturally enough, fragmented along the lines of sectional interest. The outlook remained bleak. But despite some drop in confidence in Hitler in autumn 1932 from groups which had been a backbone of his support, no political alternatives were on offer on the Right which appeared capable of creating the conditions of national renewal and imposed social harmony needed for economic recovery. For businessmen, craftsmen and small-scale producers, the Nazis held out the prospect of salvation from the economic threat posed by department stores, consumer associations, mail-order firms and mass-production. Authoritarian rule was far from an unattractive proposition. Part of its illusion was an implied return to the 'good old days' before the First World War and protection of the 'little man' from the incursions of the modern, interventionist state. Civil servants, smarting under Brüning's salary cuts, had their own illusions of a state which would restore their own traditional status – and financial position. Teachers and lawyers also looked to renewed authority once the shackles of democratic 'interference' had been removed, and to enhanced status. Doctors, too, like lawyers a social group traditionally sympathetic to the nationalist Right, had their resentment at diminished career prospects, falling earnings, and a 'leftist' imposed funding system greatly amplified during the Depression years. Many looked to a new, authoritarian regime for rescue.

For young people, the Depression years had both in material and in psychological terms been appallingly damaging. Hopes and ideals had been blighted almost before they could take shape. By the end of 1932, four consecutive cohorts of pupils had left school to miserable prospects. Those lucky enough to find work had done so in deteriorating conditions, and were usually dismissed at the end of their apprenticeships. The youth welfare system was close to collapse. Growing suicide and youth criminality rates told their own tale. Those from more well-to-do backgrounds faced greatly diminished chances of launching a career in the professions to match their ambitions. Above average support for the Nazis among university students was one indication of middle-class youth's alienation from the Weimar Republic. In fact, the attractiveness of extremist parties of Right and Left – the NSDAP and the KPD – to young people is an indication of their different forms of alienation from Weimar democracy and their readiness to resort to political radicalism. In many respects, it was a generational revolt against a system and a society that had failed them. Militant parties capable of playing to utopian expectations could fill the void produced by the alienation. Young Germans in late 1932 were still split largely along party-political lines which themselves reflected in the main class and religious divisions. The socialist, Catholic, and – taken together – the collectivity of bourgeois youth organizations still dwarfed the Hitler Youth. But the overlap of ideals and ideology with the bourgeois youth organizations, especially, offered a rich potential for expansion to the Nazi youth leader, Baldur von Schirach, should his party start to recover from its setbacks of autumn 1932, and should his Leader manage to get to power soon.

The disaffection in German society did not, it seems, divide on gender lines. The Depression heightened the discrimination against women in the jobs market that had existed throughout the Weimar Republic. Traditional prejudice that a woman's role should be confined to 'children, kitchen, and church' was strongly reinforced. The witchhunt against 'double-earners' – where both husband and wife worked and the woman was regarded as unnecessarily occupying a 'man's job' – was an indication of growing intolerance. Nazi propaganda had no difficulty in playing on such intolerance, both before and after 1933. But anti-feminism was by no means confined to Hitler's Movement. Despite its 'macho' image, the NSDAP's views on the role of women were essentially shared by all conservative and denominational parties. Women's political behaviour in the Depression was little influenced by anti-feminism or, conversely, by pro-feminist issues. Women voted, it appears, much like men did, and presumably for the same reasons. They voted in disproportionately large numbers for the conservative and Christian parties, which were anti-feminist. They voted in smaller numbers than men for the radical parties of both Left and Right. The party with the most pronounced emancipatory stance regarding women, the KPD, was the least successful of all in attracting women's votes, and was as male-dominated a party as was the NSDAP. Despite all the talk of Hitler's mesmerizing attraction for women, the elderly, statesmanlike Hindenburg, not the dynamic Nazi leader, had been their choice in the presidential elections earlier in 1932. But by the November Reichstag election, the gap between female and male voting support for the NSDAP had narrowed almost to vanishing point. Women were just about as likely as men to find the prospect of a Hitler dictatorship an attractive one. The mentalities which Nazism could build upon and exploit crossed the gender divide.

Despite the disappointment in Hitler and decline in support for the NSDAP in the autumn of 1932, such mentalities, which would benefit the Nazi regime once

Hitler had taken power, were kept alive and given sustenance by the bruising years of the Depression. Though two-thirds of the people had not voted for Hitler, many were less than root-and-branch opposed to all that Nazism stood for, and could fairly easily be brought in the coming months to find *some* things in the Third Reich that they might approve of. The loathing and deep fear of Communism that ran through some four-fifths of society was one important common denominator. Faced with a stark choice between National Socialism and Communism – which was how Hitler was increasingly able to portray it after his takeover of power – most middle-class and well-to-do Germans, and even a considerable leaven of the working class, preferred the Nazis. The Communists were revolutionaries, they would take away private property, impose a class dictatorship, and rule in the interests of Moscow. The National Socialists were vulgar and distasteful, but they stood for German interests, they would uphold German values, and they would *not* take away private property. Crudely put, this reflected a wide-spread train of thought, not least in the middle classes.

Fear, bitterness, and radicalization were part of a climate of political violence. These tensions of the Depression years had made political violence an everyday occurrence, even in the sleepiest of places. People became used to it. If it was targeted at the 'Reds' they often approved of it – even 'respectable' sections of society which decried the breakdown of 'order' in public life. Paradoxically, the party responsible for much of the mayhem, the NSDAP, could benefit by portraying itself – enhanced by the image of serried ranks of marching stormtroopers – as the only party capable of ending the violence by imposing order in the national interest. The acceptance of a level of outright violence in public life, which had been there at the birth and in the early years of the Weimar Republic and again become pronounced in the Depression years, helped to pave the way for the readiness to accept Nazi terror in the aftermath of the 'seizure of power'.

Along with this went a vindictiveness that the deprivations and tensions of the Depression years had promoted. Someone had to be blamed for the misery. Scapegoats were needed. Enemies were targeted. Political enemies were lined up for scores to be settled. Personal and political enmities often went hand in hand. If the anonymity of the big city could offer some protection, that was not the case in small towns and in villages. Here there was no hiding-place. Once the power of the state could be used to support violence, not contain it, there would be no shortage of those volunteering to participate in the bloodletting. For countless others, the social and political conflicts of the Depression years stored up personal grudges that would be paid back after 1933 through denunciation for real or fictional political 'offences'.

As regards scapegoats, the Jews were an easy target. Nazi diabolization of Jews enabled them to be portrayed as both the representatives of rapacious big capital and of pernicious and brutal Bolshevism. Most Germans did not go along with such crude images. Nor were they likely to become involved in, or approve of, physical violence directed at individual Jews and their property. But dislike of Jews extended far beyond Nazi sympathizers. No political party, pressure-group, or trade union, and neither main Christian denomination, made the defence of the Jewish minority an issue. And, when times were hard, it was simple enough to stir envy and resentment against a tiny minority of the population – 0.76 per cent in 1933 belonged to the Jewish faith – by stressing how they dominated out of all proportion to their numbers sections of business, the arts, and the professions. It was no coincidence, for instance, that one of the most viciously antisemitic Nazi sub-organizations was the Fighting League of the Commercial Middle Class (*Kampfbund des gewerblichen Mittelstandes*), where small traders campaigned against department stores that they claimed to be largely in Jewish hands. Most people during the Depression years, as we have already commented, did not vote for the NSDAP, or even join the party, primarily *because* of its antisemitism. But the widespread latent antisemitism in Weimar Germany – the feeling that Jews were somehow different, 'un-German', and a harmful influence – did not provide any deterrent to people offering their enthusiastic support to Hitler's movement in full cognizance of its hatred of Jews. And since that hatred *was* central to the ethos of a Movement which was massively expanding its membership in the early 1930s – by the end of 1932 its membership numbers had reached 1,414,975 – more and more people were becoming exposed, once in the Movement, to the full brutality and viciousness of Nazi antisemitism. The same applied to the SA, by this time numbering around 400,000 stormtroopers. Even many of the young thugs who had been attracted to it in increasing numbers were not outrightly antisemitic before they joined. But once members, they were part of an organization whose 'Fighting Song' contained the lines: 'When Jews' blood spurts from the knife, good times are once more here.'

The half-a-million-strong Jewish community – the vast majority patriotic, liberal-minded Germans, anxious to be assimilated into, not separated from, their fellow countrymen – was divided in its reactions to the upsurge of antisemitism. The main Jewish organization, the Centralverein – the 'Central Association of German Citizens of Jewish Faith' – took the danger very seriously, and put up a sturdy defence of Nazi inroads into civil rights. Others were more complacent – a feeling they often combined with a sense of helplessness. They thought the danger would blow over. Few had direct experience of racist attacks – something Jews themselves associated with Russia, Poland or Rumania, not with Germany. It was possible to accept some discrimination, avoid threatening situations, and generally keep out of trouble. It was still possible to feel 'at home' in Germany. It was still possible on the very last day of 1932, as Lion Feuchtwanger's fictional characters in *Geschwister Oppermann* did, to joke about whether 'the Führer' would end up as a market salesman or an insurance agent.

Three years of crippling Depression had left Germany a more intolerant society. A sign that the humane principles on which the Republic had been based were being whittled away during the Depression, as German society lurched towards the Right, was the reintroduction of the death penalty in the early 1930s. A few years earlier it had seemed close to abolition. The Nazis were to make it the pivot of their proclaimed restoration of 'order'. Another indicator of a changing climate in which liberal values were being rapidly eroded was the radicalization of medical views on eugenics and 'racial hygiene'. The costs of keeping mental patients in asylums at a time of drastic cuts in public expenditure brought increased pressure for legislation to introduce the voluntary sterilization of those with hereditary defects. Growing support for such measures among doctors, psychiatrists, lawyers, and civil servants led to draft proposals, supported by the German Doctors' Association, for a Reich Sterilization Law. Württemberg and Prussian Chambers of Doctors underlined their backing for such legislation in November and December 1932. Hitler's party, with a third of the voters behind it, went further and advocated *compulsory* sterilization of the hereditarily sick. In 1933, the Nazis wasted little time after coming to power in introducing notorious legislation to this effect. But the ground had been prepared by the 'experts' before Hitler took office.

(Ian Kershaw, *Hitler 1889–1936: Hubris*, Harmondsworth, Penguin, 1998, pp.404–11)

10   ADOLF HITLER: 'WAR PROPAGANDA'

In watching the course of political events I was always struck by the active part which propaganda played in them. I saw that it was an instrument which the Marxist Socialists knew how to handle in a masterly way and how to put it to practical uses. Thus I soon came to realize that the right use of propaganda was an art in itself and that this art was practically unknown to our bourgeois parties. The Christian-Socialist Party alone, especially in Lueger's time, showed a certain efficiency in the employment of this instrument and owed much of their success to it.

It was during the War, however, that we had the best chance of estimating the tremendous results which could be obtained by a propagandist system properly carried out. Here again, unfortunately, everything was left to the other side, the work done on our side being worse than insignificant. It was the total failure of the whole German system of information – a failure which was perfectly obvious to every soldier – that urged me to consider the problem of propaganda in a comprehensive way. I had ample opportunity to learn a practical lesson in this matter; for unfortunately it was only too well taught us by the enemy. The lack on our side was exploited by the enemy in such an efficient manner that one could say it showed itself as a real work of genius. In that propaganda carried on by the enemy I found admirable sources of instruction. The lesson to be learned from this had unfortunately no attraction for the geniuses on our own side. They were simply above all such things, too clever to accept any teaching. Anyhow they did not honestly wish to learn anything.

Had we any propaganda at all? Alas, I can reply only in the negative. All that was undertaken in this direction was so utterly inadequate and misconceived from the very beginning that not only did it prove useless but at times harmful. In substance it was inefficient. Psychologically it was all wrong. Anybody who had carefully investigated the German propaganda must have formed that judgement of it. Our people did not seem to be clear even about the primary question itself: Whether propaganda is a means or an end?

Propaganda is a means and must, therefore, be judged in relation to the end it is intended to serve. It must be organized in such a way as to be capable of attaining its objective. And, as it is quite clear that the importance of the objective may vary from the standpoint of general necessity, the essential internal character of the propaganda must vary accordingly. The cause for which

we fought during the War was the noblest and highest that man could strive for. We were fighting for the freedom and independence of our country, for the security of our future welfare and the honour of the nation. Despite all views to the contrary, this honour does actually exist, or rather it will have to exist; for a nation without honour will sooner or later lose its freedom and independence. This is in accordance with the ruling of a higher justice, for a generation of poltroons is not entitled to freedom. He who would be a slave cannot have honour; for such honour would soon become an object of general scorn.

Germany was waging war for its very existence. The purpose of its war propaganda should have been to strengthen the fighting spirit in that struggle and help it to victory.

But when nations are fighting for their existence on this earth, when the question of 'to be or not to be' has to be answered, than all humane and æsthetic considerations must be set aside; for these ideals do not exist of themselves somewhere in the air but are the product of man's creative imagination and disappear when he disappears. Nature knows nothing of them. Moreover, they are characteristic of only a small number of nations, or rather of races, and their value depends on the measure in which they spring from the racial feeling of the latter. Humane and æsthetic ideals will disappear from the inhabited earth when those races disappear which are the creators and standard-bearers of them.

All such ideals are only of secondary importance when a nation is struggling for existence. They must be prevented from entering into the struggle the moment they threaten to weaken the stamina of the nation that is waging war. That is always the only visible effect whereby their place in that struggle is to be judged.

In regard to the part played by humane feeling, Moltke stated that in time of war the essential thing is to get a decision as quickly as possible and that the most ruthless methods of fighting are at the same time the most humane. When people attempt to answer this reasoning by highfalutin talk about æsthetics, etc., only one answer can be given. It is that the vital questions involved in the struggle of a nation for its existence must be subordinated to any æsthetic considerations. The yoke of slavery is and always will remain the most unpleasant experience that mankind can endure. Do the Scwabing[1] decadents look upon Germany's lot to-day as 'æsthetic'? Of course, one doesn't discuss such a question with the Jews, because they are the modern inventors of this cultural perfume. Their very existence is an incarnate denial of the beauty of God's image in His creation.

Since these ideas of what is beautiful and profane have no place in warfare, they are not to be used as standards of war propaganda.

During the War, propaganda was a means to an end. And this end was the struggle for existence of the German nation. Propaganda, therefore, should have been regarded from the standpoint of its utility for that purpose. The most cruel weapons were then the most humane, provided they helped towards a speedier decision; and only those methods were good and beautiful which helped towards securing the dignity and freedom of the nation. Such was the only possible attitude to adopt towards war propaganda in that life-or-death struggle.

If those in what are called positions of authority had realized this there would have been no uncertainty about the form of employment of war propaganda as a weapon; for it is nothing but a weapon, and indeed a most terrifying weapon in the hands of those who know how to use it.

The second question of decisive importance is this: To whom should propaganda be made to appeal? To the educated intellectual classes? Or to the less intellectual?

Propaganda must always address itself to the broad masses of the people. For the intellectual classes, or what are called the intellectual classes to-day, propaganda is not suited, but only scientific exposition. Propaganda has as little to do with science as an advertisement poster has to do with art, as far as concerns the form in which it presents its message. The art of the advertisement poster consists in the ability of the designer to attract the attention of the crowd through the form and colours he chooses. The advertisement poster announcing an exhibition of art has no other aim than to convince the public of the importance of the exhibition. The better it does that the better is the art of the poster as such. Being meant accordingly to impress upon the public the meaning of the exposition, the poster can never take the place of the artistic objects displayed in the exposition hall. They are something entirely different. Therefore, those who wish to study the artistic display must study something which is quite different from the poster; indeed for that purpose a mere wandering through the exhibition galleries is of no use. The student of art must carefully and thoroughly study each exhibit in order slowly to form a judicious opinion about it.

The situation is the same in regard to what we understand by the word, propaganda.

The purpose of propaganda is not the personal instruction of the individual, but rather to attract public attention to certain things, the importance of which can be brought home to the masses only by this means.

Here the art of propaganda consists in putting a matter so clearly and forcibly before the minds of the people as to create a general conviction regarding the reality of a certain fact, the necessity of certain things and the just character of something that is essential. But as this art is not an end in itself and because its purpose must be exactly that of the advertisement poster, to attract the attention of the masses and not only by means to dispense individual instructions to those who already have an educated opinion on things or who wish to form such an opinion on grounds of objective study – because that is not the purpose of propaganda, it must appeal to the feelings of the public rather than to their reasoning powers.

All propaganda must be presented in popular form and must fix its intellectual level so as not to be above the heads of the least intellectual of those to whom it is directed. Thus its purely intellectual level will have to be that of the lowest mental common denominator among the public it is desired to reach. When there is question of bringing a whole nation within the circle of its influence, as happens in the case of war propaganda, then too much attention cannot be paid to the necessity of avoiding a high level, which presupposes a relatively high degree of intelligence among the public.

The more modest the scientific tenor of this propaganda and the more it is addressed exclusively to public sentiment, the more decisive will be its success. This is the best test of the value of a propaganda, and not the approbation of a small group if intellectuals or artistic people.

The art of propaganda consists precisely in being able to awaken the imagination of the public through an appeal to their feelings, in finding the appropriate psychological form that will arrest the attention and appeal of the hearts of the national masses. That this is not understood by those among us whose wits are supposed to have been sharpened to the highest pitch is only another proof of their vanity and mental inertia.

Once we have understood how necessary it is to concentrate the persuasive forces of propaganda on the broad masses of the people, the following lessons result therefrom:

That it is a mistake to organize and direct propaganda as if it were a manifold system of scientific instruction.

The receptive powers of the masses are very restrictive, and their understanding is feeble. On the other hand, they quickly forget. Such being the case, all effective propaganda must be confined to a few bare essentials and those must be expressed as far as possible in stereotyped formulas. These slogans should be persistently repeated until the very last individual has come to grasp the idea that has been put forward. If this principle be forgotten and if an attempt be made to be abstract and general, the propaganda will turn out ineffective; for the public will not be able to digest or retain what is offered to them in this way. Therefore, the greater the scope of the message that has to be presented, the more necessary it is for propaganda to discover that plan of action which is psychologically the most efficient.

It was, for example, a fundamental mistake to ridicule the worth of the enemy, as the Austrian and German comic papers made a chief point of doing in their propaganda. The very principle here is a mistaken one; for, when they came face to face with the enemy, our soldiers had quite a different impression. Therefore, the mistake had disastrous results. Once the German soldier realized what a tough enemy he had to fight he felt that he had been deceived by the manufacturers of the information which had been given him. Therefore, instead of strengthening and stimulating his fighting spirit, this information had quite the contrary effect. Finally he lost heart.

On the other hand, British and American war propaganda was psychologically efficient. By picturing the Germans to their own people as Barbarians and Huns, they were preparing their soldiers for the horrors of war and safe guarding them against illusions. The most terrific weapons which those soldiers encountered in the field merely confirmed the information that they had already received and their belief in the truth of the assertions made by their respective governments was accordingly reinforced. Thus their rage and hatred against the infamous foe was increased. The terrible havoc caused by the German weapons of war was only another illustration of the Hunnish brutality of those barbarians; whereas on the side of the Entente no time was left the soldiers to mediate on the similar havoc which their own weapons were capable of. Thus the British soldier was never allowed to feel that the information which he received at home was untrue. Unfortunately the opposite was the case with the Germans, who finally wound up by rejecting everything from home as pure swindle and humbug. This result was made possible because at home they thought that the work of propaganda could be entrusted to the first ass that came along, braying of his own special talents, and they had no conception of the fact that propaganda demands the most skilled brains that can be found.

Thus the German war propaganda afforded us an incomparable example of how the work of 'enlightenment' should not be done and how such an example was the result of an entire failure to take any psychological considerations whatsoever into account.

From the enemy, however, a fund of valuable knowledge could be gained by those who kept their eyes open, whose powers of perception had not yet become sclerotic, and who during four-and-a-half years had to experience the perpetual flood of enemy propaganda.

The worst of all was that our people did not understand the very first condition which has to be fulfilled in every kind of propaganda; namely, a systematically one-sided attitude towards every problem that has to be dealt with. In this regard so many errors were committed, even from the very beginning of the war, that it was justifiable to doubt whether so much folly could be attributed solely to the stupidity of people in higher quarters.

What, for example, should we say of a poster which purported to advertise some new brand of soap by insisting on the excellent qualities of the competitive brands? We should naturally shake our heads. And it ought to be just the same in a similar kind of political advertisement. The aim of propaganda is not to try to pass judgement on conflicting rights, giving each its due, but exclusively to emphasize the right which we are asserting. Propaganda must not investigate the truth objectively and, in so far as it is favourable to the other side, present it according to the theoretical rules of justice; but it must present only that aspect of the truth which is favourable to its own side.

It was a fundamental mistake to discuss the question of who was responsible for the outbreak of the war and declare that the sole responsibility could not be attributed to Germany. The sole responsibility should have been laid on the shoulders of the enemy, without any discussion whatsoever.

And what was the consequence of these half-measures? The broad masses of the people are not made up of diplomats or professors of public jurisprudence nor simply of persons who are able to form reasoned judgement in given cases, but a vacillating crowd of human children who are constantly wavering between one idea and another. As soon as our propaganda made the slightest suggestion that the enemy had a certain amount of justice on his side, then we laid down the basis on which the justice of our own cause could be questioned. The masses are not in a position to discern where the enemy's fault ends and where our own begins. In such a case they become hesitant and distrustful, especially when the enemy does not make the same mistake but heaps all the blame on his adversary. Could there be any clearer proof of this than the fact that finally our own people believed what was said by the enemy's propaganda, which was uniform and consistent in its assertions, rather than what our propaganda said? And that, of course, was increased by the mania for objectivity which afflicts our people. Everybody began to be careful about doing an injustice to the enemy, even at the cost of seriously injuring, or even ruining, his own people and State.

Naturally the masses were not conscious of the fact that those in authority had failed to study the subject from this angle.

The great majority of a nation is so feminine in its character and outlook that its thought and conduct are ruled by sentiment rather than by sober reasoning. This sentiment, however, is not complex, but simple and consistent. It is not highly differentiated but has only negative and positive notions of love and hatred, right and wrong, truth and falsehood. Its notions are never partly this and partly that. English propaganda especially understood this in a marvellous way and put what they understood into practice. They allowed no half measures, which might have given rise to some doubt.

Proof of how brilliantly they understand that the feeling of the masses is something primitive was shown in their policy of publishing tales of horror and outrages which fitted in with the real horrors of the time, thereby cleverly and ruthlessly preparing the ground for moral solidarity at the front, even in times of great defeats. Further, the way in which they pilloried the German enemy as solely responsible for the war – which was a brutal and absolute falsehood – and the way in which they proclaimed his guilt was excellently calculated to reach the masses, realizing that these are always extremist in their feelings. And thus it was that this atrocious lie was positively believed.

The effectiveness of this kind of propaganda is well illustrated by the fact that after four-and-half years, not only was the enemy still carrying on his propagandist work, but it was already undermining the stamina of our people at home.

That our propaganda did not achieve similar results is not to be wondered, because it had the germs of inefficiency lodged in its very being by reason of its ambiguity. And because of the very nature of its content one could not expect it to make the necessary impression on the masses. Only our feckless 'statesmen' could have imagined that on pacifist slops of such a kind the enthusiasm could be nourished which is necessary to enkindle that spirit which leads men to die for their country.

And so this product of ours was not only worthless but detrimental.

No matter what an amount of talent employed in the organization of propaganda, it will have no result if due account is not taken of these fundamental principles. Propaganda must be limited to a few simple themes and these must be represented again and again. Here, as in innumerable other cases, perseverance is the first and most important condition of success.

Particularly in the field of propaganda, placid æsthetics and blasé intellectuals should never be allowed to take the lead. The former would readily transform the impressive character of real propaganda into something suitable only for literary tea parties. As to the second class of people, one must always be aware of this pest; for, in consequence of their insensibility to normal impressions, they are constantly seeking new excitements.

Such people grow sick and tired of everything. They always long for change and will always be incapable of putting themselves in the position of picturing the wants of their less callous fellow-creatures in their immediate neighbourhood, let alone trying to understand them. The blasé intellectuals are always the first to criticise propaganda, or rather its message, because this appears to them to be outmoded and trivial. They are always looking for something new, always yearning for change; and thus they become the moral enemies of every effort that may be made to influence the masses in an effective way. The moment the organization and message of a propagandist movement begins to be oriented according to their tastes it becomes incoherent and scattered.

It is not the purpose of propaganda to create a series of alterations in sentiment with a view of pleasing these blasé gentry. Its chief function is to convince the masses, whose slowness of understanding needs to be given time in order that they may absorb information; and only constant repetition will finally succeed in imprinting an idea on the memory of the crowd.

Every change that is made in the subject of a propagandist message must always emphasize the same conclusion. The leading slogan must of course be illustrated in many ways and from several angles, but in the end one must always return to the assertion of the same formula. In this way alone can propaganda be consistent and dynamic in its effects.

Only by following these general lines and sticking to them steadfastly, with uniform and concise emphasis, can final success be reached. Then one will be rewarded by the surprising and most incredible results that such a persistent policy secures.

The success of any advertisement, whether of a business or political nature, depends on the consistency and perseverance with which it is employed.

In this respect also the propaganda organized by our enemies set us a brilliant example. It confined itself to a few themes, which were meant exclusively for mass consumption, and it repeated these themes with untiring perseverance. Once these fundamental themes and the manner of placing them before the world were recognized as effective, they adhered to them without the slightest alteration for the whole duration of the War. At first all of it appeared to be idiotic in its imprudent assertiveness. Later on it was looked upon as disturbing, but finally it was believed.

But in England they came to understand something further: Namely, that the possibility of success in the use of this spiritual weapon consists in the mass employment of it, and that when employed in this way it brings full returns for the large expenses incurred.

In England propaganda was regarded as a weapon of the first order, whereas with us it represented the last hope of a livelihood for our unemployed politicians and a snug job for shirkers of the modest heroic type.

Taken all in all, its results were negative.

Note

[1] Schwabing is the artistic quarter in Munich where artists have their studios and litterateurs, especially of the Bohemian class, foregather.

(Adolf Hitler, *Mein Kampf*, trans. by J. Murphy, London, Hurst Blackett, 1939, pp.156–63)

11   P. M. H. BELL, 'APPEASEMENT'

Any consideration of appeasement must begin with an attempt at definition. The word has acquired so many meanings that it is difficult to use with precision. Which states practised a policy of appeasement, and over what period of time? To what parts of the globe did it apply – only to Europe, or to Asia and the Pacific as well? What colour or resonance does the word carry with it? It has been used at different times to imply extremes of virtue on the one hand and of cowardice or foolishness on the other.

The British naturally associate the policy of appeasement principally, or even exclusively, with their own country, and especially with Neville Chamberlain in his dealings with Hitler. But France too pursued a policy of appeasement, with Georges Bonnet as its most prominent exponent. Less obviously, it can be argued that the Soviet Union was among the appeasers, and that the biggest single act of appeasement was the Soviet-German pact of August 1939, which accepted German control over a far larger area of territory than that conceded by Britain and France at the Munich conference in September 1938.

As to dates, Paul Kennedy has argued that some form of appeasement formed a continuous strand in British foreign policy from the 1860s onwards, in that there was a strong tendency to seek for peaceful, negotiated solutions to problems rather than to adopt a stance of confrontation or conflict.[1] There is some truth in this, though it is a generalization so broad as to be unhelpful for most purposes. Another starting-point has been found in 1919, when Lloyd George, the British Prime Minister, argued strongly for a moderate peace with Germany in his Fontainebleau memorandum of 25 March, and when his friend and advisor the South African General Smuts actually used the word 'appeasement' in a letter to Lloyd George on 26 March.[2] In the 1920s, British policy was frequently directed towards revising the treaty of Versailles in Germany's favour (notably by scaling down reparation payments), and towards bringing Germany back into the concert of Europe (for example, by treating her as an equal partner at international conferences). From the Locarno Treaty of 1925 onwards, the French Foreign Minister Aristide Briand directed his actions towards reconciliation between France and Germany, often using the word *apaisement* to describe his objective. Another version of the time-scale covered by appeasement takes the Manchurian crisis of 1931 as its starting-point, regarding the passive reaction by other powers to the Japanese occupation of Manchuria as the beginning of a phenomena which then extended through the decade of the 1930s. Yet another interpretation, particularly common in Britain, attaches the policy of appeasement tightly to the years 1938–9, and to the policy pursued by Neville Chamberlain, with the Munich agreement of September 1938 as its centre-piece. Some writers have claimed that this period should be extended right through the phoney war of 1939–40, taking the policy of appeasement up to the time of the fall of Chamberlain and Churchill's assumption of office on 10 May 1940.

Turning to geography, appeasement is usually regarded as a European policy, directed towards meeting the claims of Germany (and to a lesser degree Italy), with the ultimate aim of reaching a lasting settlement of European problems. Other interpretations include the Far East and Pacific within their scope, extending the term to include British, French and American policies towards Japan.

The psychological and moral implications of the word 'appeasement' have been even more varied. At the time of the Munich agreement, at the end of September 1938, it was not thought incongruous to apply to Neville Chamberlain the words of one of the Beatitudes, 'Blessed are the peace-makers.' Letters flooded in to Chamberlain with heart-felt thanks for his achievement in saving the peace of Europe.[3] Yet at the same time Churchill saw Munich as a surrender to the threat of force. '£1 was demanded at the pistol's point. When it was given, £2 were demanded at the pistol's point. Finally, the

Legend:
- Lost by Germany 1919
- Saar: League of Nations control 1919 – 1935
- Demilitarized Rhineland 1919 – 1936
- Austria-Hungary until 1918
- Plebiscite areas
- Former territory of Imperial Russia

European frontiers, 1919–37

Dictator consented to take £1.17s.6d. and the rest in promises of good will for the future.' In 1948 Churchill presented, as the theme of the first volume of his war memoirs, 'How the English-speaking peoples through their unwisdom, carelessness and good nature, allowed the wicked to rearm.'[4] Again, there has been a marked contrast between those who saw appeasement as a simple reaction against the horrors of war (for example, Daladier, the French Premier from 1938 to March 1940, had been an infantryman during the Great War, and did not want others to endure a repetition), and those who have seen it as a policy of farsighted calculation – the best means, for example, of saving the British and French empires, or a deep-laid plot to turn Germany eastwards against the Soviet Union, so that the Nazi and Communist giants might tear one another apart and leave Britain and France as spectators. Virtue approaching saintliness; cowardice or foolishness; simplicity verging on naivety; stratagems worthy of Machiavelli – all these have been attached to the apparently plain word 'appeasement'. Surely they cannot all be correct.

We must start, therefore, with a working definition. Great Britain and France were countries most closely associated with a policy of appeasement. To include the Soviet Union would have a certain logic, but would cast the net too widely for a single essay. The central scene of the policy was Europe, and its core was the British and French attempt to reach a permanent settlement with Germany, which would bring stability to Europe by means of negotiation and limited concessions. It is important to stress the words *limited concessions*. Appeasement is sometimes referred to as a policy of 'peace at any price', but this was never true for either Britain or France. It was a policy of peace at limited price, to be paid if possible by somebody else – for example, by Czechoslovakia in 1938. As to dates, the period to be examined will be that between 1935 and 1939, though with a backward glance to the First World War and the Treaty of Versailles, and a forward look at events during the phoney war and the summer of 1940. It is in the second half of the 1930s that the central events related to the policy of appeasement took place: the acceptance of the growth of German power and territory, from open rearmament in 1935, through the occupation of the Rhineland in 1936, to the *Anschluss* with Austria and the Czechoslovakian crisis in 1938. Here lies the heart of our subject.

The widely different resonances of the word itself must be reduced to the simple, workaday assumption, which was widely made at the time, that it was possible to find terms which would satisfy German aspirations (themselves often seen as legitimate) and so secure peace and stability in Europe without involving any fundamental damage to British or French interests. This was not saintly, nor was it unduly cowardly. It meant accepting the growth of German power and the expansion of German territory, up to a point, as being preferable to a policy of opposing German claims at the risk of friction and perhaps war. In the event, what happened was that the British and French permitted the growth of German power to a point where, if it was to be resisted at all, it could only be at the cost of a great war; but that was far from being their intention.

The main events

The principal events of the period 1935–9 may be rapidly summarized. In March 1935 Germany openly denounced the disarmament clauses of the Treaty of Versailles, which had imposed a limit of 100,000 on the strength of the army, to be raised by voluntary recruitment, and forbidden the existence of any air force at all. In practice, these restrictions had long been evaded, with greater or lesser degrees of concealment. But now the German government announced the introduction of conscription and the formation of an army of thirty-six infantry divisions; the first three Panzer divisions followed in October. Also in March 1935 the Germans declared publicly that a military air force (the *Luftwaffe*) was already in existence. At that time, its strength was some 2,500 aircraft, though a large proportion of these were trainers. The British and French made formal protests against these breaches of vital sections of the Treaty of Versailles, but left it at that. The British Foreign Secretary, Sir John Simon, carried on with a visit to Berlin which had been arranged before the German announcements. Moreover, in June 1935 the British government, acting solely on its own account and without consultation with France, concluded a naval agreement with Germany, accepting a German fleet of 35 per cent of the strength of the Royal Navy, and even agreeing that the Germans had the right to build up to equality in submarines if they thought it necessary. This too was a breach of the Versailles treaty, which had forbidden Germany to possess warships of over 10,000 tons, or to have any submarines at all. In short, the British took the lead in accepting the rearmament of Germany, which from 1935 onwards was pursued at great speed, especially in the air. The Nazis shrewdly seized on the *Luftwaffe* as a means of striking terror into the hearts of potential opponents; and their success in this regard had considerable effects on the policy of appeasement.

In October 1935 Mussolini, the Italian dictator, launched an invasion of Ethiopia. The links between this event and appeasement were by no means straightforward. The French government was willing to accept Italian expansion in Africa as the price of retaining Italy as an ally against Germany in Europe; that is, in crude terms, to appease one country in order to oppose another. The British government, at least in principle, claimed to oppose the Italian action in Ethiopia in order to maintain the authority of the League of Nations and the concept of collective security. Britain therefore took the lead in imposing limited economic sanctions on Italy. But at the same time the British worked secretly with the French to find terms which would give Mussolini most of what he wanted in Ethiopia, while saving some fragment of territory and independence for the Emperor of Ethiopia, Haile Selassie. These negotiations culminated in what is commonly known as the Hoare-Laval pact of December 1935, which was a characteristically 'appeasing' proposal, in that it accepted the growth of Italian territory at someone else's (i.e. Ethiopia's) expense. In the event, the Hoare-Laval proposals were leaked to the French press, denounced by a vocal section of British public opinion and rapidly abandoned. The Italians went ahead anyway with the military conquest of Ethiopia. This set a precedent for successful military adventure. The episode also provoked dissension between France and Britain, because the French had broadly speaking been willing to accept the Italian action, and felt that the British had thrown away the advantages of that policy without putting anything effective in its place. Over Ethiopia, policies of resistance to aggression (economic sanctions) and appeasement (the Hoare-Laval agreement) had both been tried, but neither had been carried through.

For the French and British, Ethiopia was far away. But the next event to shake the structure of international relations was close to home. In March 1936 the Germans moved troops into the Rhineland zone, which had been demilitarized under the terms of the Versailles Treaty, confirmed with Germany's free agreement by the Treaty of Locarno in 1925. Demilitarization meant that Germany must not station any armed forces in the Rhineland, nor construct any fortifications there, leaving the French an open door through which they could march into Germany in case of need. The closing of that door by military occupation, and later by the building of the fortifications known as the Siegfried Line, destroyed the ability of France to come to the help of her allies in Eastern Europe, and undermined the whole basis of French policy in Europe. Its consequences for Britain were less immediate, but in the long run highly significant – after all, Stanley Baldwin, the Prime Minister at the time, had earlier declared that the British frontier no longer lay on the white cliffs of Dover but on the Rhine. Yet both France and Britain accepted the German occupation of the Rhineland, and its progressive fortification, with no more than formal protest.

The Treaty of Versailles expressly forbade the union of the new state of Austria with Germany; and in the 1920s and early 1930s France and Britain several times reaffirmed their support for Austrian independence.

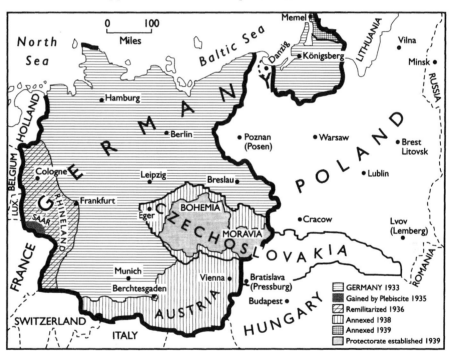

The expansion of Germany, 1935 to July 1939

On 11 March 1938 the government of Austria was taken over by nominees of Germany, under pressure exercised from Berlin – often by the simple device of threatening telephone calls. On the 12th, German troops entered the country unopposed, with bands playing and often welcomed with flowers. On 13th Hitler proclaimed the annexation of Austria to Germany. In three days a sovereign European state, supposedly safeguarded by treaties and other declarations, vanished from the map. Austria's nominal protectors made no move. Italy was the country most closely concerned, and had defended Austria in an earlier crisis; but Mussolini was now in league with Hitler. France and Britain delivered protests at Berlin, but separately and without conviction. In

Britain especially there was a strong belief that the prohibition of union between Austria and Germany had been an error and an injustice, running contrary to the principle of self-determination.

The German annexation of Austria left the state of Czechoslovakia, another creation of the peace settlement in 1919, with the head of its long, slender shape in the jaws of a German nutcracker. The country contained a minority if rather over three million German-speakers (about one-fifth of the total population), who themselves included a substantial Nazi element. The Sudeten German Nazi party, under guidance from Berlin, agitated first for autonomy within the Czechoslovakian state, and then for separation from it and union with Germany. This agitation threatened to destroy Czechoslovakia if it succeeded by disruption from within, and carried the danger of European war if it lead to German armed intervention from without. France had a treaty of alliance with Czechoslovakia; and if France were drawn into war Britain would be bound to follow. To avoid this danger, both the British and French governments put intense pressure on the Czech government to make concessions to the Sudeten Germans. Finally the British Prime Minister, Neville Chamberlain, took the bold initiative of flying to meet Hitler to find a solution through the ceding of territory by Czechoslovakia to Germany. An extraordinary fortnight of diplomatic activity in late September 1938 culminated in the Munich conference on 29 September. Hitler, Mussolini, Chamberlain and Daladier, with a Czech delegation in attendance to await the country's fate, decided on the transfer of a horse-shoe shaped slice of territory from Czechoslovakia to Germany. At the beginning of November, Poland annexed Teschen, and Germany and Italy together (without a word from France and Britain) handed another large strip of territory from Czechoslovakia to Hungary. The Czechoslovakian crisis, and especially the Munich agreement, are generally regarded as the apogee of the policy of appeasement, because on this occasion it was not a question of the British and French simply accepting the growth of German power and territory, but of them taking the initiative to ensure that Hitler got what he wanted. When people refer to appeasement, it is usually Munich they have in mind.

While these events were taking place in 1938, certain more long-drawn-out processes were also under way. Civil war broke out in Spain in July 1936, continuing until the end of March 1939. The major Powers, and several lesser ones, signed an agreement pledging non-intervention in this war. Germany and Italy, and to a lesser degree the Soviet Union, openly disregarded the non-intervention in this war. Germany and Italy, and to a lesser degree the Soviet Union, openly disregarded the non-intervention agreement, while Britain and France stood by and watched while the war was won by General Franco's Nationalists with German and Italian support. This amounted to a form of continuous appeasement. The policy also had a number of other aspects. For much of the 1930s, and especially between 1936 and 1938, Britain tried to formulate a policy of colonial appeasement, which might allow Germany to recover some of the colonies she had lost in the peace settlement of 1919, or perhaps take a share in some form of joint administration over parts of central Africa. A complicated proposal along the lines of joint administration was put to Hitler by the British government in February 1938, only to be brushed aside as irrelevant. The British also discussed schemes of economic appeasement, either on a limited scale, by conceding a German sphere of economic influence in

Central Europe (which the Germans were creating for themselves anyway), or more grandly by bringing Germany back into the world economic system and weaving her way from her policy of autarky or self-sufficiency. There was a widespread feeling that if only the Germans could be made fat and contented through economic prosperity they would not be prone to military adventures and aggression. These ideas led to various discussions between the British and German governments, which reached no conclusion. A proposal for a coal cartel between British and German producers was approaching fruition in March 1939, but was then abandoned.

These events and schemes form the body of what is known as the policy of appeasement. On most reckonings, the catalogue of concessions to Germany came to an end in March 1939, when Germany seized most of what remained of Czechoslovakia, throwing the tail-end (Ruthenia) to Hungary. Hitler's claim that he sought only to unite German-speaking peoples within the Reich was exposed as a lie, and a vital basis of the policy of appeasement was destroyed. A reaction then set in. The British and French distributed a string of guarantees across Eastern Europe (to Poland, Romania and Greece), designed to act as a deterrent against any further German expansion. The change of mind was not absolutely convincing, and there was much suspicion that Chamberlain in Britain and Bonnet in France still hankered after another Munich at the expense of Poland in 1939. Even after Britain and France declared war on Germany in September 1939, there were movements for a compromise peace (stronger in France than in Britain). In May 1940, faced with a successful German offensive in the west and the imminent intervention of Mussolini on the German side, the French government proposed an attempt to buy Italy off with an offer of territorial concessions in Africa and the Mediterranean; which may perhaps be regarded as the last useless kick of the policy of appeasement.

When these events are set out this baldly, the extent of Germany's gains between 1935 and 1939 and the paucity of any concessions made in return become strikingly apparent. What after all did the Germans concede? The Anglo-German naval agreement limited the size of their fleet, but it could be broken at any time; and in any case the limits comprised as much as the Germans wished to build at that period. Germany did not actually attack Czechoslovakia in September 1938. This was a real concession, which Hitler later regretted bitterly, resolving that he would not again be deprived of a war by an interfering British politician. Even so, merely to abstain from war would not normally be regarded as much of a concession, or a fair *quid pro quo* in a bargain. Apart from these two cases, which were of dubious value, the traffic was all one-way. At first sight, there is a good deal of explaining to be done. What were the motives behind the policy of appeasement, and why was it pursued in face of such apparent lack of success?

The motives behind appeasement

The most obvious motives probably remain the most important. There was a profound reaction, in both France and Britain, against the appalling experience of the war of 1914. It now requires an effort of imagination to understand the full depth of that emotion; but anyone who looks at the war memorials in every town and village from the north of Scotland to the Pyrenees can catch something of its force. It is above all impressive to visit the immense war cemeteries in Flanders, or to stand in a tiny French village and read a list of twenty or thirty killed, often with the same names recurring. The figures of some 1,327,000 French military deaths and 723,000 for the United Kingdom are still appalling, and were more so at the time. 'Never again' was a sentiment shared on both sides of the Channel. Everyone was therefore determined that the causes of the Great War must be understood and avoided in the future. Among these causes, in the understanding of many people in the 1930s, were the pre-1914 alliance system, arms races and economic competition. Thus British statesmen frequently said that alliances would only make Germany feel threatened; that the Anglo-German Naval Agreement of 1935 was better than the naval rivalry before 1914; and that Germany must be assured of access to raw materials for her industries and markets for her exports.

Alongside this revulsion against the last war and its perceived causes there lay a dread of the next. This fear was particularly powerful in France. The French population had suffered a sort of biological disaster in the war of 1914–18, not only through the casualties but through the tremendous fall in births during the war years. This gap in the French population (the total 'deficit' was reckoned at some 1,770,000) moved on inexorably as the years passed. School classrooms were part-empty. By 1935 there were fewer men reaching the age of call-up for military service. Later still there would be fewer men and women to marry and raise the next generation. France could not afford another catastrophe of this kind.

The British were haunted by similar fears. Their casualties had been smaller than the French, but no-one wanted to see another Somme or Passchendaele. A new terror was added with the fear of aerial bombardment. In 1934 Stanley Baldwin told the House of Commons that 'the bomber will always get through' – a simple phrase which made a deep impression on the public mind. In 1936 the Joint Planning Committee of the Chiefs of Staff estimated that London might suffer 20,000 casualties in the first twenty-four hours of a future war against Germany, rising to 150,000 within a week. The dread of air attack possessed the minds of both layman and expert. Behind such fears lurked others, amorphous but terrible. In 1928 a leading authority on war and politics wrote that the next war would be waged through 'agencies and processes of destruction wholesale, unlimited, and perhaps, once launched, uncontrollable ... Death stands at attention, obedient, expectant, ready to serve, ready to shear away the peoples *en masse*; ready, if called on, to pulverise, without hope of repair, what is left of civilisation. He awaits only the word of command.'[5] The words carried all the more weight because their author was no pacifist, and was indeed known to relish war when he was engaged in it – Winston Churchill. His prediction proved very close to the mark. Later generations, which have lived under the threat of nuclear war, should not find it difficult to appreciate the fears of their predecessors in the 1930s.

Revulsion against war was accompanied by a reaction against the Treaty of Versailles of 1919. This was much stronger in Britain than in France. During the 1920s the view took root in the British mind that the peace treaty had been harsh and unjust towards a beaten foe. Reparations, as J. M. Keynes argued in *The Economic Consequences of the Peace* (first published in 1919), were both unjust and unworkable. Disarmament, which should have been applied to all countries, was imposed solely upon Germany. The principle of self-determination, which many held sacred, was imposed when it could damage Germany but disregarded when it would help – for example, the Austrians were not allowed an official plebiscite on union with Germany. If all this (or even half of it) were true, then it followed that the Treaty of Versailles should not be enforced but revised in Germany's favour. Reparations were scaled down, and there was some relief in Britain when they were effectively abandoned in 1932. Germany should be allowed equal rights in armaments. German-speaking people in Austria or the Sudeten areas of Czechoslovakia should be allowed to join Germany if they wished to do so. These propositions had the force of truths universally acknowledged. To oppose German claims on such matters ran counter to instincts of justice and fair play, as well as creating friction and incurring the risk of war at some stage.

These deep-seated psychological motives for the policy of appeasement were reinforced by others which partook more of the nature of calculation. There were important strategic constraints on French and British policy. From the end of the war of 1914–1918, the French high command worked on the assumption that at some time there would be another war against Germany. In such a war, France would be inferior in numbers and economic resources, and would have to stand on the defensive for a prolonged period – a concept which found practical (indeed literally concrete) expression in the Maginot line, the fortified zone along the French frontier with Germany. The French army was committed to a defensive strategy and permeated by a defensive frame of mind, which in practice ruled out certain options in foreign policy – for example, a rapid strike into the Rhineland in 1936, or an offensive to help the Czechs in 1938. It was also vital for France to have allies, to counterbalance German superiority; and this meant that French policy was often constrained within the limits of what Britain would accept. Single-handed French action was ruled out – the last time it was attempted was in the occupation of the Ruhr in 1923, which came to be seen as an unhappy venture, not to be repeated.

The British too worked under severe strategic constraints, of which the gravest were those arising from Britain's world position. The British Empire in the 1930s was at its greatest territorial extent, covering about a quarter of the land surface of the globe. To defend it was beyond British economic and military resources. There were four zones of particular anxiety: the defence of the United Kingdom; the Mediterranean and Middle East; India and the Far East and Pacific. In the 1930s there were threats from Japan in the Pacific, Italy in the Mediterranean, and Germany at home; and in the background loomed a potential danger from the Soviet Union in India. It is not surprising that in 1937 the Chiefs of Staff argued powerfully that it must be the prime task of foreign policy to diminish the number of Britain's enemies. Three major enemies were too many, and their threats too widely spread, to be coped with. This was one of the most cogent reasons for a policy of appeasement. Was it not sensible to appease, even in the sense of buying off, one or more of these enemies? The logic is so powerful that the surprising thing is, not that such a policy was attempted, but that it was not pursued with even greater determination than it was.

Another important constraint of British policy in the 1930s lay in the strategic concept of 'limited liability'. After the experience of the 1914–18 war, the British had no wish to send another great army to the continent. The Committee of Imperial Defence actually warned its members in 1934 against using the words 'expeditionary force'. It would be better to confine British efforts in any future war to a limited strategy of naval blockade, aerial warfare, a small army and economic assistance to a continental ally (i.e. France). The concept, of which Neville Chamberlain was a strong advocate, placed restraints on British policy by ruling out options involving land warfare on any large scale. Indeed, in September 1938, when there was a serious danger of European war over Czechoslovakia, Britain could only offer to send two divisions to France – fewer troops, in terms of numbers, than were at that time operating in Palestine to combat Arab revolt.

In addition to these general strategic constraints, there were also specific inhibitions arising from French and British assessments of German strength at particular times. Perhaps the most dramatic case was the French General Staff's estimate of the German forces in the Rhineland zone in March 1936. They produced fairly accurate figures for the army units involved (10,000 troops, plus 23,000 armed police incorporated as infantry), but then produced an extraordinary total of 235,000 auxiliaries, supposedly organized into fifteen divisions. They then proceeded to argue, on the basis of these inflated figures, that they could not take even limited military action in the Rhineland without calling up something like a million French reservists – facing the government of the day with an alarming political as well as military problem. Again, in January 1938 French Air Force intelligence attributed to the *Luftwaffe* a strength of 2,800 first-line aircraft, as against 1,450 French, which were also of poorer quality. British estimates of German air strength were too low in 1934–5, when the Air Staff underrated the rate of German aircraft production; but by 1938 this complacency had given way to exaggeration of German airpower. In September 1938 (at the height of the crisis over Czechoslovakia) the RAF estimated the combat-ready German bomber force at 1,019, while the actual figure in August was 582.[6] In August a *Luftwaffe* report had concluded that, without bases in the Low Countries, the bombing of England was impossible. But the effect of the RAF's inflated estimate of German bomber strength was to reinforce in the government's mind the existing fears of aerial bombardment, and so give an added impulse to the desire to find an agreement which would avoid war.

Strategic constraints were accompanied by economic constraints. In France, 1935 saw the worst point of the economic depression of the 1930s, and the French economy remained stagnant until the end of 1938, when German steel production was almost four times greater than that of France. French governments were actually conscious of their industrial weakness in face of Germany, and also of their need for a British alliance to provide them with economic support. British problems were even more acute. To adopt a policy of confrontation with Germany, incurring the risk of war, would demand substantial rearmament; but any large-scale rearmament programme would mean increasing imports of the necessary raw materials, while at the same time diminishing the capacity to pay for them by means of exports. This would in turn cause a crisis in the balance of payments. Even if these problems could be overcome, there were limits on the industrial resources available for rearmament – for example, large-scale aircraft production needed factories, machine tools and skilled labour which could not be found overnight.

Behind these various economic inhibitions on British policy there lay a final crucial consideration. It was considered virtually certain that an all-out war would lead to national bankruptcy, in the sense that the country would no longer be able to pay for its imports. This situation had been faced before, during the Great War, but on that occasion the British had been saved from disaster by loans from the United States. Next time there would be no American loans, which fell under a double prohibition. First, under the Johnson Act of 1934 the United States would make no loans to any government which had defaulted on its previous debts – which included Britain. Next, under United States neutrality legislation, enacted at different times between 1935 and 1937, no loans (whether private or governmental) were to be made to any belligerent country. The same prohibitions would also apply to France, so that both countries faced the daunting prospect of having to supply and finance a great war from their own resources. It was a powerful argument for avoiding such a war if at all possible.

These three categories of motive (emotional, strategic and economic) together constituted a strong case for preserving the peace and trying to reach an agreement with Germany by making some concessions to German demands. There were also other motives at work. In France there prevailed, from 1936 to 1937 onwards, a sort of paralysis of will. French diplomats reported on the European situation with their customary lucidity. The outlines of impending doom could be clearly discerned. Yet no-one could decide how to avert it. If France chose to resist the advance of German power, if necessary by force, she would be involved in a war which could at best only result in another victory like that in the Great War; and France could afford no more victories like that. On the other hand, if the French continued to acquiesce in the German advance, the best that they could hope for was that the tiger would eat them last – after, say Czechoslovakia and Poland. The problem seemed insoluble by rational means, and there was no-one of the stature of Clemenceau or (in later times) de Gaulle to disregard reason.

A very different state of affairs prevailed on the other side of the Channel. Neville Chamberlain possessed a steely political will. When he became Prime Minister in May 1937 he was determined to impart a new drive to British foreign policy, which he thought Baldwin had allowed to drift. Alastair Parker has shrewdly reminded us that, in all the talk of constraints on British policy, it is too easy to forget that Chamberlain actually *wanted* to follow a policy of appeasement.[7] The constraints were real, but Chamberlain was not constrained into his policy. It was what he wanted to do, and he was a very tough and determined man. In this sense, the old caricature of a feeble 'man with an umbrella' is thoroughly misleading.

There were other elements at work. There was some new active sympathy with Nazism as a political doctrine and form of government – more in France, where there were a number of near-fascist groups, than in Britain, where Oswald Mosely never had much of a following and where the 'fellow-travellers of the Right' were not very influential. There was a good deal of hostility towards the Soviet Union and Communism – this time more in Britain than in France, where the slogan that one should have 'no enemies on the Left' was still powerful. The 1930s were a period of intense ideological debate and vibrancy in

Europe, and such attitudes and prejudices counted for something in the making of policy.

Finally, there was one motive behind the whole policy of appeasement which is so obvious that it can easily be missed. Those who pursued the policy *believed that it would work*. They thought that Hitler could be appeased: that he was a rational statesmen with limited aims – probably the absorption into Germany of the various German-speaking populations in neighbouring countries. This optimism was always stronger among British leaders than among French – perhaps because French politicians all had some training in philosophy, and were inclined to take political theories more seriously than the pragmatic British. It has often been asserted that, if only British and French ministers had read *Mein Kampf,* they would have known what to expect, and changed their policies accordingly. In fact, the British and French Embassies in Berlin provided perfectly competent summaries of *Mein Kampf.* The problem was not to know what Hitler had written in the 1920s, but what he was going to do in the 1930s. On the whole, the British tended to think that Hitler the Chancellor would be different from Hitler the prisoner. They often believed that Hitler represented a moderate strand in Nazism, and that if he were displaced it would be by someone more extreme. In France, even Daladier, who declared from time to time that Hitler's appetite would only grow through being fed, and that the real issue in 1938 was not the former Czechoslovakia but the fate of Europe – never pursued his own arguments to their logical conclusion. An absolutely vital premise of the policy of appeasement, on both sides of the Channel, was the assumption that it had a good chance of working. In fact, of course, it did not work. It is time to look at the other side of the argument, and turn to the case against appeasement.

The case against appeasement

The fundamental case against appeasement is extremely simple. It failed. The policy was intended to avoid war, but war came. It was intended to achieve a European settlement while preserving basic British and French interests, and above all the security of the two states. In June 1940, France lay defeated and two-thirds occupied by the Germans. The German army stood at Calais, and appeared to have a good chance of reaching Dover. German bombers were based within easy range of London. The policy of appeasement had ended in utter disaster. In these circumstances, the fact that it was also dishonourable stood out all the more starkly. To sacrifice small states – for example, Czechoslovakia – to the maw of Nazi Germany might have been acceptable if the sacrifice had attained its objective; but when it did not, the policy stood doubly condemned as dishonour plus disaster.

From this verdict there can be no appeal. Appeasement failed the acid test: it did not work. But there is another, and more elaborate, aspect to the case against, which may be summarized as the assumption that there was available another policy, simple to devise and straightforward to apply, which could have saved the world from war and from the curse of Hitler. Not for the first time we must go back to Churchill for the most forceful statement of this view. In the Preface to *The Gathering Storm* he wrote: 'One day President Roosevelt told me that he was asking publicly for suggestions about what the war should be called.

I said at once "The Unnecessary War". There never was a war more easy to stop than that which has just wrecked what was left of the world from the previous struggle.'[8] The application of a firm, consistent and courageous policy of resistance to German demands would have cut them short at an early date, and probably have got rid of Hitler into the bargain.

From this line of reasoning there has resulted much discussion of 'lost opportunities' when such results have been achieved. The favourite occasion has been the German occupation of the Rhineland in March 1936. Looking back, it was widely assumed that an immediate French intervention ('police action' was a favourite description) would have resulted in an immediate German retreat. Even before March 1936 was out, Pope Pius XII told the French Ambassador at the Vatican that if France had moved 200,000 troops into the Rhineland they would have done everyone a great service. Hitler himself later encouraged the idea of a lost opportunity in the Rhineland by saying that if the French had marched the Germans would have had to withdraw with their tails between their legs. But at the time his instructions were that troops must withdraw fighting step by step, and it is likely that they would have stood firm on the Rhine itself. The 'lost opportunity', if there was one, was not to stop Hitler *without* war but *by* war; by serious military operations, not a promenade.

Another much-canvassed occasion has been the Czechoslovakian crisis in 1938, where two 'might-have-beens' are envisaged. One is that, through a combination of a firm stance against Germany and suitable encouragement to conspirators against Hitler within Germany, Hitler might have been overthrown. The other scenario is for a war against Germany, waged by Czechoslovakia, France, Britain and perhaps the Soviet Union, and resulting in a much easier and less costly victory than that achieved in 1945 after nearly six years of struggle. Such speculations are of unending interest, and battles fought on paper can produce whatever results their manipulators require. There could, of course, have been no certainty of an Allied victory, and one shrewd and well-informed study estimates that the Czech resistance would have lasted no longer than that of Poland in 1939, though German casualties might well have been much higher than in Poland.[9]

Another strong candidate for a lost opportunity to stop Germany is found in the negotiations for a three-power alliance between France, Britain and the Soviet Union in the summer of 1939. The argument is that such a coalition would have been so powerful that even Hitler would have been deterred from further territorial expansion, and contented himself with consolidating the gains which he had made in 1938 and March 1939. There has been a strong consensus in historical writing on this affair that the British wrecked these negotiations by a combination of tardiness, incompetence and anti-Soviet prejudice. (Such accusations are not levelled against the French, who wanted to press the talks forward with all speed and ruthlessness.) The case against the British conduct of negotiations is indeed strong; for example, they repeatedly affirmed that certain points were unacceptable, only to accept them some time later. But it is by no means certain that a three-power agreement was there for the taking if the British had only shown reasonable determination and competence. The question is whether an alliance was available at a price which the British government was willing or able to pay. Stalin wished to strengthen his borders by securing a large sphere of influence in Eastern Europe, notably in eastern

Poland and the Baltic states. The British were in no position to deliver such a sphere of influence, even if they had wanted to do so. Hitler was, and did. The essence of the German-Soviet agreement of 23 August 1939 lay in a line on the map delimiting German and Soviet spheres. The case, like the others, must remain hypothetical; but it is at any rate highly questionable whether the great three-power anti-German coalition was in fact within reach.

In general, the idea of lost opportunities which has played a large part in the case against appeasement looks a good deal weaker than it once did. Certainly in 1936 and 1938 it appears that the true choice was between immediate war and the likelihood of a worse war later. Yet a war postponed might be a war averted; and the choice might well be rephrased as one between war now and a chance of peace later. It was Churchill himself who was to say, several years later and in a different context, that 'jaw-jaw is better than war-war.'

With the passage of time, the 'lost opportunities' case against appeasement has come to look much weaker. The anti-appeasers themselves are doubtless also due for reassessment. The reputation of Eden as an opponent of appeasement, which arose from his resignation as Foreign Secretary in February 1938 (which meant that he took no responsibility for the fate of either Austria or Czechoslovakia) has been severely damaged in recent years. Even Churchill's record has been sceptically reviewed, with the questions about the accuracy of his information relating to German rearmament and the soundness of his proposals for a 'Grand Alliance', which probably put too much faith in the Soviet Union. In France, there has been a new biography of Daladier, which puts him more firmly in the anti-appeasement camp, without fully explaining his swings between resistance and capitulation. Paul Reynaud awaits a biographer; yet it was he who most pungently summed up the true basis of the case against appeasement. In June 1940, when Pétain was arguing the case for an armistice with Germany, and thinking in terms of a rational discussion round a negotiating table, Reynaud told him sharply that things were not like that any more. 'Hitler is Gengis Khan!' he exclaimed. The author of this vehement and accurate remark deserves to be remembered.[10]

Argument without end

Appeasement has retained a remarkable hold on historical scholarship, and in a large part on the public mind. This is partly through its connection with the Second World War, which even fifty years after its close still commands attention and arouses controversy. The debate on appeasement is part of the wider debate on the origins of that war. Did Britain and France, by trying to appease Hitler, open the way to war and bring catastrophe upon Europe and the world? Or did they, by demonstrating beyond doubt that Hitler was unappeasable, lay the basis for the implacable resistance which eventually brought him down? Either argument can be sustained, and has been. But the questions go further and deeper, touching the long-term fate and the national identities of France and Britain.

In France, appeasement was the prelude to the defeat of 1940. Discussion of foreign policy in the late 1930s is carried on in the shadow of the most shattering event in recent French history. The titles of Jean-Baptiste Duroselle's massive histories of French foreign policy in the relevant period tell the story themselves:

La décadence, 1932–1939, and *L'abîme, 1939–1945*. Through decadence (of which appeasement was a part) to the abyss. It is no coincidence that some of the most acute and profound observations on French appeasement, and its end in the decision to go to war in 1939, are to be found in a study of the events of 1940 – Jean-Louis Crémieux-Brilhac's *Les Français de l'an 40*.[11] These events, which themselves led to the German occupation, the Vichy regime, collaboration and resistance, are still living issues in France. Professional historical writing has made some headway with them, but they remain acutely sensitive in the public mind. Appeasement forms a part of a fitful debate on France in the Second World War, which has certainly not been concluded and in some respects has scarcely begun.[12]

For Britain, the events associated with appeasement did not end in the catastrophe of defeat but in the sudden renaissance and glorious defiance of 1940. Yet appeasement and defiance alike have become part of the story of British decline in the twentieth century. In July 1940 a hastily written little book of some 120 pages was published under the pseudonym of 'Cato', which concealed a trio of authors, one of whom was Michael Foot, later leader of the Labour Party. Its title was *Guilty Men*, and its cast list of the guilty headed by the name of Neville Chamberlain. The charge was one of having led Britain to the verge of defeat (the opening scenes of the book are set on the beaches of Dunkirk) by appeasement in diplomacy and by neglect in armaments. Appeasement, therefore, was one of the causes of Britain's decline and (almost) fall. Some fifty year later John Charmley stood this interpretation on its head, by arguing that in fact Chamberlain's policy of appeasement was the last hope of arresting, or at least postponing, Britain's decline as a Great Power. According to Charmley, the fatal blow to Britain was the Second World War, which led to national bankruptcy, economic and political subordination to the United States, and, in the not very long run, the loss of Empire. Therefore, Chamberlain, in trying to avoid that deadly conflict, was pursuing a policy which would have preserved British power. Between these two radically different diagnoses lie many historical discussions in which the decline (or sometimes collapse) of British power is a recurrent theme. The subject itself has been something of an obsession for politicians, journalists and historians.[13] While the debate on British decline continues, appeasement is not likely to vanish from the historical agenda.

In addition to these considerations, the word appeasement has acquired a life of its own, by frequent repetition and appeal to analogies during later crises in international affairs. Repeatedly statesmen argued that appeasement had failed in the 1930s, and led to a terrible war. Therefore resistance to an aggressor rather than an attempt to negotiate with him was the best and ultimately safest course. President Truman applied this line of reasoning when deciding in 1950 to oppose the North Korean attack on the South. Anthony Eden of Britain and Guy Mollet in France appealed to the same analogy when deciding to use force against President Nasser of Egypt after he nationalized the Suez Canal in 1956. In the 1960s the United States government invoked the precedent of appeasement, and especially the Munich conference, to explain and justify the war in Vietnam. Much later, in 1991, similar arguments were used in the United States, Britain and France at the time of the Gulf War. Saddam Hussein of Iraq was cast as Hitler, with Kuwait as a sort of Austria or Czechoslovakia. It is significant that these very different episodes involved both Democratic and Republican presidents of the United States; Conservative prime ministers in Britain (Eden and Major); and Socialist leaders in France (Guy Mollet as Premier in 1956, and François Mitterrand as President in 1991). Appeals to the appeasement analogy spanned political differences with ease. This is partly because of the appealing simplicity of the idea, but even more because of the moral element which has become firmly embedded in the appeasement debate. After appeasement had become indelibly stained with dishonour as well as disaster, the idea of a reversion to such a policy became abhorrent right across the political spectrum. The issue here is not whether the analogy was universally valid, or whether the appeal to the precedent of the 1930s was always justifiable or useful; but only that the appeal was made, and was widely accepted. Appeasement has been not merely a subject of historical study, but a part of current political discussion. This remained true during the prolonged crisis in the former Yugoslavia in the early 1990s, when references to precedents in the 1930s – to appeasement and Munich – were frequent in both the British and French press. The political echoes of the appeasement debate still persist; and as long as that is the case, the subject will continue to exercise a particular magnetism.

Where do we stand now? Appeasement is under review and revision, as it always has been. There is a sense in which all history is revisionist history, and the rise of so-called 'revisionist schools' is no more surprising than the presence of waves on the sea. There were contemporary debates in parliaments and the press in 1938, after the Munich conference. The *Guilty Men* thesis attracted replies during the war – Quintin Hogg declared that *The Left was never Right.* After the war, many of the participants stated their case in their memoirs – Hoare, Simon, Halifax in Britain; Reynaud and Bonnet in France, among a host of others. In Britain, the introduction of the Thirty-Year rule for access to government records meant that in 1968 documents from 1938 became available to historians; and valuable collections of private papers often (though not always) followed the same rule. In France the opening of the archives was less systematic, but over the years the files of the Quai d'Orsay, and of some individuals, have been opened for research. The result of this has been, over something like a quarter of a century, an increasing grasp of detail and of the process of decision making which had been previously impossible. There has also been a marked change of emphasis and attitude. Historians who work long hours on government documents absorb, almost without noticing it, a frame of mind similar to that of the politicians and officials they are studying. The fierce, and often essentially political, attacks on appeasement tended to give way to explanations of the policy, and of the constraints within which hard-pressed governments had to work.

At the same time, and simply with the passage of years, there was a change from the generation of historians who had been closely involved in the events themselves to others who had no memory of the 1930s, and so progressively to other generations putting different questions. In Britain, the stronger the case for appeasement has come to seem, through the examination of government documents, the more attention has shifted to the question of why the policy was changed. After all, if the motives behind the policy were as powerful as they now appear, why was it abandoned?

The process of revision and rethinking will not come to an end, except in the unlikely event of the subject falling into complete oblivion or (more simply) out of fashion. The great wave of new evidence in Britain has probably passed, but in France there is certainly fresh documentation to be opened and exploited. New interpretations can confidently be expected, if only because each generation writes its own history. It may even come about that, at some stage, appeasement will cease to be a political subject and become solely a matter for the historians – like, for example, the Peloponnesian War. Thucydides, writing his history of that war, declared that: 'My work is not a piece of writing designed to meet the taste of an immediate public, but was done to last for ever.'[14] It was a daring claim, but he has yet to be proved wrong. We have yet to see who will be the Thucydides of the policy of appeasement, capturing both its events and its essence for readers far in the future.

Notes

[1] P. M. Kennedy, *Strategy and Diplomacy, 1870–1945; Eight Essays* (London, 1983); see ch. 1, 'The tradition of appeasement in British foreign policy, 1865–1939'.

[2] W. K. Hancock, *Smuts: The Sanguine Years, 1870–1919* (Cambridge, 1962), p. 512.

[3] K. Feiling, *The Life of Neville Chamberlain* (London, 1946), pp.370–81, gives something of the flavour.

[4] W. S. Churchill, *The Second World War*, vol. 1, *The Gathering Storm* (London, 1948), p.256 (speech in the debate on Munich), p. ix (theme of the volume).

[5] Ibid., p.33, quoting from the same author's *The Aftermath*, written in 1928 and published in 1929.

[6] J. A. Gunsberg, *Divided and Conquered: The French High Command and the Defeat of the West, 1940* (Westport, CT, 1979), p.53. E. L. Homze, *Arming the Luftwaffe: The Reich Air Ministry and the German Aircraft Industry, 1919–39* (Lincoln, NB, 1976), p.241.

[7] R. A. C. Parker, *Chamberlain and Appeasement: British Policy and the Coming of the Second World War* (London, 1993).

[8] Churchill, *The Gathering Storm*, p.viii.

[9] W. Murray, *The Change in the European Balance of Power, 1938–1939* (Princeton, NJ, 1984); see ch.7, and especially pp.217–34.

[10] On Eden, see D. Carlton, *Anthony Eden: A Biography* (London, 1981), for a critical account; David Dutton, in *Anthony Eden: A Life and Reputation* (London, 1997) provides a perceptive and balanced reassessment. On Churchill, see D. C. Watt, 'Churchill and Appeasement', in *Churchill*, ed. R. Blake and W. R. Louis (Oxford, 1993), ch.12. E. Du Réau, Edouard Daladier, 1884–1970 (Paris, 1993) contains much new material. Reynaud's remark is quoted in P. M. H. Bell, *A Certain Eventuality: Britain and the Fall of France* (Farnborough, 1974), p.57.

[11] J. –B. Duroselle, *La décadence, 1932–1939* (Paris, 1979); and *L'abîme, 1939–1945* (Paris, 1982). J.-L. Crémieux-Brilhac, *Les Français de l'an 40*, vol.1, *La guerre, oui ou non?*, vol.2, *Ouvriers et soldats* (Paris, 1990).

[12] For example, the best studies we have on Bonnet and Gamelin are by British historians: A.P. Adamthwaite, *France and the Coming of the Second World War, 1936–1939* (London, 1977); M. S. Alexander, *The Republic in Danger: General Maurice Gamelin and the Politics of French Defence, 1933–1940* (Cambridge, 1992).

[13] J. Charmley, *Chamberlain and the Lost Peace* (London, 1989); and *Churchill: The End of Glory* (London, 1993). See also C. Barnett, *The Collapse of British Power* (London,

1972). The *International History Review*, 13, no.4 (1991) devoted the whole number to articles on 'The decline and fall of Great Britain'.

[14] Thucydides, *History of the Peloponnesian War,* trans. Rex Warner, revised edn (London, 1972), p.48.

(Martin Pugh (ed.), *A Companion to Modern European History 1871–1945*, Oxford, Blackwell, 1997)

12   H. W. KOCH, 'HITLER'S "PROGRAMME" AND THE GENESIS OF OPERATION "BARBAROSSA"'

Hitler's foreign policy is still in an area of widespread interest – particularly the question of its inner coherence. The present consensus goes back to the early 1950s and 1960s, when the German attack upon Russia was viewed as one stage in Hitler's quest for European hegemony or even world domination. While Alan Bullock viewed Hitler as an opportunist, Hugh Trevor-Roper in his Essay of Hitler's war aims interpreted Hitler's invasion of Russia as a systematic step in Hitler's programme.[1] Since then this model has been highly refined and systematized, notably by Andreas Hillgruber,[2] who argues that Hitler's foreign policy programme had already been formulated long before he came to power, particularly in *Mein Kampf* and Hitler's *Second Book*. On this model National Socialist foreign policy was programmatically fixed and Hillgruber goes as far to say that Hitler's programme 'alone determined the great line of German policy in general' and that he devoted all the energies available to him to realizing it.[3] Yet even before Hillgruber had formulated the model, case studies were available which appeared to contradict its inner coherence and logic.[4] Serious objections have also been raised by Martin Broszat, who describes Hitler's idea of an eastern empire as a 'metaphor and utopian figure of speech'.[5]

Certainly, from an early stage Hitler had based the content of his foreign policy pronouncements upon racial, biological and geographical principles. In Hillgruber's view, Hitler's programme, his *Stufenplan*, envisaged first of all the consolidation of the NSDAP within the Reich, then re-establishment of military sovereignty in the demilitarized zone of Germany, followed by an aggressive foreign policy which in stages would ultimately achieve for Germany world hegemony. However, one major problem is presented by the available sources, or rather the way sources have been used. Hillgruber, who in 1964 had published a brilliant essay on sources and source criticism in the history leading up to the Second World War, in his own work ignores the very warnings which he had given.[6] The most recent challenge to Hillgruber's thesis of Hitler's long-term aim of carrying out the 'Final Solution' of the Jewish problem by way of genocide has come from none other than Martin Broszat.[7]

It cannot be the task of his essay to dismantle Hillgruber's thesis piece by piece. However, the analysis of the genesis of operation 'Barbarossa' serves as a test and an example demonstrating how questionable apparently closed and logical models of explanation are. Within the scheme of the *Stufenplan*, the conclusion of the Russo-German Non-Aggression Pact represented the necessary precondition which enabled Hitler to conduct his war against an isolated Poland, which he is alleged to have deliberately engineered. It is conveniently forgotten that the initiative for a bilateral German-Polish settlement over the Danzig and the Corridor question had come at the height of the Munich crisis from the Poles and not from the Germans. The solution then outlined by Hitler was the same as that put forward by Ribbentrop from November 1938 onwards; he picked up the threads which the Polish ambassador in Berlin, Lipski, had begun to spin the previous September.[8]

Also other important motives for Germany's rapprochement with Russia are ignored. Firstly, in view of the Anglo-French-Soviet military talks Hitler could hardly afford to remain passive, since he could not exclude the possibility of a coalition between the three powers. Secondly, and more important, the conclusion of the Russo-German Pact on 23 August 1939 was the motive not to provoke war, *so oder so*, but by means of the agreement to exert such pressure upon the Poles that they would accept the compromise proposals put forward by Hitler and Ribbentrop for the solution of the Danzig and the Corridor problem. Immediately, though unsuccessfully, from the time of the conclusion of the pact until 3 September, Germany sent request upon request to Moscow, firstly to send a Soviet military mission to Berlin and, secondly, to move strong Russian troop concentrations among Poland's eastern frontier.[9] In other words through pressure from the east and west the Poles were to be coerced into realizing the hopelessness of their position and accepting the German proposals. A man determined to erase Poland from the political map was hardly likely to have recourse to this wide range of political pressure in order to prevent a war which allegedly he was set upon provoking.[10]

Naturally the Russo-German pact caused also considerable surprise inside Germany. But it is important to distinguish between various important groupings in Germany, since the myth of the German monolith dominated by the Führer has crumbled into dust long ago.[11] Firstly, of course, there was Hitler himself, often erratic and indecisive, difficult in making up his mind, but once made up carrying through a decision relentlessly. Secondly, there was Ribbentrop, foreign minister since 1938 and, contrary to the orthodoxy current in the latter half century not simply a cypher and his master's voice, but according to the results of recent research a man capable of devising his own concept of foreign policy, even if this initially did not accord with Hitler's own ideas on the subject.[12] Ribbentrop after his return from his London embassy was convinced that Great Britain would oppose any German expansionist course in Europe. His summing-up report about his ambassadorial activities in London, which the Nuremberg prosecution team, despite repeated requests, withheld from the defence, while it rested peacefully in the archive of the Foreign Office, provides a very realistic assessment of official British attitudes towards the Third Reich.[13] From the moment of becoming foreign minister Ribbentrop consistently worked at achieving one objective: the creation of a continental, even Eurasian bloc against Great Britain, which was to keep it in check on a global scale and allow Germany to reach what had eluded her in 1914: the status of a world power. Such a continental bloc included Italy, but it was also to include Japan and Soviet Russia. The Russo-German pact was not something that for the Germans just luckily dropped out of the blue, but was part of Ribbentrop's scheme for forging a continental bloc directed against great Britain. It was defensive in the sense of preventing Great Britain from pursuing her traditional balance-of-power policy in Europe, but offensive in the sense that it aimed at establishing German hegemony in central and eastern central Europe with sufficient weight to exercise pressure upon Great Britain and France to make concessions to Germany's colonial ambitions.[14]

Thirdly, there was the army, which in spite of Hitler achieving supremacy over it as a result of the Blomberg/Fritsch crisis of 1938, had for some years come to enjoy relative autonomy and some of whose leaders belonged to the circle of opposition to Hitler.[15] Until the winter crisis of 1941/1942 they, especially the chief of the general staff, General Halder, exerted decisive influence in military policy making and on occasions showed no hesitation in ignoring or even forgetting about Hitler's orders.[16]

II

The Russo-German pact came as an utter surprise to the members of the German opposition, especially to General Beck, who as chief of the general staff had resigned during the Czech crisis in 1938, not on moral grounds, but because he was sure it would lead to another world war for which Germany was not armed. Out of his retirement Beck continued to pour out a flood of memoranda in which he criticized Hitler's policy and strategy, so much so that General von Tippelskirch asked 'Does this memorandum originate from an Englishman or a German? In the latter case he is over-ripe for a concentration camp.'[17] Halder was a complete disciple of Beck's and so were his closest associates.[18] He was a staunch anti-Bolshevik and shared Beck's anxiety that the Russo-German pact would open the door to the Soviets for expansion into the Baltic and Black Sea areas, an anxiety shared by members of the German Foreign Office.[19]

One other important factor was the way in which Hitler set about dealing with problems, which Halder aptly summarized as: 'when it appeared to him [Hitler] unavoidable to deal with an emerging problem, he used, as far as possible, to enter simultaneously upon all the avenues which would lead to the solution of the problem, in order to have some practicable solution at hand in case of a final decision'.[20]

This does not mean that between September 1939 and July 1940 Hitler considered the Soviet Union as a problem in the short term. There is no evidence that Hitler occupied himself with this problem. Indeed until the late summer of 1940 there existed no offensive plan against the Soviet Union in the German general staff. All we have is a record of a discussion with the chief of the OKW, General Keitel, of 17 October 1939 concerning the situation in Poland: 'Our interests consist in the following. Preparations are to be made, since the territory has military significance for us as a forward *glacis* which can be used for military assembly. For this reason railways, roads and communications must for our purposes be kept in order and used.' In the [Polish] General Government the preconditions for military movements were to be maintained, but the Soviet Union was not mentioned directly or indirectly, let alone that a war should be prepared from Polish soil against the Soviet Union.[21]

From Hitler's point of view the campaign in the west had its objective to deprive Great Britain of its 'continental sword'; for the protagonists of Hitler's 'programme' it was the necessary precondition before smashing Russia. The compromise peace expected with Great Britain would consolidate Germany's position in the west and allow the German armies to turn east. Halder in his diary noted a remark made by the liaison officer between the OKH and the foreign office, Hasso von Etzdorf: 'We are looking for feelers with England on the basis of the division of the world.'[22] This comment does not reveal from whom the idea originated and lacks any concrete indication as to what the 'division' was to look like. To this quotation another is frequently added, reported by General Sodenstern, chief of staff of army group A, according to whom Hitler had said on 2 June 1940: 'If England, as I expect, now gives up and is prepared to make a reasonable peace, then finally I will have my hands free for my really great task: the conflict with Bolshevism.' This evidence is complicated by the fact that Sodenstern withheld it 'for political reasons' until 1954 and that it was not published until 1958.[23] However, when Hitler was alleged to have made this remark, at the headquarters of army group A at Charleville, others were present, including General Blumentritt, who maintains that Hitler had mentioned in passing Russia's build-up of forces in her western border areas and that therefore it would be desirable to conclude a sensible peace with England.[24]

Interestingly enough, it was not Hitler but Halder and the foreign office, notably its secretary of state von Weizsäcker, who recognized a threat to Germany's position through Russian troop assemblies in the Baltic states and to the south, opposite Bessarabia. On 23 May reports of strong Russian troop movements reached the German foreign office and Weizsäcker forwarded them to Ribbentrop, noting in his diary, 'in the east there will be probably a further reckoning',[25] while General Jodl, chief of the Wehrmacht's leadership staff in the OKW, noted in his own diary a day later: 'Because of Russian troop assembly position in the east is threatening.'[26] When the news was reported to Hitler he replied saying that Russia in response to his request would limit herself to Bessarabia. But from 25 May onwards Russia created a series of crises in Lithuania, Estonia and Latvia, all three of which were occupied by Russia and incorporated in the USSR by 21 July 1940. Precisely during that period Hitler planned a drastic reduction of the German army. 'A precondition for this directive is the assumption that with the immediate final collapse of the enemy the task of the army has been fulfilled and that we can carry out in peace this reconstruction in enemy country, as the basis for future peacetime organization',[27] noted Halder on 15 June 1940. Russia's moves were felt as an inconvenience by Hitler, since they threatened Germany's supplies of raw materials. On 23 June Russia had demanded the concession for the nickel ores at Petsamo from Finland and four days later participation in the defence of the Aaland Islands or their demilitarization. This was followed by Russia's invasion of the northern Bukovina on 28 June 1940. There is nothing to indicate that Hitler envisaged at that stage a campaign against Russia; instead he gave priority of armaments to the Luftwaffe and the Navy.[28] On 25 June Hitler had still sounded optimistic:

> The war in the west has ended. France has been conquered, and I shall come, in the shortest possible time, to an understanding with England. There still remains the conflict with the east. That, however, is a task which throws up world-wide problems, like the relationship with Japan and the distribution of

power in the Pacific, one might perhaps tackle it in ten years' time, perhaps I shall have to leave it to my successor. Now we have our hands full for years to come to digest and to consolidate what we have obtained in Europe.[29]

Nothing was mentioned of an eastern campaign to be launched in 1940 or 1941. The directives just issued concerning army manpower and equipment for the armed forces would have been contrary to such a plan. It is quite incorrect to assert; 'as soon as it was clear that France was defeated, Hitler's eyes turned eastwards'.[30] It was not Hitler's eyes that turned eastwards, but those of Halder.[31] While on 26 June Halder expressed his opinion that the Bessarabian question could be solved without any warlike complications (an opinion confirmed a day later by Russia's unopposed occupation of that territory),[32] by 3 July 1940 Halder saw two problems, first how to deal with England and secondly the question of the east: 'The latter will have to be considered from the point of view of how a military stroke can be executed against Russia to force it to recognize the predominating role of Germany in Europe. Besides special considerations like the Baltic and the Balkan countries may cause variations.'[33] This was to counter Russia's moves to extend its power and influence in areas vital for Germany's war economy. Already on 30 June without instructions from Hitler Halder had ordered his staff to examine the possibilities of a campaign against Russia. It was not until 21 July 1940 that Hitler himself became active in the planning of such a campaign. The reason is not difficult to discern: the British peace offer did not come.[34] Why did England hold out? The answer to Hitler was simple, American support and 'Stalin courts England to keep her in the struggle to tie us down and to gain time to take what he wants to take and which cannot be taken anymore once peace ensues. He will be concerned that Germany does not become too strong. But there are no signs of Russian activity against us.'[35] Hence his directive, 'Russian problem is to be tackled. Mental preparations to be made.'[36]

III

The question which arises is what caused Hitler to change his mind and, following his chief of the general staff, to turn his eyes to the east? The Russo-German pact contained a consultative clause which compelled both partners to consult on issues touching mutual interests. When Germany had occupied Denmark and Norway, she had failed to consult the Soviet Union first. But Ribbentrop managed to explain it away by saying that Scandanavia would have become a theatre of war and, more important, that by allied action the Finnish question would have been resurrected. The Kremlin's fear that Sweden might be drawn into the conflict proved unfounded. Russia, which had stopped its deliveries of grain and oil, resumed its supplies to Germany.[37] But the lesson was not lost in Germany where the ugly word 'Soviet blackmail' made its rounds. Russia's conflict with Finland, settled in March 1940, had also threatened the nickel supplies from Petsamo, essential to the German war economy. It was therefore of paramount interest for the German leadership to contain the conflict in Norway, and bring it to an end as quickly as possible. What applied to Finland applied in equal measure to south-eastern Europe, to Rumania in particular, whose oil supplies represented the mainstay of Germany's oil imports until August 1944. Consequently most of the Balkans became for the Germans a security zone within which the allies would have to be prevented from establishing bases which could be used in the launching of air raids against the Ploesti oilfields, or gain a foothold in the Balkans to mount a land operation in this direction. In the question of oil supplies the Soviet Union occupied a critical position both as a supplier of oil itself and as the power nearest to Rumania's oil. Molotov's proclamation in December 1939 to the effect that Russia's great aims lay in south-eastern Europe and the Black Sea, whose attainment required a quick end to the Russo-Finnish conflict,[38] was bound to have been received with unease by the German leadership whose paramount interests in the Balkans as well as north-eastern Europe was to maintain calm and peace. Another power with traditional Balkan interests was Italy and Hitler urged upon Mussolini the necessity to keep still in the region, which Mussolini promised to do.[39] However, as a result of the Paris peace treaties of 1919, Rumania was surrounded by three 'revisionist' powers, Soviet Russia, Bulgaria and Hungary, each anxious to regain territories lost to Rumania. This course was realized in Germany, but for the moment the launching of the western campaign dominated the thinking of Germany's political and military leaders. Once Germany had launched its offensive, Stalin was not slow in following it up with his own demands, namely Bessarabia. On 22 May 1940 Germany received the news of the Russian demands on Rumania but, as we have seen already, Hitler believed they would be satisfied with Bessarabia.[40] King Carol of Rumania, who had expected this, had already addressed a letter to Hitler a week before, asking for his support and help in building fortifications on Rumania's eastern frontier. Hitler did not bother to reply.[41] But the German army leaders recognized the danger, so did the *Seekriegsleitung*.[42] On 25 May the German foreign office drew Russia's attention to the fact that her moves against Rumania at this point were highly inconvenient to Germany and Italy.[43] Great Britain, aware of the difficulties in the Balkans, announced the dispatch of Sir Stafford Cripps as envoy extraordinary to Moscow, a move whose effect the German ambassador in Moscow, Count von der Schulenberg, did his utmost to minimize with a success confirmed by a *Tass* communiqué of 30 May stating that the Soviet government could not receive Cripps or anyone else in the capacity of special or extraordinary plenipotentiary.[44] However, King Carol, when confronted by the Russian pressure, opted for Germany and on 27 May signed the oil pact which Germany had pursued for more than two years.[45]

In the meantime Russia liquidated the Baltic states, a process completed before the campaign in the west had ended and watched with disquiet by the Germans, especially as the Russians occupied a small territorial strip around Mariampul in Lithuania which had originally been consigned to the German sphere of influence in 1939. With that the Russians bolted the door to German access to the Baltic countries. Russia's annexations also had economic consequences. Seventy per cent of the exports of these three countries had been absorbed by Germany, mainly wheat, butter, pork, dairy produce, flax, wood and oil. A German foreign office assessment of the situation recorded that 'the stabilization of the Russian influence in these territories signifies a serious danger for us in so far as these essential supplies are concerned'.[46]

Rumours of Russian troop movements circulated in Berlin, which were immediately denounced by *Tass* as lies.[47] The Russian action in north-eastern Europe was also correctly interpreted as an overture to the solution of the

Bessarabian question.[48] Hitler, and Ribbentrop for that matter, had interpreted 'spheres of interest' rather literally, neither of them expecting the total destruction of sovereignty of the states concerned. Hitler therefore emphasized Germany's economic interest in Rumania.[49] On 23 June Molotov informed the German ambassador that the question of Bessarabia would no longer brook any delay, furthermore Soviet demands extended also to the Bukovina whose population he alleged to be Ukrainian.[50] Schulenburg was surprised at the speed of Russia's action. He was also surprised that Russia had successfully sought Italian backing. Relations between Russia and Italy had considerably improved during May 1940, and Italy, which in 1939 had still promised aid to Rumania in case of a Russian attack, stepped into accord with Russia, ostensibly to solve the Bessarabian problem with Germany.[51] Ribbentrop tried to counter this development, especially Italy's involvement in the Balkans, because the status quo there was not to be disturbed. He informed the Soviets that Germany had no objection to Russian claims for Bessarabia provided the claims could be realized in a way which would not result in war-like complications. Nevertheless the Italians could not be kept out of the game altogether. Ambassadors were exchanged between Moscow and Rome. This step was welcomed by Ribbentrop because it was in line with the foreign policy aims he had had since 1938.

In principle, harmony with the Soviet Union and Italy was one of Ribbentrop's desiderata, as long as this harmony was not at the expense of the tranquillity of south-eastern Europe. Yet when the Italian ambassador Rosso visited Molotov in the Kremlin on 17 and 20 June, Molotov picked up precisely those issues which were likely to produce conflict. Molotov declared his support for the territorial demands of Bulgaria and Hungary, namely the Dobrudsja and access to the Aegean Sea; Hungary's demands on Rumania he felt justified, and in the background of Molotov's elaborations was the unspoken aim of Russian expansion via Bulgaria to the Straits.[52] This, as Molotov pointed out, produced tensions with Turkey, the sources of which needed to be removed, but with due regard for German and Italian interests there. He furthermore acknowledged Italy's predominance in the Mediterranean, provided Italy would do the same as regards Soviet Russia and her claims in the Black Sea.[53]

The country that was expected to pay the highest price for these arrangements was Rumania. The German foreign office felt ill at ease in face of Moscow's call to Bulgaria and Hungary to state their claims against Rumania. Molotov was obviously a man in a hurry, and he made his demands at a time when a total of a hundred Soviet divisions on Russia's western frontier confronted a weak German covering force. As a result Halder on 25 June increased the German forces in the east to twenty-four divisions, including six armoured and three motorized divisions, a force still small compared with that of Russia.[54] Also Stalin's demand for the Bukovina had made Hitler angry, since it was of strategic importance.[55] Flanking the Moldavian territory, it controls the river Pruth from its source to its mouth, quite apart from the closer proximity of the Russians to the Ploesti oilfields. Hitler was bound to feel that his dependence on Russia was increasing.

Ribbentrop tried to counter the Russian demand for the Bukovina and Molotov ostensibly gave way on 26 June, restricting his claim to the northern Bukovina with the city of Czernowicz which provided the Soviet Union with the important rail link from Bessarabia via Czernowicz to Lvov. The following day Russia issued her ultimatum demanding the cession of Bessarabia and northern Bukovina.[56] The effects of the ultimatum were profound. Rumania, which so far had tried to steer a neutral course between the warring groups in Europe, had to take sides and chose Germany in the hope of German intervention. King Carol was prepared to fight, but Ribbentrop advised Rumania to accept the Russian demands in order to avoid war. Only one power could benefit from a war in the Balkans: Great Britain. More important, Rumania's oil production was bound to suffer. Therefore Ribbentrop and Hitler could do no other than to hold back the Rumanians. Rumania, on the other hand, asked for a German guarantee of its frontiers and for a German military mission. Hitler failed to reply immediately but ordered that security measures for the oilfields be reinforced.[57] Nevertheless on 1 July Rumania renounced all the guarantees previously given by the western powers and on 11 July 1940 left the League of Nations.

IV

The OKH, especially the general staff under Halder, had watched the developments in Rumania with apprehension, even with some alarm. Thus Halder recorded on 26 June that Russia wanted Bessarabia, in which Germany was not interested. But 'the question of the Bukovina thrown in by the Russians is new and exceeds the agreements arrived at between Russia and ourselves. But we have the greatest interest that there should be no war in the Balkan countries.'[58] And 'in foreign policy Russia's attitude stands in the foreground. The opinion predominates that the Bessarabia question can be solved without war.'[59] This was followed a day later with a sigh of relief when it became known that Russia had moved into Bessarabia without a struggle.[60] But a new note of alarm was raised, while the Russians now seemed to keep quiet, the Hungarians raised their territorial claims on Rumania resulting in the massing of troops on both sides of the Hungarian-Rumanian border, while at the same time news was received of increasing Russian activity in Estonia.[61] As early as 9 July Halder had noticed the increasingly unstable situation in Rumania, while Russia's attitude remained unclear and his aims to take control over the mouth of the Danube became more and more suspect. That the Russian moves would also have their impact upon the designs of Bulgaria and Hungary towards Rumania was noted, as well as Rumania's attempt to move closer to Germany, pretending that it enjoyed German protection. Russia's seizure of Bessarabia and also rumours that Rumania was evacuating the southern Dobrudsja elicited strong reactions within Rumania, especially among the Fascist Iron Guard under Horia Sima.[62]

The policy of russification of the Baltic states was viewed by the German general staff with dismay. More alarming, however, were rumours of a rapprochement between Great Britain and Russia: 'England and Russia look for closer relations with one another. An agreement over Iran cannot be excluded and could provide the basis on which 'bear and whale' find an understanding as in 1908.'[63] In the Balkans it was noted that the Dobrudsja had been evacuated for Bulgaria while Hungary had been advised by the Germans to hold back. But how long this could be maintained was a matter of speculation: 'The danger that Rumania and thus the whole of the Balkans is exposed to an internal crisis cannot be dismissed. With this England's interests would be served.'[64] On 13 July Halder noted Hitler's observations on the general situation. Hitler intended to bring Spain into line against Great Britain, to build up a front from the North Cape of Morocco. Hitler recognized that it was in Russia's interest for Germany not to become too powerful, but still unaware of the Russo-Italian conversations, he thought that Russia's drive for the Bosphorus would provide discomfort to the Italians. As far as the Balkans were concerned Hitler was sure that Rumania would have to foot the bill since Hungary would want its spoils while Bulgaria was taking the Dobrudsja, at the same time seeking access to the eastern Mediterranean at the expense of Greece. Hitler also made reference to the letter written to him by King Carol in which the latter put himself under Germany's protection. He considered that Rumania could easily sacrifice something to Hungary and Bulgaria, but:

> the Führer is most preoccupied with the question of why England does not want to step on to the path of peace. Like us he sees the answer to the question in the hopes which England puts upon Russia. He therefore reckons to have to force England to make peace. But he does not like it very much. Reason: if we smash England militarily, the British Empire will collapse. Germany will not benefit from this. With German blood we would obtain something whose beneficiaries would only be Japan, America and others.[65]

On 21 July the supreme commander of the German Army Field Marshal von Brauchitsch, had a conference with Hitler in Berlin the contents of which he reported to Halder the following day. The main theme was how to tackle Great Britain. A military operation against Great Britain might become necessary; Hitler was very unsure of its nature and expected the chiefs of the three services to put forward adequate proposals, but regarded an amphibious operation as a very serious risk:

> England sees perhaps the following possibilities: to cause unrest in the Balkans, via Russia to deprive us of our fuel supplies and thus ground our air fleet. The same purpose could be achieved by turning Russia against us. Aerial attacks upon our hydrogenation plants. Rumania: King Carol II has paved the way for a peaceful solution. Letter to the Führer. If England wants to continue the war, then politically everything will have to be harnessed against England: Spain, Italy, Russia.[66]

In other words Hitler slowly began to move towards the idea of the Eurasian bloc as advocated by Ribbentrop. Nevertheless, since Stalin appeared to be courting England, military preparations against Russia were to be taken in hand,[67] a decision which, as we have seen, Halder had already anticipated.[68]

In point of fact, Hitler was in a corner. He did not know how to put an end to the war. Without realizing it yet, he had lost the *political* initiative. Obviously the most direct way of dealing with the problem was to attack Great Britain, but in spite of laborious staff and logistics work carried out, Operation 'Sea-Lion' was stillborn. On 13 July the army had submitted its first operational study for cross-Channel invasion,[69] in response to Hitler's Directive no. 16 of 16 July 1940 concerning a German landing on British soil. During his conference with Brauchitsch he pointed out that it was 'not just a river crossing, but the crossing of a sea dominated by the enemy'.[70] He also added that if preparations could not be completed with certainty by the beginning of September it would be necessary to consider alternative plans.[71] By 31 July the requirements of the army and the inability of the navy to meet them had become so apparent that Raeder proposed that 'Sea-Lion' be postponed to the spring of 1941. Hitler gave no clear-cut assent to this proposal, but instead stated that the Luftwaffe should subject the south of England to eight days intensive bombardment: 'If the effect of the Luftwaffe is such that the enemy air-force, harbour, naval forces and so on are smashed then 'Sea-Lion' should be carried out in September. Otherwise postponement to May 1941.' At the same time Hitler emphasized that England's hopes rested with Russia and the U.S.A. Hence Russia would have to be smashed, the quicker the better. Consequently military preparations for the campaign against Russia should be continued.[72]

In effect Hitler's decision envisaged the postponement of 'Sea-Lion' and ultimately its abandonment. However, the continuation of military planning against Russia as such did not settle the final *political* decision that it should be attacked. Indeed, a day prior to the *Führerbesprechung* the alternatives to 'Sea-Lion' were considered by the OKH, which included the containment of Russia by diverting its attention towards expansion to the Persian Gulf. Other alternative steps were considered.[73]

> In case a decision against England cannot be enforced, the danger arises that England will ally herself with Russia, the question then arises of whether one should conduct a two-front war resulting from such an alliance, first against Russia; this is answered in that it would be better to keep friendship with Russia. To visit Stalin would be desirable. Russia's aims in the Straits and in the direction of the Persian Gulf do not disturb us. In the Balkans, which economically comes into our sphere, we can avoid one another. The Italians and Russians won't hurt one another in the Mediterranean.[74]

Thus German military planning went in all directions, while the number of political alternatives in Hitler's mind were gradually reduced to two. On the one hand there was a political solution in close collaboration with Russia and its participation in a continental bloc, a solution emphatically endorsed by Ribbentrop; on the other hand, in case of the failure of the continental bloc, plans for a quick decisive campaign against Russia in order to deprive Britain of her last 'continental sword'. This is not to say that Hitler cherished the first alternative, especially since Russia's actions continuously increased his suspicions. North-eastern Europe had been divided into spheres of interest, not so the Balkans. From June 1940 onwards it had become that which Hitler attempted to avoid: a source of unrest. While the German military presence in northern Europe was strong, this was not so in south-eastern Europe. Any upset of the status quo there would benefit Great Britain, and it could be triggered off by only two persons: Stalin and Mussolini. The latter he believed would follow his advice. But how far could Hitler afford to give way to Stalin's pressure without becoming more dependent upon him? If Hitler attempted to stop him, he was likely to drive him into the arms of Great Britain. Hence to integrate the USSR into the continental bloc seemed one way out of the dilemma, short of actually fighting her.

From 25 June Sir Stafford Cripps was British ambassador in Moscow. Stalin received him in early July and the German ambassador was informed of the conversations, which Schulenburg reported to Berlin. Cripps had put his finger on the crucial point, namely that His Majesty's Government was of the opinion that it was up to the Soviet Union to rally and lead the Balkan states for the purpose of maintaining the *status quo* there. Under the present circumstances this serious mission could only be undertaken by the Soviet Union.[75] Stalin was careful in his reply to this point, saying that the Soviet Union could not claim an exclusive role in the Balkans, but that nevertheless it was very interested in Balkan affairs.[76] This conversation was received with some alarm in Berlin and no doubt was at the root of Hitler's exposition of 21 July 1940. On the same day the Baltic states were formally annexed and incorporated into the Soviet Union.[77] Also Russia had resumed exerting pressure on Finland. In response Finland ostentatiously granted Germany 60 per cent of the annual output of nickel, which caused serious protest by the Russians.[78] Inevitably the German leadership interpreted the Russian move as one designed to increase Germany's dependence on Russia.

Throughout July, however, the main problem remained Rumania. Only on 15 July did Hitler reply to King Carol's letter of 2 July. He offered a German guarantee of Rumania's frontiers, dependent on Rumanian concessions to Hungary and Bulgaria.[79] This was tantamount to Hitler taking the initiative of reordering the Balkans, it was his response to Russia's moves – a response further nourished by the dispatches sent by the Yugoslav ambassador in Moscow, Gavrilovich, to Belgrade which were intercepted by the Germans. They pointed to a closer rapprochement between Russia and Yugoslavia, while the German ambassador to Belgrade summarized the views current there, 'after the present war is terminated a Russo-German conflict, sooner or later, is inevitable. If Germany succumbs she will be attacked by Russia.'[80]

Upon Ribbentrop's initiative, Hitler in the conference held on 31 July proposed to breathe new life into German-Japanese relations, essentially for two reasons: firstly in the case of the Russo-German conflict, to divert Great Britain's attention to south-east Asia; secondly if that conflict could be averted, to recruit Japan to the Eurasian continental bloc against Great Britain.[81] But before any final decision regarding an attack against Russia was made, relationships between the two countries should first be clarified *politically*. As far as Hitler's attitude to the Soviet Union at this point of time is concerned, no evidence whatsoever exists that it was motivated by his postulates about *Lebensraum*. Instead it was determined exclusively by political factors, predominately those operating in north-eastern and south-eastern Europe.

On 1 August Molotov addressed the Supreme Soviet in Moscow and drew up a balance sheet. He praised the improvement of Anglo-Russian relations as well as those with Finland, but with regard to the latter indicated the possibility of their deteriorating again. He demanded the full mobilization of Russia's resources so that no surprise of its enemies would meet it unprepared. But, most significantly, he described the successes achieved so far as being of limited value only and that new and greater ones would have to be achieved.[82] But where could the new achievements be attained? Mainly in the Balkans, the Straits and Finland. There is no record of a German reaction to this speech, but if there was one it can hardly have been favourable.

Still, in spite of continuing military planning against Russia, the Luftwaffe and the Navy retained priority in raw materials allocations and production programmes. On the diplomatic front Ribbentrop was convinced of the need for a speedy settlement of Hungary's and Bulgaria's territorial claims in Rumania, the need to fan the glowing embers of the conflict between Russia and Turkey to prevent an Anglo-Russian rapprochement under Turkey's mediation and to prevent bilateral agreements between Italy and Russia – aims the achievement of which should be crowned by an overall political settlement with Russia within the framework of a Berlin-Rome-Moscow-Tokyo agreement.[83] But under any circumstances peace would have to be maintained in the Balkans. Mussolini and his foreign minister Count Ciano had let it be known that they planned an attack on Greece and Yugoslavia, a plan which Hitler vociferously opposed.[84] On 24 August in a letter to Hitler, Mussolini promised not to venture anything in the Balkans, but instead to take the offensive in North Africa and, furthermore, that he could help to improve Russo-Japanese relations in the interest of the Axis policy.[85]

But Germany's policy of keeping the peace in the Balkans at almost any price was being threatened by the rapid deterioration of the relationship between Rumania and Hungary. King Carol had requested Germany on several occasions to dispatch a German military mission. Upon Hitler's initiative Rumanian-Hungarian negotiations had begun on 16 August but collapsed on the 24th. War threatened.[86] Germany was further alarmed by news of Russian troop movements in Bessarabia and in the northern Bukovina.[87] It quickly became clear that the Russians aimed at the occupation of the southern Bukovina, which Stalin had only given up under Hitler's pressure on 26 June.[88] The OKW on 25 August immediately decided to transfer demonstratively ten divisions to the east, including two armoured divisions which should ensure the possibility of 'quick intervention for the protection of the Rumanian oilfields'.[89] An exasperated Halder noted on 27 August:

> Conference with ObdH ... one intends to take Spain into harness, without realizing the economic consequences, one counts North Africa as a theatre of war against England ... one wants to secure Rumania without trying as yet to provoke the Russians too much. One wants to be prepared in the north (Petsamo) in case Russia attacks Finland. The army should be prepared for everything without receiving any clear-cut orders.[90]

However, by 29 August preparations for the occupation of the Rumanian oilfields were running at full speed,[91] and Jodl declared that the Führer had now decided that after the determination of the new frontiers between Hungary and Rumania he would dispatch a German military mission to Bucharest.[92] Ribbentrop invited the Hungarian, Rumanian and Italian foreign ministers to Vienna for 29 August and a day later the Vienna Arbitration Treaty was signed as a result of which Rumania ceded the northern part of Transylvania to Hungary. Germany and Italy now guaranteed the territorial integrity of Rumania.[93] Thus Germany for the first time countered Russian moves in south-eastern Europe by the overt threat of force of arms. Russo-German relations were clearly deteriorating. The treaty had serious consequences inside Rumania. King Carol abdicated, handing over his crown to his son Michael, and the government to Marshal Antonescu.[94]

At the same time the crisis continued to develop in north-eastern Europe. In the secret protocol of the Russo-German pact Finland had been assigned to the Russian sphere of influence. When new tensions between Russia and Finland began to develop from the end of July 1940 onwards, Hitler changed his mind, not least because of a memorandum from the war economy and armaments office which pointed out that Pestamo's nickel was as important to Germany's war effort as was the oil from Ploesti.[95] War was threatening between Russia and Finland, which inevitably would result in Russia's capture of Pestamo. Germany concluded a transit agreement with Finland which allowed the transport of German forces through Finland to the extreme northern part of Norway, Kirkenes. The German military delegation which had negotiated this agreement in Helsinki had been received with full military honours and great public enthusiasm. The agreement itself was signed on 22 September.[96] This does not mean that German forces were actually stationed in Finland. Until May 1941 only German forces in transit entered Finland. But in northern Norway mountaineering forces were placed in a state of readiness, so as to occupy Petsamo immediately, if the situation should require this.[97] A period of lull seemed to intervene but was disrupted by news received by the OKW that Russia had made new demands on Finland.[98] General von Falkenhorst was personally entrusted with guaranteeing the security of Petsamo.[99] Hitler also sanctioned the supply of weapons of all kinds to Finland, a step he had previously blocked.[100] Furthermore, he decided upon a public demonstration directed against Russia by assembling 88 mm flak batteries and their crews, fully uniformed and guns for all to see to be transported through Finland to Norway.[101] The Vienna Arbitration treaty, the 'public' transport of fully armed German forces through Finland as well as the transit agreement were a clear signal to Russia: *So far and no further!* Neither over the arbitration treaty nor the transit agreement had Ribbentrop consulted the Russians; it was his reply to Russia's proceedings in the Baltic countries, Bessarabia and the Bukovina. On the question of the transit agreement he left it to the Finnish government to inform the Russians. He subsequently informed Molotov about the contents of the arbitration treaty, justifying the speed with which it had been concluded by the imminent danger of war.[102] He did not hide his anger about Russia's Balkan policy, pointing out that the year before Russia had expressed merely her interest in Bessarabia. Although Germany had declared her lack of political interest, her economic interests were of vital importance in view of the connexion with oil and grain supplies. Apart from that Germany had not been consulted over the annexation of the Baltic states, nor the occupation of the strip of Lithuania which should have fallen to Germany.[103] Molotov accepted the note, promising a written reply, but cryptically assuring the German ambassador that nothing had changed the Russian attitude.[104] Molotov gave his written reply on 21 September 1940. In it he rejected the German arguments point for point and thus put an end to common Russo-German policy as it had been inaugurated on 23 August 1939.[105] Germany did not realize this immediately, though Hitler was more sceptical than Ribbentrop. Whilst the latter still worked for a joint Russo-German policy, Hitler doubted that it could be realized, though he did not exclude a political arrangement between the two countries until two months later. Hitler's scepticism was fully justified in view of the Kremlin's continuation with its previous policy. It supported Bulgaria's claim for the southern Dobrudsja, and what was all the more alarming to Hitler was that Bulgaria had appealed to Russia directly.[106] On 14 September Hitler had convened a conference whose major topic was 'Sea-Lion'. Hitler stated that a landing was not fixed for a specific time and was not constrained by any special set of circumstances. But one could not deny that the longer the war lasted, the greater would become the political tensions. Russia had expected Germany to bleed herself white in the west. The result had been a disappointment for Moscow. Hence Russia's speedy pressure upon Finland and the Balkans, whereas Germany was interested in maintaining a stable situation in north-eastern and south-eastern Europe: 'A long duration of the war is not desired. All that which is of practical value to us we have already obtained. Politically and economically the bases gained are sufficient.'[107] As far as 'Sea-Lion' was concerned he admitted that the pre-conditions for it had not been achieved, but it should not yet be cancelled. The Luftwaffe's chief of staff, Jeschonnek, demanded the bombardment of British residential areas, a demand which Hitler rejected, emphasizing that decisive targets would be railways, water and gas supplies. The bombing of the population must be a threat, a final resort.[108] It was a confession that Hitler did want to end the war, but did not see any way of how to do so. Instead of decreasing, complications increased. Early in October the Russians raised new demands for concessions in the Pestamo nickel mines. Ribbentrop advised the Finnish government to use delaying tactics.[109] He was playing for time in the course of which he hoped to come to a general settlement with the Soviet Union, by way of Molotov's visit to Berlin.

Rumania provided further cause for friction in the form of a German military mission consisting of army and Luftwaffe officers, to which were attached training units of both services. Germany did so on the explicit request of Marshal Antonescu.[110] While the Germans wanted only a force strong enough to protect the oilfields, Antonescu really desired a sizeable German contingent in order to train the Rumanian army for what he considered to be the inevitable conflict with Russia.[111] At this stage Hitler turned down the request making only one division available for Rumania. The function which the German troop transit through Finland was to achieve vis-à-vis Russia, one German division, plus Luftwaffe detachments were to achieve in the Balkans.[112] But Russia was not the only power German military presence was aimed at. It was aimed equally at Great Britain, from whom Hitler feared a direct intervention in Greece and Crete.

V

Although the east was beginning to dominate Hitler's attention, the forging of a continental bloc against Great Britain also required that he turn his attention to the west. Vichy-French forces on 23 September had successfully repulsed a British attempt to land at Dakar. France seemed a likely recruit for the continental bloc. So was Spain, where a successful attack by the Germans of Spanish-German forces upon Gibraltar could block the western entry into the Mediterranean. The Hitler-Franco meeting on 23 October at Hendaye proved a fiasco. Franco was not prepared directly to commit himself.[113] Hitler then went on to Montoire to meet Marshal Pétain. The results were equally inconclusive.[114] It is quite probable that in principle neither Franco nor Pétain would have had any objection to joining Germany provided Great Britain had been forced to her knees. By October 1940 this was obviously less likely than it had seemed during the previous early summer months. Moreover America's economic weight came increasingly to play in support of Great Britain and exerted pressure on Spain and Vichy. Still, Hitler retained the impression that at the right time under the right circumstances these two countries could be welded into the projected continental bloc. The surprise he received came from Mussolini, whom he met on 28 October and who informed him that Italy had just commenced its attack upon Greece. The OKW had anticipated this move: German forces in Rumania and later Bulgaria were reinforced.[115] Still, it was an unpleasant surprise to Hitler who had warned Mussolini against taking this step. Its results were disastrous and brought to nought Hitler's intention to preserve the peace in the Balkans. The OKW's prophecy came true; Italy's forces were contained by the Greeks and ultimately German forces had to come to their rescue.[116] The most immediate consequence was that Italy's action provided the British with the opportunity to establish bases in Greece and Crete.

In the meantime military preparations in the east went ahead, as did Ribbentrop's endeavours to forge his bloc. Once Hitler had become convinced that peace with Great Britain could not be obtained, he abandoned his notion of restoring the General Government of Poland into a German satellite state.[117] Instead came the order *Aufbau Ost*, frequently considered as a preparatory measure for 'Barbarossa'.[118] This interpretation has been strongly contradicted by Keitel, Raeder, von Brauchitsch, Jodl and Halder.[119] It served two ends, first the securing of sufficient training bases for the German army as storage areas for equipment to be removed from areas accessible to the RAF., and secondly as a blunt indicator to Russia that Germany could defend her interests in the Balkans.

Quite apart from that, the OKW's work and that of the OKH was not dominated by preparations for an eastern campaign. A host of other projects were worked on.[120] What did take place was a transfer of substantial forces into the southern corner of the General Government, so as to have a strong force in reserve to intervene in Rumania to protect the oilfields. There were now only 8 divisions in East Prussia compared with 16 divisions in the Cracow area.[121] Moreover, these troop movements were not carried out in any concealed fashion but *openly* to ensure that the Russians would take due notice of them.[122] On the contrary, the transfer of German forces from the west to the east:

> must not create in Russia the impression that we are preparing an offensive in the east. On the other hand, Russia will recognize that strong, high-quality German troops are in the [General] Government, in the western provinces as well as in the Protectorate and they will draw the conclusion that we can protect our interests – notably in the Balkans – at any time with strong forces.[123]

The size of the German forces was nevertheless inferior to those of the Russians. Between 1 September 1939 and 31 December 1940 Russia had doubled her forces from two to four millions on her western frontier.[124]

The diplomatic sphere was now dominated by the consequences of Mussolini's action in the Balkans, by the increasing activity of the USA and its deliveries of war material and foodstuffs to Great Britain. However, upon Hitler's orders German U-boats were prohibited from attacking American shipping, even if it sailed for British harbours.[125] For in 1940 there was no fear of any direct intervention of the USA in Europe, as it was election year and the promise of non-intervention a major plank in the election platforms of both Democrats and Republicans.[126]

Therefore the attempt had to be undertaken either to keep the USA out of the war or divert its attention to the Pacific. Once again Ribbentrop's concept of a Eurasian bloc came into play, at first in the form of the German-Italian-Japanese Tripartite Pact.[127] Ribbentrop's estimate of the American military potential and the speed with which it could be mobilized was somewhat more realistic than that of his Führer.[128] Russia could interpret the Tripartite pact as another version of the Anti-Comintern pact, despite Ribbentrop's endeavours to mediate between Russia and Japan. The result could well be driving Stalin into the arms of Germany's enemies. Therefore, from Ribbentrop's point of view, the new alliance would make sense only if Russia were included. Early in August 1940 the prospect of such a pact seemed rather remote because of Hitler's still prevailing scepticism towards it. But when on 17 August Roosevelt and the Canadian prime minister Mackenzie King met in Canada and agreed to joint staff talks and Canada made bases available along Nova Scotia for the US navy and air force,[129] following the conclusion of the Land-Lease agreement between the USA and Great Britain,[130] Hitler drastically changed his mind. He sent his special envoy Stahmer to Tokyo, who arrived on 7 September.[131] The Japanese prime minister Konoye shared Ribbentrop's view that Germany, Japan, Italy and Soviet Russia should join in one common front in spite of unresolved differences between Japan and Russia going back to the treaty of Portsmouth of 1905.[132] Mussolini, who during the initial sounding had been ignored, was informed personally by Ribbentrop who brought a personal letter from Hitler to Rome. Ribbentrop, in the course of his conversations with the Duce, admitted that the Tripartite pact ran the risk of driving Russia towards Great Britain and the USA, but Germany intended to divert Russia towards the Persian Gulf and to India. He welcomed the Italo-Russian rapprochement, though he shared Hitler's view that in any dealings with the Russians the spheres of interest would have to be defined very clearly and precisely. The only alternative to Russia's present Balkan policy would be to tie Russia even closer to the Axis powers, by which he meant having Russia join the alliance.[133]

In September 1940 Hitler had hoped that the Vienna arbitration treaty and the conclusion of the Tripartite pact would act as a deterrent to Russia's Balkan ambitions (as well as to America's further involvement in the war).[134] This was the primary reason why he urged the speedy conclusion of the pact rather than waiting until negotiations aimed at bringing Russia into the bloc (negotiations which, as Hitler knew, were bound to be lengthy) were completed. The pact was signed on 27 September 1940; from Hitler's point of view the foundation had been laid for a structure which, as we have already seen, he intended to extend to the west in the following months. Ribbentrop informed Russia two days before the pact was signed. According to Ribbentrop's instructions it was to be emphasized that the treaties concluded by the three powers with Russia, especially the Russo-German pact, would remain fully in force. Furthermore Ribbentrop would address a personal letter to *Herr* Stalin in which he would in detail and confidence put down the German opinion about the present political situation. The letter would also contain an invitation for Molotov to visit Berlin in order to discuss important questions concerning common political aims for the future.[135] The secretary of state von Weizsäcker also informed the Russian ambassador in Berlin accordingly.[136] Ribbentrop, and the somewhat more sceptical Hitler, aimed at a 'once-and-for-all' settlement of the open questions between Germany and Russia not outside the tripartite pact but within it – supplementing it with an alliance with Russia and with other European countries and thus creating a consolidated front against Great Britain and for that matter against the USA. The German chargé d'affaires von Tippelskirch was kept waiting because Sir Stafford Cripps had a rather lengthy interview with Molotov. When he was finally received, Molotov received the news without great surprise and appeared pleased about the news of the impending letter to Stalin. But he did ask for the text of the agreement and for information about any secret agreements.[137] Ribbentrop let it be known that no secret agreement existed and that according to article 4 of the pact none of the existing agreements of the signatory powers affected the political status which existed between them and the Soviet Union.[138] It soon became evident that Molotov in reality was more concerned than he showed.[139]

Both Hitler and Ribbentrop were now set upon bringing about a general clarification of the relations between Germany and Russia. That this would not be an easy task was obvious in the light of existing tensions. But both the German foreign office and the OKW were of the opinion that these tensions were of a transient nature only, that relaxation in Russo-Finnish relationships could be observed and that Moscow was stopping its forward policy in the Balkans.[140] On 24 October Halder noted that Brauchitsch, as a result of conversation with Hitler, expected Russia to join the Tripartite pact and again on 1 November that Hitler hoped 'to build in' Russia to the front against England.[141]

Yet in this period of high hopes new difficulties arose, this time over the Danube. The International and the European Danube commissions had ceased to exist and Ribbentrop convened a new European one, however omitting Russia, which in the meantime had gained a foothold on the mouth of the Danube. On balance it seems that he had overlooked Russia, because when the Soviet Union on 12 September submitted its protest, Ribbentrop immediately extended his invitation to her. Molotov demanded the reconstitution of the European commission but only by states along the Danube. This would have meant the exclusion of Italy. Now Ribbentrop protested and Molotov gave in. A preparatory conference was to meet on 29 October in Bucharest.[142] But three days before, the Russians unexpectedly occupied those islands in the Danube Delta which controlled the entire navigable mouth of the Danube and its traffic.[143] While the OKW took due notice of this step as well as the arrival of four Russian officers in Bucharest to observe the German forces there,[144] Hitler ignores this step, which amounted to a consequent continuation of Russia's Balkan policy, in the hope that this would be one of the many issues to be dealt with by the Russians during Molotov's visit. The conference in Bucharest prorogued itself on 21 December, never to meet again.

VI

Molotov's visit was not necessarily ill starred, but it did take place at a time when Russo-German relations were burdened by heavy liabilities. This is reflected in Hitler's directive No. 18, worked out by the *Wehrmachtsführungsstab* under Jodl. The OKW and the OKH had observed the gradual massing of the Russian forces on her western frontier, and in response the 30 German divisions in the east were increased up to 100. 'Russia would bite on granite; but it is not probable that Russia puts herself in opposition to us, "in Russia men rule with reason"'.[145] Also the fact that Rumania and Bulgaria wished to join the Tripartite pact was registered with satisfaction with the aim of a 'continental front against England',[146] and then a little later, 'Molotov on 10 November in Berlin. Reply by Stalin to letter by the Führer. He agrees with him. Molotov is coming to Berlin. Then one expects Russia's entry into the Tripartite pact.'[147] Also Hitler's attempts were registered to have Russia exert pressure on Turkey in order that the latter maintain her neutrality.[148] But the precondition for that was the continuation, indeed the intensification of Russo-German collaboration. This in turn caused Brauchitsch and Halder to enquire what the real intentions of Germany's political leadership were. But Russia 'remains the great problem of Europe. Everything must be done for great reckoning.'[149] Against this background Directive No. 18 was drafted.[150] It stands out from all other directives in listing operations the premises for which were as yet questionable or incomplete. In the form of a military directive it was the concept of a European coalition against Great Britain, in which Russia was expected to take part after Molotov's visit. To combine Germany, Italy, France, Spain and Japan was part of the scheme from which the attempt to draw Russia into it cannot be separated. Directive No. 18 reflected these endeavours.[151] After France, the Iberian peninsula, Italy and the Balkans, Russia was mentioned in the fifth point: 'Political talks with the aim of clarifying Russia's attitude in the near future have been introduced. Irrespective of what the results of these talks may be, all orally ordered preparations against the east are to be continued. Directives about this follow as soon as the basic lines of the operational plan of the army have been submitted and approved by me.' But then follows point six: 'Due to *changes* in the *general situation* [author's italics] the possibility or the necessity may arise that in the spring of 1941 we still come back to Operation 'Sea-Lion', consequently all three branches of the Wehrmacht must seriously endeavour to improve the foundations of such an enterprise in every respect.'[152] Halder in his entry from 4 November had already noted that one had to be prepared for 'Sea-Lion', but parallel to it preparations for the east would have to be continued. In other words Hitler was making provisions for both contingencies, as Directive No. 18 clearly shows, especially when one does not take point 5 in isolation but reads it with point 6; 'Sea-Lion' without Russian co-operation would have been impossible.

Ribbentrop's letter to Stalin had been handed over to Molotov on 17 October. It was a lengthy document, based on the premise that the war against Great Britain was already won. Molotov received it with reserve. He could not reply to the invitation yet, he would withhold his answer until Stalin had studied the letter.[153] But already on 19 October Molotov indicated a favourable response.[154] On 21 October the reply was given.[155] While Ribbentrop had suggested a joint meeting between the foreign ministers of Germany, Russia, Italy and Japan, Stalin expressed his preference, at least initially, for a joint Russo-German meeting between 10 and 12 November.[156] Molotov also refused publication of the date of his visit until the moment of his departure. As Hungary, Rumania, Bulgaria and Slovakia were about to join the Tripartite pact, the German ambassador pressed for publication of this news to be withheld until after Molotov's visit.

Molotov arrived in Berlin on 12 November. Already at midday on the day of his arrival, Molotov and the deputy people's commissar for foreign affairs, Dekanosov, shortly to be ambassador in Berlin, met Ribbentrop, who wanted to brief him about what Hitler intended to talk about in the afternoon.[157] According to Ribbentrop England was beaten; even the entry of the USA. would not change this fact. Germany was about to unite the European states into an anti-British coalition. The tripartite pact was the suitable instrument which otherwise served peaceful purposes. Ribbentrop's personal aim was to bring about a rapprochement between Russia and Japan. In the same way in which spheres of influence between Germany and Russia had been defined, this should be possible between Russia and Japan. It was the Führer's aim to specify the spheres of influence between Germany, the USSR, Japan and Italy. This should present no great difficulty since the main interest of all countries concerned lay in a southern direction. The German Reich tended towards central Africa, Italy to North and East Africa and Japan into the southern Pacific. The real question was whether or not Russia could see that its true interests lay in southern expansion. Germany was interested in Russia's expansion towards India and the Persian Gulf, this would take pressure from the Baltic and the Straits.[158] Ribbentrop's exposition, painted with broad strokes on a white canvas, shows that the wish was father to the thought. Molotov was quick to detect the weakness in Ribbentrop's argument. But to remain conciliatory Ribbentrop pointed to the possibilities in the Dardanelles such as the revision of the Montreux Convention, but ruled out any suggestion of Russian naval bases at the Bosphorus. Molotov's reply was concise. With the exception of the Finnish question to which he would come shortly, the laying down of spheres of interest in 1939 had only been a partial solution which had been overtaken by the events of 1940. Much to Ribbentrop's discomfort he continued in this vein for some time.[159]

In the afternoon Molotov was received by Hitler, who went out of his way to charm him and make him comfortable.[160] Hitler talked quietly, making no attempt at intimidation. He pointed out that Germany was not seeking direct military help from the Soviet Union; the war and its development had forced Germany into areas in which it had primarily no political or economic interest. But as long as the war lasted, the Reich was dependent upon certain raw materials which it could not do without. Then he turned to the question of how in the future the collaboration between Germany and Russia could be more clearly defined and strengthened. Germany's most important problem had been that of living space, but in the course of the war it made conquests which it would take a century to digest, also Germany was interested in Central Africa because of the raw materials there. In addition there were certain areas in which Germany could not allow any rival to have air or naval bases. On none of these points existed any reason for conflict between Germany and Russia. Although the USSR and Germany could never be one world, there were good preconditions for co-existence. Hitler admitted that there were a number of points that touched the interests of both countries. Germany desired to break out of the North Sea, Italy out of the Mediterranean and Russia, too, was striving for access to the open seas. The question was whether or not there was the possibility of achieving this without these countries coming into conflict with one another. With France he had settled everything in a manner to put an end to the age-old historical conflict. Germany had no interest in the Balkans, although there were important raw materials there and consequently the Reich would do everything to prevent the British from gaining a foothold in that region. For this reason the presence of German forces would be temporarily necessary. He, Hitler, wished for peace because war is a bad business. The long-term threat originated from the USA. For that reason he was in touch with France to formulate a European Monroe Doctrine. In other areas in which Russia was primarily interested she should be a privileged power and her interests would dominate. Out of this situation emerged a power grouping, whose cohesion might well be difficult, but should not represent an insurmountable obstacle. Naturally Germany would assist Russia in the revision of the Dardanelles question.[161]

Hitler's exposition had been rather more specific than that of Ribbentrop. But there remained points over which Hitler was vague and imprecise, as for example over the time when German forces would be withdrawn from the Balkans.

Molotov's answer was relatively short, but to the point. At the outset he declared that Stalin and he were of the same opinion. He agreed with the Reich chancellor that the Russo-German treaties had brought advantages to both sides. And he underlined the fact that Germany's advantages were in no small measure due to the loyalty of Russia. He ignored Hitler's reference to the Dardanelles question. Instead he immediately raised the Finnish problem. The Finns had fulfilled the Moscow Treaty but for one point. Molotov asked Hitler whether the Russo-German agreement of 1939 still applied to Finland. Apart from that these agreements were only partial solutions. Other problems had moved to the fore and demanded solution. What did the German Reich understand by the establishment of a new order in Europe and Asia? To what extent were Russian interests, especially in Bulgaria, Rumania and Turkey touched by it? What was one to make of the Greater Asia Co-Prosperity Sphere? Certainly these were details he could discuss with Ribbentrop in Moscow, but he was anxious to hear the Führer's own opinions.

Hitler was slightly annoyed by the directness of Molotov's questions since they touched upon problems he would rather have deferred dealing with, or ignored altogether, especially those concerning the Balkans and Finland. At this point he became vague. Not Russo-German relations but Franco-German relations had been his most difficult problem. Now that he had resolved the latter, he would return to the former. The first stage of co-operation of the nations of western Europe had been achieved. It was a policy which also envisaged co-operation with the east, with Russia and Japan. The main problem was to keep the USA from Europe, Africa and Asia. Molotov noted well that Hitler was avoiding a direct answer, but expressed his general agreement and readiness for Russia to co-operate with the Tripartite pact, as long as she would partner and not object.[162]

The second meeting between Hitler and Molotov was, as far as Hitler was concerned, determined by the conviction he had gained that the position of the Soviets could not be shifted. Russia concentrated on two aims: Finland and Rumania. This meant, sooner or later, the annexation of Finland and the extension of Russian influence over the Balkans. Hitler in his talk with Molotov emphasized that on the question of respective spheres of interest Germany had strictly adhered to the Russo-German agreements, something which Russia in some cases had not done, especially in Lithuania and the Bukovina. Hitler then touched on the Finnish problem. In principle Germany had no interest there, but as long as the war lasted it was dependent on Finnish supplies of timber and nickel. Therefore Germany did not desire a new conflict in the Baltic region. With regard to Russo-Finnish relations he pointed to the widespread sympathies of the German public for the Finns in the Russo-Finnish conflict and the difficult stand he had had then. He did not wish in the foreseeable future to be put in a similar position again. As long as the war lasted Finland was as important to Germany as was Rumania, although these areas belonged to the Russian sphere of influence. Molotov interjected that the Russo-German agreement had concerned a first stage, the second stage had come to an end with Germany's victory over France, and now the third stage was being confronted. Germany must show sympathies for Russia's claim for the southern Bukovina. Hitler blocked this demand and underlined his wish to avoid war in the Baltic and Balkan regions. Otherwise previously unforeseen complications could arise. To avoid war there did not by any means imply a breach of the Russo-German agreement. Nor was it a breach when Germany guaranteed the territorial integrity of Rumania.[163]

Molotov remained unimpressed. He returned to the Finnish problem, which led to a short but sharp exchange between him and Hitler. Hitler put an end to it by asking Molotov how he envisaged the solution of the Finnish problem. Molotov blandly replied that he saw it in much the same way as in the Baltic countries and Bessarabia. Thus Molotov had put his cards on the table. Hitler replied that there must be no war in the Baltic region. Molotov demanded that Germany adopt the same attitude which it had adopted during the winter of 1939/40. Thus both positions had been clearly defined, especially Russia's expansionism to the south, a solution which Hitler by that time seems to have lost faith in, though not Ribbentrop, who also submitted a draft treaty for Russia to join the Tripartite pact which he handed to Molotov.[164] Molotov produced one last shock, namely the question of Russia's free access from the Baltic. Ribbentrop, at first at a loss for an answer, replied that for the duration of the war the *status quo* in the Baltic would have to be preserved. Molotov then remarked that he would submit the draft treaty to Stalin and discuss it with him.[165] For Hitler the conversations with Molotov had been a 'test', whether Germany and Russia 'stood back to back, or chest to chest.[166]

Even after Molotov's departure some weak hopes remained; Hitler and Ribbentrop waited for Stalin's answer. But Hitler's scepticism was justified when on 18 November Molotov warned the Bulgarian envoy against accepting a German guarantee without the participation of Russia.[167] Shortly thereafter news reached Berlin that Hungary's, Rumania's, Bulgaria's and Slovakia's accession to the Tripartite pact had not met with Russian approval.[168] Finally on 25 November Molotov handed Russia's official reply to the German ambassador. Russia made her joining the Tripartite pact conditional on the withdrawal of all German forces from Finnish soil. All economic obligations towards Germany by Finland would be assumed by Russia. Furthermore, Russia insisted on bases for land and naval forces at the Bosphorus and the Dardanelles. Thirdly the Kremlin demanded Germany's recognition of Russian claims to the territory south of Baku and Batum in the direction of the Persian Gulf. Lastly Japan would have to cede to Russia its concessions for the exploitation of oil and coal resources in North Sakhalin. And last but not least, Moscow demanded the abrogation of the Russo-German secret treaties in its favour.[169] Hitler read the note, put it on his desk and did not bother to reply. The dice had been cast.

Was 1941 meant to be a preventative stroke, or was it simply an act of aggression? It was both. Hitler could under no circumstances risk Soviet intervention in Finland. He could not afford to expose himself further to the Russian threat of blackmail, irrespective of whether it was Finland, Rumania or any other Balkan country. Against the background of the Soviet attitude and actions adopted since June 1940 he was convinced that Stalin would not keep to the letter of any agreement, but from time to time, according to the prevailing situation, tighten the thumbscrews in order to gain further concessions from Germany, territorial or political. Russia's entire policy in 1940 had aimed at predominance in south-eastern and north-eastern Europe, a policy consistently pursued until 22 June 1941. Hitler was not prepared to accept the risk of conducting war in which he was dependent on the goodwill of Stalin, whose ambitions he asserted rather more realistically than either Churchill or Roosevelt. Without doubt, in August 1939 Hitler, as was so often the case, had fixed his eyes upon one aim only, this time Poland, without taking into consideration the ultimate consequences of a German dependence upon Russia. He calculated that the end of this dependence would come at the latest after the defeat of France and Great Britain, or at the earliest as a result of these two powers failing to enter into a European war in the light of the power constellation as it existed on 23 August 1939. Only stage by stage did he recognize the Soviet aims and their effect upon Germany's position in Europe. It was only as a last resort that he found himself forced in the interest of Germany and Europe, as he interpreted it, to point to the Soviets the limits of their power. Thus 25 November 1940 becomes the key date in Russo-German relations as well as in German military planning aimed at attacking the Soviet Union. On 5 December Brauchitsch and Halder submitted the first operation plan of the German attack against Russia. Hitler baptized it 'Barbarossa'.[170] Operation 'Sea-Lion' 'can remain outside our consideration'.[171] Seven days later in Directive No. 21, 'Case Barbarossa', Hitler stipulated that decisive importance was to be placed upon the German preparations for the attack in the east not being recognized.[172] Whereas before, Hitler, in order to contain Russian ambitions, had carried out German troop movements in north-eastern and south-eastern Europe demonstratively, this was now no longer the case.

The war against Poland, as Ernst Nolte argued, was in its inception a war of national restitution, that in the west one of the revision of Versailles.[173] The war against Russia, however, was an attempt also to impose Germany's 'Manifest Destiny' under the slogan 'Eastwards the course of Empire': the attempt to transpose upon Germany the process of territorial expansion analogous to that experienced by the USA. and Russia in the preceding century. Only Germany did not face fragmented Indian tribes, tartars or Mongolians whose subjugation and even extermination was relatively easy to accomplish, about whose disappearance hardly anyone cared. To transpose the American and Russian experience by Germany upon eastern Europe meant the subjugation of over 200 million people. Hitler's own ideology, largely left in limbo since 1933, came to full fruition. Theory and practice coincided. Both preventive war and ruthless territorial aggrandizement, accompanied by mass enslavement and extermination on a scale which Stalin apart, no one in Europe had practised in modern times merged into an orgy of destruction.

VII

This study of Russo-German relations in 1940, however, demonstrates how mistaken it is to see in Hitler's aims a detailed 'programme', conceived long before 1933, executed with remorseless logic and consistency. Hitler, like any other statesman, could only act and react within the context of the changing political constellation. Until the late summer of 1940 a compromise with, or a defeat of, great Britain stood at the centre of Hitler's aims. However, these were subject to gradual change in the face of Soviet actions in north-eastern and south-eastern Europe. But even at a time when he had begun to recognise the cloud on the horizon, he still believed he could leave it to 'a successor' to deal with. And, even more important, at the moment when there could be no longer any doubt about Soviet intentions in Europe, he and Ribbentrop tried to contain or absorb them within the framework of the Tripartite pact, or to divert them into other regions as well as harness Russia into a common front against Great Britain. All the alternatives available to the Third Reich were put into play, but Stalin and Molotov rejected them. Germany's arsenal of traditional diplomacy was exhausted. Not fate, but old ambitions, German and Russian alike, rekindled and refashioned, took their course.

Notes

[1] A. Bullock, *Hitler. a study of tyranny* (London, 1952); H. R. Trevor-Roper, 'Hitler's Kriegsziele' in *Vierteiljahrhefte für Zeitgeschichte (VfZg)*, 1960.

[2] A. Hillgruber, *Hitler's Strategie und Kriegsführung* 1940–41(Frankfurt 1965); Ibid. *Deutsche Grossmacht und Weltpolitik im 19. Und 20. Jahrhundert* (Düsseldorf 1977); K. D. Bracher, *Die deutscher Diktatur* (Cologne, 1969); H.-A. Jacobsen, *1939–1945: Der Zweite Weltkrieg in Chronik und Dokumenten* (Darmstadt, 1965); E. Jäckell; *Hitlers Weltanschauung Entwurf einer Herrschaft* (Tübingen, 1969); A. Kuhn, *Hitlers aussenpolitisches Programm, und Entwicklung 1919–1939* (Stuttgart, 1977); K. Hildebrand, *Deutsche Aussenpolitik 1933–1945. Kalkül oder Dogma* (Stuttgart, 1970); J. Thiess, *Architekt der Weltherrschaft. Die Endziele Hitlers* (Düsseldorf, 1976).

[3] Hillgruber, *Hitlers Strategie*, pp. 564ff.

[4] J. Gehl, *Austria, Germany and the Anschluss 1931–1938* (Oxford, 1963); W. Rosar, *Deutsche Gemeinschaft. Seyss-Inquart und der Anscluss* (Vienna, 1971); W. Schieder, 'Spanischer Bürgerkrieg und Vierjahresplan' in U. Engelhardt, V. Sellin, H. Stuke (eds.), *Soziale Bewegung und politische Verfassung. Beträge aur Geschichte der modernen Welt* (Stuttgart, 1976), pp. 162–90; W. Conze, *Die deutsche Nation. Ergebnis der Geschichte* (Göttingen, 1963), p. 144.

[5] M. Brosazart, 'Soziale Motivation und Führerbindung' in *VfZg*, 1970; for a perceptive discussion of the ambivalent terms 'world power', world dominion' and 'world domination' see D. Aigner, 'Hitler und die Weltherrschaft' in W. Michalka (ed.), *Nationalsozialistische Aussenpolitik* (Darmstadt, 1978), pp. 49–69.

[6] A. Hillgruber, 'Quellen und Quellenkritik aur Vorgeschichte des Zweiten Weltkrieges' in Wehrwissenschaftliche Rundschau, 14, 1964.

[7] A. Hillgruber, 'Die Endlösung und das deutsche Ostimperium als Kernstück des rassenbiologischen Programms des Nationalsozialismus', in Hillgrüber, *Deutsche*

Grossmacht, pp. 252–75; M. Broszat, 'Hitler und die Gebesis der Endlösung' in *VfZg* 1977; Broszat, while rejecting D. Irving's nonsense on the subject, convincingly argues and demonstrates that the 'Final Solution' was not the product of a programme but based on a number of *ad hoc* decisions by local SD and NSDAP officials on the spot which in course of time became institutionalized. Broszat's arguments receive confirmation from a surprising quarter, none other than Adolf Eichmann in his posthumuous memoirs, *Ich, Adolf Eichmann* (Leoni, 1980) in the introduction of which he explicitly declares himself guilty as an accessory to murder.

[8] T. Desmond Williams, 'Negotiations leading to the Anglo-Polish Agreement of 31 March 1939' in *Irish Historical Studies*, x, 59–93 and 156–92; *Documents and materials relating to the eve of the Second World War* (Moscow, 1948), pp. 176–83.

[9] *Document on German Foreign Policy* (DGFP), Series D, vii, docs. Nos. 360, 383, 387, 388, 413, 414, 424, and 446. See also *Generaloberst Halder Kriegstagebuch* (Halder-KTB) (Stuttgart, 1962), 1, entry 29 Aug. 1939.

[10] H. W. Koch, 'Hitler and the origins of the Second World War; second thoughts on the status of some documents' in *Historical Journal*, 1968; some additional material has since come to light which shows that Hitler's speech to his generals on 23 May 1939 was put on paper only in early November 1939 of that year and D. Kluge's study, *Das Hossbachprotokoll: Die Zerstörung einer Legende* (Leoni, 1980) conclusively proves, at least to this author, that the document submitted at Nuremberg under that name is a falsification. W. Bussmann's contribution on the origins of the Hossbach Memorandum (*VfZg*, 1968) adds nothing to the debate, while W. Baumgart's analysis of Hitler's speech to his generals on 22 August 1939 was put on the hypothesis tentatively put forward by the late Gerhard Ritter, that in fact there mat have been two speeches, a hypothesis firmly contradicted by such participants in the conference as Admiral Böhm and General Halder in his diary. See *VfZg*, 1971. For the most recent source criticism see B. Stegmann, 'Hitler Ziele im ersten Kriegsjahr 1939/40. Ein Beitrag sur Quellenkritik', in *Militärgeschichtliche Mitteilungen* I/1980, and for a summary criticism of Hitler's 'programme' N. Stone, *Adolf Hitler* (London, 1980), passim.

[11] See for instance M. Broszat, *Der Staat Hitlers* (Munich, 1969); A. Speer, *Erinnerungen*, (Berlin, 1969); ibid. *Der Slavenstaat* (Berlin 1980); H. Höhne, *Der Orden unter dem Totenkopf*, (Gutersloh, 1969); P. Hüttenberger, 'Nationalsozialistiche Polykratie' in *Geschichte und Gesellschaft. Zeitschrift für historische Sozialwissenschaft* (Göttingen, 1976).

[12] W. Michalka, *Ribbentrop und die deutsche Weltpolitik 1933–1940* (Munich, 1980); idem, 'Von Antikominternpakt sum Euroasiatischen Kontinentalblock: Ribbentrops Alternativkonzeption zu Hitlers aussenpolitischen Programm' In Michalka, *Nationalsozialistische Aussenpolitik* (Darmstadt, 1981), pp. 474–92.

[13] Ribbentrop's Hauptbericht London A 5522, 28 December 1937' reprinted in full in Annelies von Ribbentrop, *Die Kriegsschuld des Widerstands* (Leoni, 1974), pp. 64ff, also his *Schlussfolgerungen* 2 Jan 1938, ibid. pp. 75ff. Michalka, *Ribbentrop*, pp. 224ff.

[14] Michalks, 'Von Antikominternpakt', pp. 477ff.

[15] See G. Ritter, *Carl Goerdeler und die deutsche Widerstandsbewegung* (Munich, 1964); P. Hoffmann, *Widerstand, Staatsstreich and Attentat* (Munich, 1969). For a more critical and differentiated assessment of the army opposition see K. Müller, *Armee, Politik und Gesellschaft in Deutschland 1933–1945* (Paderborn, 1979), especially his essay 'Die deutsche Militäropposition gegen Hitler. Zum Problem ihrer Interpretation und Analyse' and, by the same author, *General Ludwig Beck* (Boppard/Rhein, 1980).

[16] Hitler in the summer of 1942 realized the sector was vulnerable to a Soviet breakthrough. He issued orders to reinforce them by anti-tank defences in depth and the transfer of one Panzer Division from France. Halder did nothing The Russian breakthrough in November 1942 occurred at precisely the point predicted by Hitler. See W. Warlimont, *Im Hauptquartier der Wehrmacht 1939–1945* (Frankfurt, 1962),

p. 266; M. Kehrig, *Stalingrad: Ana;yse und Dokumentation einer Schlacht* (Stuttgart, 1974), passim.

[17] Quote from H. Groscurth, *Tagebücher eines Abwehroffiziers 1938–1940* (Stuttgart, 1970), p. 478. But see also B. A. Leach, *German strategy against Russia 1939–1941* (Oxford, 1973), pp. 533ff. And Ritter, *Goerdeler*, pp. 209ff.

[18] Such as General Karl-Heinrich von Stülpnagel, the deputy chief of the general staff, General Wagner, the quartermaster-general, General Fellgiebel, the inspector-general of signals, and Colonel (later Geberal) von Treskow, staff officer Ia of the operations department of the general staff, as well as members of the OKW, like the chief of the *Abwehr* Admiral Canaris, General Oster, one of his departmental heads, and General Thomas, head of the war economy and armaments office.

[19] Groscurth, *Tagebücher*, pp. 490–9.

[20] F. Halder, *Hitler as Feldher* (Munich, 1950), p. 47.

[21] *Halder-KTB*, I, 18 Oct. 1939.

[22] Ibid. 21 May 1940.

[23] K. Klee, Das Unternehemen 'Seelöwe' (Göttingen, 1958), p. 189.

[24] W. Ansel, Hitler confronts England (Durham, N. C., 1960), p. 108.

[25] L. E. Hill (ed.), *Die Weizsäcker Papiere 1933–1950* (Berlin, 1974), p. 204.

[26] *Jodl-Diary* quoted by *Jacobsen*, 1935–1945, p. 145.

[27] *Halder-KTB*, I, 15 June 1940.

[28] Ibid. 28 May; 7 June; 12 June; 16 June and 19 June 1940; also G. Wagner (ed.), *Lagevorträge des Oberbefehlshabers der Kriegesmarine vor Hitler 1939–1945* (Munich, 1972), 14 June 1940.

[29] H. Böhme, Der deutsch-französische Waffenstillstand im Zweiten Weltkrieg. T. I. Entstehlung und Grundlagen des Waffenstill standes von 1940 (Stuttgart, 1966), p. 79.

[30] Leach, *German strategy*, p. 55.

[31] *Trial of the major German war criminals before the International Military Court* (Nuremberg, 1947), xx, 576–7 (IMT).

[32] *Halder-KTB*, 26 and 27 June 1940.

[33] Ibid. II, entry for 3 July 1940.

[34] Public Record Office (P. R. O.) London, War Cabinet minutes, May–June 1940, CAB65/67; July–August 65/8; Premier: miscellaneous correspondence on peace negotiations I 1940, PREM 1/443. Private papers of Lord Halifax (1938–40), FO 408/70; *Foreign relations of the United States* (FRUS) I, *General* (Washington, 1959); II, *General relations of the United Sates* (Washington, 1957); III, *The British Commonwealth*, and IV, *The Far East* (Washington, 1955). E. L. Woodward, *British foreign policy in the Second World War* (London, 1962), and subsequent multi-volume versions of the same work maintain a discreet silence over the tensions and divisions within the British cabinet and government at the time over the issue of a negotiated peace, although there is ample evidence in the P. R. O. and the relevant volumes of the *FRUS* as well as in the Swedish archives. The latter have closed access since the embarrassing revelations of the Swedish ambassador in London at the time, Björn Prytz. The best and only volume dealing with this complex matter is Bernd Martin's *Friedensinitiativen und Machpolitik im Zweiten Weltkrieg* (Düsseldorf, 1974), parts IV and V, pp. 234–370.

[35] *Halder-KTB*, II, Brauchitsch's report on the Führer's conference of 21 July 1940 in Berlin, p.32.

[36] Loc. cit.

[37] A. Seidl (ed.), *Die Beziehungen zwischen Deutschland und der Sowjetunion 1939–1941* (Tübingen, 1949), doc. Nos. 127, 128. This collection of official documents comes mainly from the Nuremberg Trials. Part of it has been reprinted in *DGFP*, though the bulk of the material is now in the *Politisches Archiv* of the Bonn Foreign Office. Information supplied to the author by the *Politisches Archiv*, July 1974.

[38] *IMT*, xxxiv, Assmann diary, entry 22 May 1940, p. 682.

[39] *Jodl-Diary*, *IMT*, xxxviii, 414.

[40] *Halder-KTB*, I, entry 22 May 1940.

[41] A. Hillgeuber, *Hitler, König Carol and Marshall Antonescu: die deutsch-rumanischen Beziehungen 1938–1944* (Wiesbaden, 1954), p. 71.

[42] Assmann in *IMT*, xxiv, 685 and also Hillgruber, Hitler, *König Carol*.

[43] Seidl, *Die Beziehungen*, doc. no. 149.

[44] J. Degras (ed.), *Soviet documents on foreign policy*, III, 1933–41 (London, 1953), p. 450; Seidl, *Die Beziehungen*, doc. no. 134; *Soviet Documents*, p. 452.

[45] *DGFP*, series D, ix, p. 459.

[46] Seidl, *Die Beziehungen*, doc. no. 134.

[47] Ibid. doc. no. 138.

[48] Ibid. doc. no. 139.

[49] Ibid. doc. no. 149.

[50] Ibid. doc. no. 137.

[51] *DGFP*, series D, ix, doc. nos. 344, 349, 359.

[52] Seidl, *Die Beziehungen*, doc. no. 142; *Soviet documents*, p. 457.

[53] *Soviet documents*, loc. cit.

[54] *Hakder-KTB*, I, 25 June 1940.

[55] *IMT*, x, Ribbentrop evidence, p. 331.

[56] Seidl, *Die Beziehungen*, doc. no. 141.

[57] Ibid. doc. no. 145.

[58] *Halder-KTB*, I, 25 June 1940.

[59] Ibid. 26 June 1940.

[60] Ibid. 27 June 1940.

[61] Ibid. 5 July 1940.

[62] For the Iron Guard and Horia Dima see E. Nolte, *Die faschistischen Bewegungen* (Munich, 1968), pp. 168ff., also Hillgruber, Hitler, *König Carol*, passim.

[63] *Halder-KTB*, II, 9 July and 11 July 1940.

[64] Ibid. 11 July 1940.

[65] Ibid. 13 July 1940; see also Raeder notes on this conference in Klee, Das Unternehmen, p. 240; Jacobsen, 1939–1945, p. 157 and *IMT*, xxxiv, 713.

[66] *Halder-KTB*, II, 22 July 1940.

[67] Loc. cit.

[68] See note 31 above.

[69] R. Wheatley, *Operation Sea Lion: German plans for the invasion of England 1939–1942* (Oxford, 1958), pp. 32–5.

[70] See note 60; also Wagner, *Lagevorträge*, 21 July 1940.

[71] , *Lagevorträge*, loc. cit.

[72] Ibid. Besprechung beim Führer am 31 Juli auf dem Berghof, pp. 125–8; *Halder-KTB*, II, 31 July 1940.

[73] Such as an attack on Gibraltar via Spain, the support of the Italians by German armoured units in North Africa to capture Egypt and the Suez Canal, striking as far north as Haifa.

[74] *Hakder-KTB*, II, 31 July 1940.

[75] Seidl, *Die Beziehungen*, doc. no. 148.

[76] Loc. cit.

[77] B. Meissner, 'Die kommunistische Machtübernahme in den Baltischen Staaten' in *VfZg*, 1954.

[78] *DGFP*, Series D, x, doc. no. 221.

[79] Ibid. doc. no. 171.

[80] Ibid. doc. nos. 215 and 238.

[81] See note 72.

[82] *Soviet Documents*, III, 46Iff.

[83] *DGFP*, series D, x, doc. nos. 348, 349, 353.

[84] Ibid. doc. no. 129.

[85] Ibid. doc. no. 388.

[86] Ibid. doc. nos. 154, 384.

[87] See note 55.

[88] *Bundesarchiv-Militürachiv* (BA-MA), Freiburg, Nachlass Greiner, fo. 17, *DGFP*, series D, x, 541, note I; also doc. no. 389.

[89] H. A. Jacobsen (ed.), *Kriegstagebuch des Oberkommandos der Wehrmacht* (*KTB-OKW*), I, (Frankfurt, 1965), 25 and 29 Aug. 1940.

[90] *Halder-KTB*, II, 29 Aug. 1940.

[91] *Soviet documents*, III, 462.

[92] *KTB-OKW*, I, 29 Aug 1940.

[93] *DGFP*, series D, x, doc. no. 413.

[94] For detailed discussion see Hillgruber, *Hitler, King Carol*.

[95] Nuremberg document no. PS-2353, copy in *Institut für Zeitgeschichte*, Munich.

[96] G. Mannerheim, *Erinnerungen* (Zürich, 1952), p. 425; *Halder-KTB*, II, 22 Aug. 1940; *DGFP* Series D, xi, doc. no. 86.

[97] *Halder-KTB*, II, 22 Aug. 1940; Klee, *Das Unternehemen*, p. 184.

[98] *BA-MA*, Nachlass Greiner, fo. II. Surprisingly, this and several other entries have not been included in the *KTB-OKW.*

[99] *KTB-OKW*, I, 14 Aug. 1940 and 29 Aug. 1940.

[100] Ibid. 30 Aug. 1940.

[101] Ibid. 10 Sept. 1940.

[102] Seidl, *Die Beziehungen*, doc. no. 154.

[103] Ibid. doc. nos. 157, 158, 159.

[104] Ibid. doc. no. 160.

[105] Ibid. doc. no. 162.

[106] *Soviet Documents*, III, 468.

[107] *Hakder-KTB*, II, 14 Sept. 1940.

[108] Loc. cit.

[109] Seidl, *Die Beziehungen*, doc. no. 168.

[110] *KTB-OKW*, I, 19 Sept. 1940.

[111] Ibid. 19 Sept. 1940; *Halder-KTB*, II, 9 Sept. And 19 Sept. 1940.

[112] Hillgruber, *Hitler, König Carol*, pp. 101ff.

[113] *DGFP*, series D, xi, doc. no. 227.

[114] Ibid. doc. no. 246.

[115] *KTB-OKW*, I, 22 Oct. 1940.

[116] Ibid. 9 Nov. 1940.

[117] Ibid. 2 Aug. 1940.

[118] G. L. Weinberg, 'Der Deutsche Entschluss zum Amgriff auf die Sowejetunion' in *VfZg*, 1953.

[119] *IMT*, x, 589ff.; xiv, 117ff.; xx, 629ff.; xv, 428ff. For the sheer dilettantism, the haphazard and improvised nature of *Aufbau-Ost* see the details provided by E. Helmdach, former group commander of the Wehrmacht's 'Fremde Heere Ost' (he was personally responsible for the Soviet Union) in *berfall: Der deutsch-sowjetische Aufmarsch* (Neckargemünd, 1975), and also his *Täuschungen und Versäumnisse* (Berg am See, 1979).

[120] Operation 'Felix' (the capture of Gibraltar, the Azores, the Canary and Cape Verde Islands); Operation 'Marita' (the support of the Italians in Greece); Operation 'Attila' (the occupation of Vichy-France if the need should arise); the defence of the Rumanian oilfields are but a few of the projects.

[121] *BA-MA*, Schematische Gliederung der Kommandobehörden und Truppen 1940 vom 9 June 1940 bis zum 21 Dec. 1940, no. H 10–3/33 1–51.

[122] *KTB-OKW*, I, 29 Aug. 1940; Hitler made the point that the German military measures had already had a 'braking effect' upon the Russians in Finland and the Balkans.

[123] *KTB-Greiner*, 5 Sept. 1940 in *IMT*, xxvii, 72, doc. no. 1229-PS. Again this entry has been omitted in the published version of the *KTB-OKW*.

[124] *KTB-OKW*, I, 30 Jan. 1941.

[125] *Kriegstagebuch der Seekriegsleitung* (KTB-SKL), 2 Jan. 1940 in *IMT*, xxxii, 178.

[126] S. Alder, *The isolationist impulse: its twentieth-century reaction* (New York, 1957), pp. 25off.

[127] For this aspect see Alder, op. Cit. And W. L. Langer and S. E. Gleason, *The undeclared war 1940/41* (New York, 1953); S. Friedländer, *Hitler et les Etats-Unis (1939–1941)*

(Geneva, 1963); E. L. Presseisen, *Germany and Japan, a study in totalitarian diplomacy 1933–1941* (The Hague, 1958); P. W. Schroeder, *The Axis-Alliance and Japanese-American relations 1941* (New York, 1958).

[128] Joachim von Ribbentrop, *Zwischen London und Moskau* (Leoni, 1953), p. 218.

[129] *DGFP*, series D, x, doc. nos. 333, 362: Presseisen, *Germany and Japan*, p. 255.

[130] Langer-Gleason, *Undeclared war*, p. 702.

[131] *DGFP*, series D, xi, doc. no. 44; Presseisen, *Germany and Japan*, pp. 265ff.

[132] *IMT*, xxviii, doc. no. 2842-PS, p. 570.

[133] Ibid. See also Alder, *Isolationist impulse*, passim.

[134] *Halder-KTB*, II, 23 Sept. 1940.

[135] Seidl, *Die Beziehungen*, doc. no. 129.

[136] *DGFP*, series D, xi, doc. no. 129.

[137] Seidl, *Die Beziehungen*, doc. no. 167.

[138] *DGFP*, series D, xi, doc. no. 118; see also J. M. Menzel, 'Der geheime deutsch-japanische Notenaustausch zum Dreimächtepakt' in *VfZg*, 1957.

[139] *IMT*, xxxiv, Assmann evidence, p. 691; Wagner, *Lagevorträge*, p. 142, contains a detailed report of the views put by Raeder to Hitler on 26 Sept. 1940. Russian concern was not mentioned; Russia in fact was mentioned in passing only, the main issues being the Mediterranean, the prospective talks with Franco and Pétain and colonial problems. The report contradicts Assmann's evidence. As to the reception of the tripartite pact within the diplomatic circles in Moscow see G. Grafencu, *Europas letzte Tage* (Zürich, 1946), pp. 133ff.

[140] *IMT*, xxiv, Assmann evidence, pp. 690, 692.

[141] *Halder-KTB*, II, 24 Oct. 1940, also Nov. 1940.

[142] *DGFP*, series D, xi, doc. nos. 50, 53, 56, 274, 188, 201, 236, 280, 281 and 299; also Grafencu, *Europas letzte Tage*, p. 92; Hillgruber, *Hitler, König Carol*, p. 104.

[143] *DGFP*, series D, xi, doc. no. 236.

[144] *KTB-OKW*, 28 Oct. 1940.

[145] *Halder-KTB*, II, 15. Oct. 1940.

[146] Ibid. loc. cit.

[147] Ibid. 24 Oct. 1940.

[148] Ibid. 4 Nov. 1940.

[149] Ibid. loc. cit.

[150] *DGFP*, series D, xi, doc. no. 172.

[151] W. Hubatsch (ed.), *Hitlers Weisungen für die Kriegsführung 1939–1945* (Munich, 1965), pp. 81ff.

[152] Ibid.

[153] Seidl, *Die Beziehungen*, doc. no. 172.

[154] Ibid. doc. no. 175.

[155] Ibid. doc. no. 178.

[156] Ibid. doc. nos. 178–179.

[157] *DGFP,* series D, xi, doc. no. 325.

[158] Ibid. loc. cit. See also G. Hilger, *Wir und der Kreml* (Frankfurt, 1955), pp. 297ff., P. Schmidt, *Statist auf der diplomatischer Bühne* (Bonn, 1954), pp. 525ff.

[159] See note 157.

[160] Hilger, *Wir und der Kreml,* p. 302.

[161] *DGFP,* series D, xi, doc. nos. 326, 328.

[162] Ibid.

[163] Ibid. doc. nos. 329, 348.

[164] Ibid. doc. no. 309.

[165] See note 163.

[166] Thus Hitler to his army adjutant Major Engel, quoted by Hillgruber, *Hitler's Strategie,* p. 356.

[167] DGFP,. series D, xi, doc. no. 379.

[168] Ibid. doc. no. 405.

[169] Ibid.

[170] *KTB-OKW,* I, 5 Dec. 1940; *Halder-KTB,* II, 15 Dec. 1940.

[171] *Halder-KTB,* loc. cit.

[172] Hubatsch, *Hitlers Weisungen,* Weisungen Nr. 21: Fall, 'Barbarossa', pp. 97ff.

[173] E. Nolte, *Der Faschismus in seiner Epoche* (Munich, 1963), p. 433.

(*The Historical Journal,* vol. 26, no. 4, 1983, pp.891–920, reprinted with permission from Cambridge University Press)

13   LOTHAR KETTENACKER, FROM *GERMANY SINCE 1945*

2   Drifting apart: the two republics

The response of the West to the worsening of the Cold War in 1948 was to set up the West European Union, to this day the only purely European defence alliance, and to press ahead with the foundation of a West German state. After the demise of the Control Council it was France that stood in the way of further progress, fearing that her neighbour might again become too powerful. However, West Germany without the French Zone would make no sense. Britain and the Social Democrats favoured a decentralized state with a federal government firmly in control. France would have preferred a loose confederation of fairly independent states, not unlike the German Bund. A compromise between these two postions had to be found.

Again the chief impetus came from General Clay, who visualized something like the United States of Germany, both as strong and decentralized as the States. The compromise worked out at the Six Power Conference in London in the spring of 1948 centred on some kind of international control of the Ruhr,

Germany's industrial heartland. This did not augur well for the future, because German politicians were now facing separation in the East and West, as well as a weak government in between. The recommendations for the formation of a West German state under Allied supervision, which were agreed upon in London, are generally referred to as the 'birth certificate' of the Federal Republic. These documents were handed over to the Minister-Presidents on 1 July 1948 as the only political representatives of Germany at the time. The party leaders had no comparable standing and were not much liked by the Military Governors. The Minister-Presidents were summoned to Frankfurt, seat of the Economic Council, and instructed – not invited – to convene a National Assembly in order to work out a proper constitution, democratic and federalist in character. Furthermore they were to make recommendations for a realignment of the *Länder* with a view to producing a lasting equilibrium. Last but not least, they were told to accept an Occupation Statute which was to circumscribe Allied prerogatives in the fields of foreign policy, foreign trade and reparations, and related matters. In other words, West Germany was to become a self-governing dominion under Allied supervision.

The chiefs of the *Länder* met a week later near Koblenz to discuss the position. None of the German politicians wished to be identified with the formal division of his country. Would they not appear to be mere puppets of or collaborators with foreign powers who planned to create a separate German state? Carlo Schmid, a close adviser and confidant of Schumacher, warned that any initiative towards a separate state would be reciprocated in the East.[1] The Germans could not be expected to build a proper house, but only an emergency shelter which would provide protection for the time being. The Minister-Presidents agreed that no constitution for a permanent state should be drafted or any elected assembly convened. Instead, an organizational framework called the 'Basic Law' (*Grundgesetz*) was to be worked out by a Parliamentary Council of *Länder* delegates. The real constitution, it was argued, was the Occupation Statute, which made clear who really was in charge, and which therefore ought to precede the promulgation of the Basic Law. For the first time, but not the last, German politicians disliked the responsibilities forced upon them. The inclusion of the French Zone and more self-government was all they aspired to achieve. That Germans wished for fewer powers than the Allies were prepared to concede struck Clay as 'odd in the light of history'.[2] The term 'Basic Law' was quite an understatement for what was to become the most successful and enduring constitution Germany has ever enjoyed. The German reservations did not please General Clay, who had set his mind on creating a proper German state, as though it were a new army he had been ordered to build up in no time. Later on, Foreign Secretary Dean Acheson wondered whether the idea of a West German state was 'the brainchild of General Clay', rather than the outcome of a government decision.[3]

While General König, the French Governor, was quietly satisfied with this state of affairs, Clay and Robertson lobbied the German leaders to be more forthcoming and accept the inevitable. The mayors of Hamburg and Bremen, Max Brauer and Wilhelm Kaisen, and the heads of the smallest states, as well as Hans Ehard, Minister-President of Bavaria, were among the first to realize that the road to state-building was the right one under the prevailing conditions. The most influential supporter of Clay was the newly elected Governing Mayor of

Berlin, Ernst Reuter, who, facing the blockade, knew what was at stake. He persuaded his colleagues to drop their reservations by arguing that 'the division of Germany is not being created; it is a fact.'[4] He was not fighting for the restoration of the *status quo ante*, but for recognition of the fact that politically and economically Berlin was part of the free West. In this he proved to be right against all the odds. Eventually, a compromise was reached in that the Allies accepted the German proposals for terminology and procedure.

The Minister-Presidents, now the only collegium speaking for Germany as a whole, convened a meeting of experts, mostly constitutional lawyers, to the tranquil island of Herrenchiemsee in order to prepare a draft constitution. To the party bosses, this looked like a devious scheme of the regional chieftains trying to safeguard their rights at the expense of central government. It was nothing like that. In the history of constitutional assemblies the work of Herrenchiemsee – the draft constitution and a report completed within a fortnight – was an outstanding achievement, just because the experts shunned party politics. Their ideas and problems inspired the debates in the Parliamentary Council. It was due to the convention of Herrenchiemsee that crucial elements were enshrined in the Basic Law – unalterable human rights, the two-chamber system, a strong executive, the Constitutional Court, to name but a few – which were to determine the political culture of the Federal Republic. One of the most hotly debated issues was whether the German state had actually ceased to exist in 1945 or its main functions had only been suspended for the time being. In the latter case, supported by the majority of experts, the German nation was called upon to exercise its democratic right of self-government. Otherwise it would be up to the individual states to form a new federation. Today the whole issue might appear to be irrelevant. However, the theory of continuity implied acceptance of full responsibility for Germany's past, especially *vis-à-vis* Israel. The SED [Socialist Unity Party] regime in the East, allegedly born without the 'original sin of fascism', was never prepared to share this burden.

The Parliamentary Council did have all the hallmarks of a constitutional assembly, except for the lack of popular assent. The 65 Deputies were chosen by the *Länder* in accordance with the last elections and on the basis of one seat per 750,000 inhabitants. Although the two main parties, the CDU/CSU [the Conservatives or Christian Democrats] and SPD [the Social Democrats], could muster the same number of Deputies, 27 each, the splinter parties (Liberals: 8; Deutsche Partei: 2; old Centre Party: 2) contributed to a safe conservative, or rather anti-Socialist, majority. The average age of 56 years, as well as the fact that 61 per cent were public servants, contributed to the conservative outlook of this assembly. This was a blessing in disguise because most Deputies had vivid memories of the Weimar Republic and how it came to grief; eleven Deputies had been members of the Reichstag. Never before could lessons learned from a disaster be applied so quickly and thoroughly as in this case. In the Parliamentary Council party politics played a more important role than at Merrenchiemsee. It turned out to be a shrewd move by Konrad Adenauer to accept the chair, which under normal circumstances would not carry much clout. However, as the first and only leader of the West German population after the war, its incumbent rose to prominence. Soon Adenauer was a national figure: his features, strongly resembling those of a Red Indian chief, his age and experience as Governing Mayor of Cologne, his Rhenish dialect and sense of humour, coupled with a paternalistic demeanour, made a deep and lasting impression on the traumatized minds of post-war Germans.[5] Of course, nobody at the time anticipated that this hearty old man of 72 would dominate German politics in a benevolent but autocratic manner for the next fifteen years, until his country was securely anchored in the Western world. Adenauer was an old cynic. He had no faith in the common man, he once admitted to Carlo Schmid.[6] He certainly looked upon his fellow countrymen as unruly children who needed a strong hand, while everyone else felt that the Germans were too disciplined to be good democrats.

The Parliamentary Council met in Bonn and Adenauer was at pains to ensure that the city also became the capital of the new state, even though he too originally favoured Frankfurt as a city more steeped in history. The decisive vote on 10 May 1949 was no foregone conclusion, but the result of Adenauer's successful scheming and lobbying. A popular legend has it that the proximity of Adenauer's home in Rhöndorf was crucial. According to another theory, Bonn was more appropriate as the capital of a provisional and fragmentary state than the old imperial city of Frankfurt. The truth is probably more banal: the passionate support for Frankfurt by the Social Democrats who controlled the city council tipped the scales in favour of Bonn. The CDU/CSU was more sympathetic towards the Catholic Rhineland and its westward orientation. Moreover, Bonn would not outshine the *Länder* capitals or undermine the federal structure of the new state. In the end Bonn came to symbolize the peaceful and somewhat provincial character of the Federal Republic.

The shadow of Weimar hovered over the proceedings of the Parliamentary Council. The Allies had already removed one of the main faultlines by dismembering Prussia and providing for a more balanced union of member states. They insisted on power-sharing between the centre and the constituent parts. This was their main concern. Among the Deputies of the Parliamentary Council mistrust of the electorate was widespread. The President was not to be elected by popular vote or endowed with special executive powers. All plebiscitary elements of the Weimar constitution were expunged. Faced with the choice between a Senate as the second chamber or an assembly of delegates from the *Länder*, the Deputies opted for the latter. The position of the Parliament was strengthened in as much as it had the right to elect and dismiss the Federal Chancellor. The most far-reaching device was the so-called 'constructive vote of no confidence': a new Chancellor could only be elected in mid-term if a majority of Deputies voted his successor into office, so that the country would never be without a government. The stability of government was much enhanced compared to Weimar. The electoral law also helped in this respect: parties had to muster at least 5 per cent of the vote to get into the Bundestag. The result was fewer parties and less haggling over coalition policies. As compensation, proportional representation gave the smaller parties such as the Liberals a better chance than elsewhere. As a matter of fact, the FDP participated in most governments from 1949 onwards.

The most contentious issue was the relationship between the central government and the individual member state which had already been established and which enjoyed the support of the occupying powers. While the Bundestag was legislating for the whole of the country, it was the *Länder* which would be in charge of administration. Now that the Military Governors had insisted that the *Länder* should also hold the purse strings, they would raise most of the taxes. For Schumacher and the SPD this was totally unacceptable. A future government could not be at the mercy of the *Länder*. The conservatives, including Adenauer, were prepared to throw in the towel when the crisis deepened and it became clear that the Germans faced the unusual alliance of the American and French Military Governers. Clay, a Southerner and as such no friend of power concentrated in the capital, objected to the legislative prerogative of the central government, especially in financial matters. He suspected that the SPD feared for their nationalization programme, more reason for him not to yield. Schumacher's motives were probably more honourable than that. Although he accepted the Western state, he did not wish the SPD to be used as a tool of foreign and particularist interests. Only a strong central government could hope to overcome the division of the country. Schumacher's intransigence paid off and helped to create a viable central government, even though it was not to be controlled by his own party for some time to come. With the foundation of NATO on 4 April 1949, which assuaged French security anxieties, the overall political climate changed in favour of a more generous attitude towards the Germans. Technical difficulties could not be allowed to hold up the formation of a German state and a bulwark against Soviet aggression. Due also to British mediation, Clay was forced by his own government to give in. Subsequently a sensible compromise was worked out.

The name of the new state was less controversial, but nevertheless significant for its identity. Here a suggestion by the federalist lobby of the CDU/CSU (Ellwanger Kreis) met with general approval: *Bundesrepublik Deutschland*. Quite a few conservative Deputies were clinging to the ominous 'Reich'. Carlo Schmid, chairman of the SPD in the Parliamentary Council, dismissed this idea out of hand by pointing out that for Germany's neighbours 'Reich' implied a claim to supremacy and domination.[7] A clear majority of Deputies wished to see the new Germany completely divorced from this tradition, even if it meant that the 'Reich' founded by Bismarck would vanish for ever. In the end the 'Reich' only survived as an oddity because the East German Railway stuck to its old name of 'Reichsbahn'. The fact that there was so little argument over the national symbols needs some explanation. For the founding fathers of the Federal Republic nationalism and all its paraphernalia were thoroughly discredited. The colours of the new state were to be those of the liberal and democratic movement which led to the Frankfurt Parliament of 1848: *Schwarz-Rot-Gold*. Of the old national anthem, only the third verse was considered appropriate, referring as it did to *Einigkeit und Recht und Freiheit* (Unity, Right, and Liberty). Of paramount importance was that Germany should not, as the first verse of the anthem seems to suggest, stand *über alles* (i.e. above all else). When the Basic Law was finally promulgated on 23 May 1949 the members of the Parliamentary Council stood up and sang a sentimental German *Lied* of the early nineteenth century which expressed a longing for the German fatherland of the future. In his final address Adenauer maintained that they all believed they had made an essential contribution to the reunification of the whole of the German people.[8] No doubt, many Deputies had great reservations about their role in creating a liberal and democratic state which left their East German countrymen in the cold. But they did not see any viable alternative. The Basic Law had been approved by all the *Länder* Diets a week earlier, except for

Bavaria, which rejected it but then agreed to succumb if two-thirds of the other states passed it. Bavaria, which called itself a *Freistaat*, was most anxious to emphasize its supposedly special status within the new union.

Even with its own constitution, the new German republic remained under Allied occupation. On 12 May 1949 the Military Governors had handed the Basic Law with their consent to a delegation of the Parliamentary Council, thus demonstrating their overall supremacy. They might as well have passed over the details of the Occupation Statute which they had announced earlier. The Germans would have preferred this procedure so as to absolve themselves from bringing about the division of their country. However, this had to wait until the election and until a new government was firmly in place. Nevertheless, the occupation regime changed its character. Military Government and zonal division were suspended. Henceforth control was exercised by a High Commission composed of the representatives of the three powers: John McCloy, who took over from General Clay; Sir Brian Robertson, who changed into civilian clothes; and André François-Poncet, the French Ambassador to Berlin before the war. German laws could only come into force if no objections were raised by the High Commission within twenty-one days. The principle of Allied unanimity, as in the former Control Council, strengthened the German position. West Germany was to become a self-governing Allied Protectorate.

The smooth passage of the Basic Law was made possible because the most contentious element, the social and economic order of the Federal Republic, was left to the free interplay of political forces. Both the CDU/CSU and the SPD had hopes of becoming the leading party which would be able to determine this issue in future.

While the Economic Council in Frankfurt handled everyday business up to the last minute, West Germany experienced its first, shortest and most crucial election campaign. The political landscape was so diverse that there were no clear pointers to the future. Altogether sixteen parties campaigned for seats, and seventy independent candidates, but only four were represented in all *Länder*: apart from the big two, the Liberals and Communists. The CDU/CSU, on the advise of Adenauer, simply dropped its legendary 'Ahlener Programme', which had rejected capitalism in favour of Christian Socialism, and now opted for Erhard's social market economy. Round-faced Erhard, not yet a member of the CDU, exuded confidence and optimism. However, the economic miracle had not yet materialized and unemployment was still at 19 per cent, a level quite staggering at that time. Nevertheless, the Social Democrats lost the battle for nationalization and for the soul of the country because they misjudged the public mood. Adenauer could afford to sit back and simply watch them ruin their chances. Schumacher re-introduced the language of class struggle and appealed to national sentiments by attacking the victorious powers and their grip on German industry in the Ruhr. He also made a grave mistake by referring to the churches as the 'fifth occupation power'.[9] Nor did his venomous attacks on Adenauer endear him to the German public, who were no longer used to the occasionally outrageous rhetoric of a democratic election campaign. Adenauer, though more restrained and statesmanlike, not only exploited the blunders of his opponent but also claimed that the Social Democrats had joined forces with the Communists in the East and that a socialist Germany would be 'no dam against Communism'.[10] This was blatantly unfair, but probably quite effective.

The Liberals steered a clever course between the two main antagonists as they had already done in the Parliamentary Council. They wooed the voters who rejected the CDU's dependence on the churches in educational matters and opposed the economic programme of the SPD. Moreover, they made sure that they would be an indispensable partner in government. In a way, the German Liberals now made up for their missed opportunities in the past. With 11.2 per cent of the votes and 52 seats they achieved one of their best electoral results in the history of the Republic. Their influence was decisive in tipping the balance against the grand coalition much favoured in nationally minded quarters of both big parties. A grand coalition might have set the pattern for the following decades, with potentially disastrous effects for the fledgling democracy.

In the election of 14 October 1949 the CDU/CSU gained 31 per cent of the votes as against 29.2 per cent for the Social Democrats. Together with the FDP and the Conservative splinter parties (*Bayern-Partei* (BP), *Deutsche Partei* (FP), and the Zentrum) Adenauer could muster 235 votes for a right-wing coalition. He was indeed voted into power on 15 December with the smallest of margins (his own vote: 202 out of 404). Against the advocates of a grand coalition within his own party he argued that an overall majority of the electorate had had enough of controls and shortages and had opted for a free market economy. The first cabinet, still small in comparison with later governments, consisted of a coalition of the CDU/CSU, the FDP, and the DP, who supplied the Minister of Transport, Hans-Christoph Seebohm (1949-66). Part of the deal was the Theodor Heuss, chairman of the Liberals, would become the first President of the Republic. The genial Swabian professor, who exuded a *tranquilitas animi* and a rare sense of humour, proved to be Germany's most popular politician.[11] Of the two grandfathers who ruled the country, he was the more liberal and good-natured. Heuss was elected on 12 September, not by the people as under Weimar constitution, but by the Bundesversammlung, consisting of the Bundestag and an equal number of Deputies to be elected by *Länder* Diets.

What was to be the official birthday of the Federal Republic? It is highly significant that the date chosen was not the first meeting of the Bundestag (7 September), or the formation of the first government under Adenauer (15 September), but 23 May 1949, when the Basic Law was officially and ceremonially promulgated. The Basic Law was to be the Magna Carta of modern Germany, which would help to overcome the feeling of insecurity and helplessness of its citizens. In 1949 democracy had not yet taken root and the economic miracle was still a long way off. The *Rechtsstaat*, however, was home-grown and something to be proud of. To live again under the rule of law, extended by a catalogue of human rights and supervised by an independent constitutional court, was for most Germans a great achievement, which reconciled them to the division of their country.

The development of the Soviet Zone into a separate state has been depicted as a reluctant response to the state-building process in the West. However, this in itself was the outcome of failed ambitions. After the war the hard-core emigré Communists had great hopes of turning the whole of Germany into a 'people's democracy', i.e. pursuing an independent path to socialism, another kind of National Socialism, as it were (though this term was, of course, taboo). It was the first of many illusions. Neither their master in Moscow nor the German electorate were inclined to go along with this venture. Stalin did not want a self-possessed German Communist state on his doorstep. For him East Germany was a means to an end, possibly a neutralized Germany, not an end in itself.[12] Nor did the Germans feel like swapping one kind of pseudo-socialism for another, which would again serve as the ideological platform for a one-party state. The German Communists arriving from Moscow misjudged the mood of the people at home. Realizing that they had no popular following they turned to manipulation from above and a constant appeal for national unity, first under the guise of a 'popular front' approach, then in the name of 'democratic centralism'.

As early as November 1946 the steering committee of the SED submitted a draft constitution for a 'German Democratic Republic' which, of course, was meant to cover the whole of Germany. In the end it was only adopted by the *Länder* parliaments of the Soviet Zone. Regional parliaments in the Western zones passed constitutions for their own territorial jurisdiction. The ever-widening gulf between pretensions and realities was the significant feature of the East German state right from the beginning. It is difficult to ascertain at which point the SED abandoned plans for control of the whole country and chose to obstruct the emergence of a West German state. As in Nazi Germany, propaganda and policy were all too often inseparable. Perhaps more can be learned about this from the SED archives which are now accessible. By the time the SED launched the movement towards a People's Congress, in November 1947, it was clearly in support of Soviet intentions to abort the West German state. The invitation to the First Congress suggested as an agenda the formation of a delegation to the London Conference of Foreign Ministers. This group of supposed representatives of the German people, amongst them Walter Ulbricht and Wilmelm Pieck, was meant to back up Molotov's position. When Pieck submitted that the delegation should get a fair hearing by the Foreign Ministers of the West, the conference was adjourned without any agreement on reconvening it. Later, the Second and Third Congresses served as a camouflage for the establishment of a separate East German state. The manipulative character of the procedure was revealing: large numbers (2,000 and more) of political appointees, who were prepared to follow the party line, rather than democratically elected delegates. They were hand-picked from political parties and mass organizations like the Free German Youth (FDJ) and the Free German Trade Unions (FDGB), with only a comparatively small number of delegates from the Western zones (20 per cent or fewer). The potential for corruption inherent in any language was fully exploited: the use of 'democratic', 'free', 'German', etc. was as common as it was fraudulent. When the chairmen of the Eastern CDU, Jakob Kaiser and Ernst Lemmer, refused to countenance the People's Congress they were, under pressure from SMAD, replaced by the more co-operative Otto Luschke and Georg Dertinger.

In spite of the SED's poor showing in the West a Second Congress for 'unity and a just peace' was convened, which claimed to be representative of the German people and was again carefully orchestrated by the SED. A 'People's Soviet' (*Volksrat*) consisting of 400 members was constituted, which was to be in session between Congress meetings. Evidently the Volksrat was the counterpart of the much smaller but more competent and democratically elected Parliamentary Council in the West. As a constitutional assembly it was large enough to be turned into the first East German parliament without the inconvenience of free elections. On 11 May 1949 the Volksrat approved the draft constitution for the German Democratic Republic, worked out by a committee under the chairmanship of Otto Grotewohl, the leader of the emasculated Eastern SPD. According to its phraseology, the constitution appeared to be as democratic as any in the West, including a catalogue of basic and human rights, except for the fact that there was no provision for a legitimate opposition or an independent judiciary. One omnibus article against slander (*Boykotthetze*) gave the government the power to harass and persecute all those who opposed what amounted to one-party rule in the guise of permanent coalition government.

The Third People's Congress in May 1949 coincided with the promulgation of the Basic Law in the West. The points were now set for the two lines to separate altogether. The election was a farce because there was no chance to vote for individual parties and candidates. The only option was a block vote for pre-selected candidates from various parties and mass organizations such as the 'Democratic Women's Federation' and the 'Cultural Federation for the Democratic Reconstruction of Germany', all creatures of the SED. The voter had to agree or disagree with the statement: 'I am in favour of German unity and a just peace. Therefore I vote for the following candidates'.[13] Altogether 66 per cent of the voters made their mark as expected. This was a more credible result, especially in view of the many abstentions, than later elections, where the supposed proportion was 99 per cent. A quarter of the Deputies (528 out of 1,969) were recruited from the Western zones with the help of the KPD. The Congress confirmed the new constitution – confirmation and acclamation were the standard procedures – and elected the 'Second German Soviet', which had no delegates from the Western zones. On 7 October its 400 Deputies were transformed into the 'Provisional People's Chamber of the German Democratic Republic'. Wilhelm Pieck became the first President of the new German state and Otto Grotewohl, the convert from the SPD, the first Prime Minister. Congratulations from Comrade Stalin, referring several times to the unitary, democratic, independent, peace-loving Germany which had been created, put the final seal on the birth of yet another German state.[14]

The whole procedure for setting up a puppet regime in the East was so farcical and phoney that today it is hard to believe that political leaders in the West were in such deadly fear of a Communist takeover of the whole of Germany. Maybe too many were reminded of the Nazi seizure of power and believed that Germany had paid too dearly for underestimating the dangers ahead. Others no doubt were afraid of the intimidating practices of SMAD backed by the Red Army. Others again, like Adenauer, did not have much confidence in the political wisdom of the German people, whom they felt might fall for empty promises of national reconciliation and reunification.

In the following years, while the Federal Republic increased its scope for action by a process of incremental improvement, the GDR was subjected to a Stalinist regime imposed by the SED. The SED revealed its true nature in the same measure as all attempts to block the West German state had proved futile. First the popular-front approach was abandoned; then the claim to a specifically German road to socialism was dismissed as 'social democratic aberration'. No doubt Tito's independent stand *vis-à-vis* Moscow played an important role. In August 1949 Yugoslavia was officially branded as an 'enemy of the Soviet Union', just because Tito pursued an independent foreign policy, seeking a *rapprochement* with the West. Everywhere Titoism was to be exterminated, by way of highly publicized show trials against its real or alleged adherents, in Poland (Gomulka), Czechoslovakia (Slansky), and Hungary (Rajk). The pattern was too clear to be lost on the SED, the assiduous follower of the satellite parties. In 1951–2 more than 150,000 Party members were dismissed as agents of the 'Schumacher circles', i.e. closet Social Democrats. State, society, and the economy were remodelled under the direction of the SED, who now openly took on the mantle of Marxism-Leninism and pretended to be the avant-garde of the working class, 'the highest form of class organization of the proletariat'. The rituals of the Party bordered on the ridiculous. Was the membership card, 'the most precious thing a man can own in his life', to be carried in a satchel around the neck or fastened to the underwear?[15] These and other such topics were debated in earnest.

At the First Party Conference of 28 January 1949 the principle of 'democratic centralism' was officially adopted and meant that every twist and turn of official policy, all measures of any significance, had to be approved by the Politbüro, the highest organ of the Party machine. Naturally, the Party had an interest in extending its hold on the economy by nationalizing more and more assets. Thus a vicious circle was set in motion: the forced pace to 'socialism' depressed the economy, which resulted in a massive exodus of the population to the West (447,000 from January 1951 to April 1953). This in turn persuaded the Party to tighten its grip on the population for fear of losing control, which then made things worse. All means of coercion were systematically expanded and strengthened: the political bias of the judiciary; the extension of the 'Kasernierte Volkspolizei' (standing police force, i.e. in barracks) to 50,000 in 1951; the setting up of a Ministry of State Security (8 February 1950) with a countrywide surveillance system, which was to become the most distinctive feature of the German Democratic Republic in the decades to come. In 1952 the five *Länder* were replaced by fourteen new districts, and thus the last vestiges of federalism were removed. The idea was to fuse Party and state into one and the same control machinery. The Party boss of the district (*Sekretär des Rates*) was the most powerful local chief in all Party as well as administrative matters.

This process went on beyond Stalin's death (March 1953) until the fuse finally blew and the people rose up against their oppressors on 17 June 1953. After that the Party relented somewhat and switched back to the familiar propaganda tune of national unity and the need for a peace treaty.

The uprising of 17 June 1953 was the most traumatic event in the history of the GDR. Like the Wall erected in 1961, it came to symbolize the division of Germany: the West Germans enjoyed a public holiday, while the East Germans were reminded that their first attempt at self-determination was brutally suppressed by Russian tanks. The historiography is also revealing. According to the SED version, the uprising was a counter-revolution instigated by Western agents; its treatment by West German historians reflects the transition from Cold War to détente.[16] Thus the *Volksaufstand* (people's uprising) of the mid-1950s was relegated to a mere *Arbeiteraufstand* (workers' uprising) and the intervention of the Red Army was interpreted as responsible and restrained, given that 'only twenty-one' people were killed. Up to the present day there is no consensus among West German historians as to how many people actually were killed and whether the appearance of Russian tanks was the decisive turning-point.

The immediate causes are well known: in order to cope with an economy fast deteriorating as a result of enforced collectivization of farms and nationalization of private enterprises, the SED raised productivity targets by 10 per cent: in other words, demanded more work for the same pay. However, following Stalin's death, the new Soviet leadership favoured a more lenient approach in the East German buffer state, popular with the peasants, small businessmen, and artisans. The SED bosses dutifully adopted the new course, which was in flagrant contradiction of their previous policies and thus exposed the Party as the puppet of a foreign power. However, when it transpired that this more relaxed attitude did not apply to the new production targets and that they were not, after all, to be lifted, the workers rose up in protest, led by the builders constructing the Stalin Allee, the would-be showpiece of East Berlin. On 16 and 17 June strikes and unrest spread throughout East Germany and soon developed their own momentum. When, by 2 p.m. on 17 June, the cabinet relented and reduced the production targets the masses in Berlin and elsewhere raised the stakes and demanded free and secret elections, price reductions, free trade unions, and no persecution of the strike leaders. Some of their slogans were too much for the Party leaders, who took refuge in the Red Army headquarters: '*Wir wollen Freiheit, Recht und Brot, sonst schlagen wir die Bonzen tot*' ('We want freedom, rights, and bread, or else we'll strike the bosses dead').[17]

Two young East German historians, Armin Mitter and Stefan Wolle,[18] who have been thoroughly researching this sorry chapter of their history since the archives were opened, come to the conclusion that the events leading up to 17 June amounted, to all intents and purposes, to a 'people's uprising', even though workers were in the forefront of events. They think it is misleading to focus attention on the events of 16 and 17 June while ignoring the overall picture: the desertion of collectivized farms and the mass exodus of professionals and skilled workers, the general unrest since the regime had closed the border with the West by installing a five-kilometre-wide exclusion zone from which all unreliable people were deported in the most brutal fashion. In May 1952 the border was sealed off so that Berlin remained the only escape route until this gap was closed in August 1961. In 1957 westward migration was denounced as *Republikflucht*, a crime punishable by up to three years in prison. In a letter to Otto Grotewohl, the Prime Minister, the German Protestant Church took up these grievances: 'Things must be in a really bad way if the peasant is prepared to leave his home and land and the tradesman his workshop to face an uncertain future.' According to Mitter and Wolle, the general situation in February 1953, brought about by enforced nationalization, resembled an 'overheated, uncontrollable steam engine smashing everything in its way and ready to explode at any time'. Their casualty figures for 17 June are also remarkably different from those in previous West German accounts: fifty killed in clashes with the Soviet occupation and German police forces; twenty demonstrators summarily executed by the Russians, along with at least forty Russian soldiers who refused to raise their arms against the demonstrating masses; three SED functionaries killed. All in all, more than 500,000 people demonstrated in over 350 places in an attempt to bring the Communist regime down. 'Without the intervention of Soviet troops', they conclude, 'the GDR would have collapsed in

June 1953 within a few days.' This is the reason for the widespread purges afterwards, the eagerness of the SED to extinguish all memories, and the embarrassment of West Germans who looked on helplessly, agonized, and then resorted to the politics of symbolism, of official rather than personal remembrance. Among those purged were two prominent SED functionaries – Rudolf Hernstadt, the editor of the Party paper *Neues Deutschland*, and Wilhelm Zaisser, head of the Ministry of State Security – for conspiring to get rid of Ulbricht with the help of Moscow, not because they sided with the demonstrators. After the rising, the Soviet leadership saw no alternative but to back Ulbricht.

Notes

[1] Carlo Schmid, *Erinnerungen* (Munich, 1980), 328–9.

[2] *Tagesspiegel*, 15 July 1948.

[3] *Foreign Relations of the United States* (FRUS), 3 (1948), 82-4. See also John H. Backer, *Winds of Change: The German Years of Lucius Du Bignon Clay* (New York, 1983).

[4] Ernst Reuter, in Eschenburg, *Geschichte der Bundesrepublik Deutschland*, i. 469.

[5] Apart from his memoirs, Konrad Adenauer, *Erinnerungen*, 4 vols. (Frankfurt am Main, 1965–8), see the most authoritative biography of the first Chancellor by Hans-Peter Schwarz, *Konrad Adenauer: A German Politician and Statesman in a Period of War, Revolution and Reconstruction* (Providence, RI and Oxford, 1995). Schwarz also contributed the two volumes on the Adenauer era in the prestigious *Geschichte der Bundesrepublik*: vol. ii (covering 1949–57) and vol. iii (covering 1957–63) (Wiesbaden, 1981 and 1985).

[6] Schmid, *Erinnerungen*, 358.

[7] Eschenburg, *Geschichte der Bundesrepublik Deutschland*, i. 506.

[8] Adenauer, *Erinnerungen*, i. 176.

[9] Merseburger, *Der schwierige Deutsche*, 434–6.

[10] Quoted by Benz in Eschenburg, *Geschichte der Bundsrepublik Deutschland*, i. 533.

[11] See Horst Moeller, *Theodor Heuß, Staatsmann und Schriftsteller* (Bonn, 1990)

[12] See now Wilfried Loth, *Stalins ungeliebtes Kind: Warum Moskau die DDR nicht wollte* (Berlin, 1994).

[13] Kleßmann, *Die doppelte Staatsgründung*, 206.

[14] *Neues Deutschland*, 14 Oct. 1949.

[15] Herman Weber, *DDR: Grundriß der Geschichte 1945–1990* (Hanover, 1991), 52.

[16] Arnulf Baring, *Der 17. Juni 1953*, new edn. (Stuttgart, 1983); Axel Bust-Bartels, 'Der Arbeiteraufstand am 17. Juni 1953', *Aus Politik und Zeitgeschichte*, 25 (1980), 24-54.

[17] Quoted by Bust-Bartels, 'Der Arbeiteraufstand', 45.

[18] Armin Mitter and Stefan Wolle, *Untergang auf Raten: Unbekannte Kapitel der DDR-Geschichte* (Munich, 1993), 27–162. See also the impressive documentation (unpublished documents, interviews, and photos) by the West German labour historian Gerhard Beier, *Wir wollen freie Menschen sein* (Frankfurt am Main, 1993).

(Lothar Kettenacker, *Germany Since 1945*, Oxford, Oxford University Press, 1997)

14   MACGREGOR KNOX, 'CONQUEST, FOREIGN AND DOMESTIC, IN FASCIST ITALY AND NAZI GERMANY'

between Germany and Italy there exists a community of destiny .... [Germany and Italy] are congruent cases.

(Benito Mussolini, 1936)

The brown shirt might perhaps not have arisen without the black shirt.

(Adolf Hitler, 1942)

Fascism, generic and historic

Mussolini and Hitler have not been alone in emphasizing the common origins, features and destinies of Fascism and National Socialism. Theories of 'fascism' – that elusive generic phenomenon with a small *f* – have proliferated with abandon ever since the 1920s.[1] Definitions have ranged from the Third International's 'open terroristic dictatorship of the most reactionary, chauvinistic, and imperialistic elements of finance capital' through Ernst Nolte's militant anti-Marxism, to the modernization theorists' 'mass-mobilizing developmental dictatorships under single-party auspices'. Voices of caution have occasionally sounded, urging the 'deflation' of a concept that 'exists in faith and is pursued by reason', or suggesting that fascism fails to encompass adequately the ultimate evil of National Socialist Germany.[2]

But the notion is still with us, even if no two theories of fascism coincide. [...] After sixty years of debate, the scene resembles a desert battlefield littered with the burnt-out, rusting hulks of failed theories. What alternatives exist? One largely unexplored possibility, which combines both breadth and reasonable closeness to the evidence, is comparative history. [...] Inevitably, the obvious candidates for comparative treatment are the two principal 'historic fascist' regimes of Italy and Germany. Both arose in relatively advanced societies – northern Italy was different from Bavaria, but no more backward economically. Both were in part responses to affronts to the self-esteem of nations that were relative latecomers to unification and industrialization, and that suffered from deep social, regional, and, in Germany, religious cleavages. Finally, both were the creation of leaders who combined conspicuous talents as agitators, political tacticians, and ideological visionaries.

This last quality inevitably implies a collision between vision and reality. Comparison of those visions and of their respective collisions with reality may offer new insight into the nature of both movements and regimes, and into possible distinctions between them and other varieties of political evil. But any attempt to analyze Fascist and National Socialist ideologies and final goals raises several questions. Did the movements have ideologies worthy of the name? If they did, whose pronouncements are authoritative sources, and which of those pronouncements are irrelevant, which are tactical, and which are fundamental? Attempts to answer the first question have frequently fallen into two pitfalls: 'mirror-imaging' and radical skepticism. Victims of the first pitfall have unreflectively applied conventional categories of liberal and Marxist social thought to phenomena that liberalism and Marxism are ill-equipped to explain. They have attempted to understand Fascist and National Socialist ideologies as social ideologies expressing the attitudes of particular classes, and addressing the problems those classes faced in adapting to industrial society.

Unfortunately for this approach, Fascist and National Socialist ideologies were not expressions of particular classes and groups, but – like Marxism – above all the creation of individuals: Mussolini and Hitler. Despite Rosenbergs and Gentiles, Feders and Himmlers and Bottais, the two dictators were the sole unimpeachable creators and interpreters of the doctrines of their movements. The dictators were the doctrine, the word made flesh, and understanding the success of their ideologies requires both appreciation of the role of charismatic leadership in hammering doctrine home, and analysis of the context in which they flourished. No pat social interpretation ('the revolt of the petite bourgeoisie') can help explain extreme nationalist political religions, the first principle of which was the denial of class, and which appealed to all classes, although in varying degrees.

Nor has the widespread assumption that an ideology must be social encouraged fruitful enquiry. Commentators have seized on whatever scraps of doctrine fit their assumptions about what an ideology must contain, especially Mussolini's 'Doctrine of Fascism' essay, written in collaboration with Giovanni Gentile. But that pompous exercise had less to do with Fascist ideology than with Mussolini's intermittent tactical attempts to achieve intellectual respectability. And even the Mussolini-Gentile essay proclaimed that the true test of manhood and nationhood was war – a curiously antisocial social ideology.[3] As for Fascist corporativism, which the regime itself touted as the answer to the social needs of the age, it remained a sickly plant in which Mussolini himself took little interest. In the German case, nothing even resembling a conventional answer to the social problems of industrial society ever emerged. Only recently have scholars begun to take Hitler's 'status revolution' seriously, although without relating it adequately to his wider ambitions.

Discarding the assumption that an ideology must be a variety of conventional social thought makes it possible to examine Fascist and Nazi ideology and goals in their own terms. But any such attempt inevitably comes up against the second pitfall: the temptation to dismiss everything as propaganda. In the Italian case, radical skepticism has been especially fashionable. [...] In the German case, scholars have tended to take Hitler's ideological efforts more seriously. The man did, after all, write a book. But some historians have gamely continued to deny that Hitler had ideas, or to argue that whatever ideas he had were irrelevant to his political course.[4]

The case of the radical skeptics would be stronger if Hitler and Mussolini had displayed the sort of erratic behavior consonant with the absence of ideology and the nihilistic pursuit of power. But in both cases the dictators expressed at the beginning of their careers coherent ideologies that were not necessarily entirely popular or plausible, and continued to profess those ideas both publicly and privately throughout. The steady radicalization of their policies suggests an attempt to bring practice into line with theory, and implies that their increasingly rare moderation was tactical, and their extremism genuine. In the end, both provoked catastrophe by persisting, against steadily increasing risks, in their attempts to bend the world to fit the idea. If that was opportunism and nihilism, it was clearly a strangely elaborate and consistent variety.

From mission to program

The Italian case is admittedly the more ambiguous of the two. Mussolini's pilgrimage from socialism to Fascism, and his apparently sincere although private criticisms of Hitler as a doctrinaire, imply an unwillingness to take principles seriously.[5] [...] Both as socialist and Fascist, [Mussolini] had a world view that rested on one underlying assumption, and two political myths. The fixity of these ideas suggests that they were not simply Nietzschean conceits or expressions of a nihilist will to power, but ideas in which he actually believed. What Mussolini did not do was to assemble his ideas into an all-embracing intellectual system or a monocausal, teleological philosophy of history. He may have been a visionary, but unlike Hitler he was not a doctrinaire.

The later Duce's underlying assumption [...] was that life was struggle. History was an endless succession of conflicts between elites, states and tribes. In each epoch a particular elite or state set the tone. By definition, dominant elites or states were the fittest, a conception Mussolini took not as rationalization for resignation, but as a call to battle.[6]

Mussolini's two myths, revolution and the nation, determined the nature of that battle. The first was inevitably that of revolution.[7] This was the myth of Mussolini's childhood and youth in the red Romagna, a myth that a career as a socialist journalist-agitator, and reading Marx and Sorel, reinforced. Not that Mussolini was the most orthodox of Marxists. The Marx he preferred was Marx the revolutionary; for Marx the philosopher of history, the economic theorist, the historian, the German patriot or the heir of the Enlightenment, Mussolini had little use. These latter Marxes he identified with the unadventurous stodginess of the reformist socialists. What Mussolini instead proclaimed was Sorel's 'barbarous notion of socialism', a revolution by an elite of primitives to inaugurate a 'new civilization' of joyous paganism.'[8] This was precisely what Mussolini later attempted as a Fascist. Even the terminology, the goal of a new civilization, remained the same, as did most of Mussolini's enemies: the reformist socialists, the bourgeois establishment, the monarchy, the military hierarchy, and the Church.

Mussolini's second fixed idea was that of the nation and the national mission, an idea also acquired in his socialist youth. Revolutionary expectations and adaptation to prevailing socialist dogma prompted occasional antinational outbursts, such as his famous 1910 exhortation to plant the Italian flag in a dunghill, or his neutralist September 1914 party manifesto. But behind protestations that the proletariat had no fatherland lurked the convictions of a radical nationalist. The Socialist Mussolini displayed an unsocialist reverence for Mazzini, as well as public approval of Giuseppe Prezzolini and his circle of quasi-nationalist litterateurs. [...] Finally, from 1909 if not earlier, Mussolini was an 'assiduous and devoted reader' of the eccentric nationalist philosopher-historian Alfredo Oriani. Oriani was a bloodthirsty recluse ('blood will always be the best warm rain for great ideas') who insisted that only war could make post-Risorgimento Italy whole, and demanded that the nation take up Rome's historic mission in Africa and the Mediterranean. This last enthusiasm did not possess

Mussolini until the war years, but he could scarcely have called himself *un orianista,* as he did in 1909, without sharing much of Oriani's world view.[9]

It was the shock of European war in 1914 that removed the theoretical opposition between the myths of revolution and the nation. Mussolini greeted the collapse of the Socialist International with something approaching relief. When his attempt to lead the Socialists into support of a 'revolutionary war' failed, his last speech to his comrades before they expelled him from the party in November 1914 was pure Oriani:

> If Italy remains absent, it will be once more the land of the dead, the land of cowards. I tell you that the duty of socialism is to shake this Italy of priests, pro-Austrians, and monarchists .... Despite all your howls of protest, the war will flatten the lot of you [vi travolgerà tutti].

In the following months, the myths of revolution and of the nation fused. War, and war alone could undermine the old Italy of priests, kings, and fainthearted Socialists, assuage the national inferiority complex, and make the nation whole. 'A nation old with fifty centuries of history and young with fifty years of national life' could not behave like 'a nation of rabbits'. War must destroy 'the ignoble legend that Italians do not fight, it must wipe out the shame of Lissa and Custoza, it must show the world that Italy can fight a war, a great war; I say again: *a great war'.* No longer would foreigners see Italy as a land 'of travelling storytellers, of peddlers of statuettes, of Calabrian *banditi'.* And war could also be a kind of revolution. The day Italian bayonets crossed the Ringstrasse in Vienna, 'the Vatican's death knell [would] sound'.[10]

Under the sign of perpetual struggle, internal and foreign policy, revolution and war merged. The barbaric new man of Mussolini the socialist became the 'impatient and generous youth', the 'young rebels' of *interventismo.*[11] And despite stalemate and Caporetto, the war, as Mussolini put it in early 1918, had proved that this 'small, despised people', this 'army of mandolin players', could fight. Combat, and the fact that Italy had willed it by deliberately entering the war, in turn confirmed the nation's historic mission and claim to 'higher destinies'. And it was the myth of Rome that shaped Mussolini's conception of those destinies. In December 1918, while proclaiming Italy's right to expansion, he insisted that Rome would 'once again become the beacon of civilization for the world'.[12] Italy might of course choose to become an 'archaeological bordello or an Anglo-Saxon colony'. But the example of Rome, which had 'laid out roads and drawn boundaries and given the world the eternal laws of its legal codes' placed modern Italians under 'another universal duty'.[13] No one, in Theodor Mommsen's words, could 'remain at Rome without a universal idea'. Rome must again become 'the leading city of the civilization of all of Western Europe', and Italy 'the leading nation of world history'.[14]

The political content of this 'new civilization' was clear from very early in Mussolini's career as a Fascist. The world, Mussolini announced in 1921 and 1922, was moving towards the right; as for Fascism, it was 'scarcely at the beginnings of its mission'.[15] By mid-1925, Mussolini had taken to characterizing Fascism as 'one of the few creative ideas of this tormented historical period'. In early 1926 he described Italy, the last of the great powers to achieve maturity, as the first to construct a truly modern state. Like the French Revolution, the Fascist revolution would have world-wide influence and epochal significance. By late

1926, the Duce had become self-assured enough to claim that his movement was the bearer of a 'new type of civilization'. The twentieth century would not merely be the 'century of Italian power', it would also be the century of universal Fascism.[16]

If Mussolini's fundamental ideas were not entirely unsystematic, Hitler's 'rock-hard convictions' amounted to a genuine philosophy of history, an all-embracing, all-explanatory system of belief. Its first principle, from which Hitler never wavered after his first recorded enunciation of it in 1919, was pseudo-biological racism, the 'anti-Semitism of reason'.[17] Race, he claimed in January 1921, was 'the driving force of world history'; later, in *Mein Kampf* he described it as 'the key not only to world history, but to all human culture'. History was the history of race struggle. National Socialism was ultimately a science.[18]

[...] Hitler's ideas were at least as systematic as those of the Marx who asserted that history was the history of class struggle. Both Marxism and Hitler's ideology were millenarian religions of world salvation: salvation for man as a species reborn from the proletariat in one case, salvation for the reborn Aryan species of man in the other.[19] Both required the pitiless elimination of groups: the class enemy for Marxism, the racial enemy for Nazism. [...]

But despite its fixity and coherence, even Hitler's system did not spring suddenly from the aspirant Führer's brow, although scholars have sometimes overestimated the length of time Hitler took to weld his ideas together.[20] Much later, Hitler conceded to his entourage that 'in the early days of the movement I found myself compelled to act from intuition'. Only during his post-Putsch imprisonment in 1924, he maintained, did he have the time to 'confirm his ideas by the study of natural history [den Gedanken naturgeschichtlich zu begründen].[21] Hitler's early speeches suggest it required roughly three years, from the fall of 1919 to the winter of 1922, for the 'anti-Semitism of reason' to harden into a genuine world-system, complete with a visionary program for action, of which more later.

Hitler's starting-point was the 'recognition' (English cannot do justice to the force of the German *Erkenntnis)* that the 'race-tuberculosis of nations', the Jews, were responsible for the 1918 revolution and thus for Germany's defeat in the Great War. By the late spring of 1920 [...] Hitler began to enunciate an all-embracing interpretation of world history. He now recognized the Jews from Moses to Lenin, or 'from Joseph to Rathenau, as the essence of triumphant evil from the Bronze Age to the Weimar Republic. Jewish 'robber nomads', the 'most national race of all the ages', lived by parasitically corrupting other peoples while seeking world mastery for themselves. Only Germany stood in the way: 'Jewry ... knew well that its domination could only be broken by a national force as strong as itself, and that would be the German *Volk*.' Hitler's solution, as early as April 1920, was simple and drastic: he proclaimed 'the inexorable resolve to strike the evil at its root and exterminate it root and branch'.[22] That this was at least potentially a project on a world scale was clear from the insistence with which Hitler spoke of the Jews' own 'world power plans' and 'eternal Jewish goal – world domination'. His remarks about German aims widened correspondingly, from the conventional nationalist (and Party program) demand for the unification of all Germans in one state 'from Memel to

Pressburg, from Königsberg to Strassburg', to the more grandiose if vaguer project of creating a 'germanic empire of the German nation'.[23]

By March 1921 he had gone far beyond merely pointing out that Germany was the main obstacle to alleged Jewish plans. His aim was no longer defense, but offense: it was Germany's mission to 'heal' a sick world.[24] In the spring of 1922, Hitler began to make this claim a major element in his speeches. Only two alternatives existed: 'either victory of the Aryan side or its annihilation and victory of the Jews'. Germanic blood was gradually becoming exhausted, and the future of the world was grim unless Germany 'made itself free'. The nation's 'greatest deed' lay ahead of it: 'to be leader [Führer] in the coming battle of the Aryans against the Jewish world peril'. Germany, he insisted in the next months, must be 'the foundation of an Aryan world order'. This was Germany's 'historic mission'.[25]

Implicitly, Hitler's 'Aryan world order' would mean an end to history in the conventional sense. In *Mein Kampf* he made this implication explicit:

And so the folkish philosophy of life corresponds to the innermost will of Nature, since it restores that free play of forces which must lead to a continuous mutual higher breeding, until at last the best of humanity, having achieved possession of this earth, will have a free path for activity in domains which will lie partly above it and partly outside it.

Even the iron law of struggle might fall into abeyance: the pacifistic-humane idea is perfectly all right perhaps when the highest type of man has previously conquered and subjected the world'.[26] Mankind would achieve biological apotheosis. Hitler had fused pseudo-Darwinist anti-Semitism and German nationalism into a religion of world redemption. All that remained was to work out the practical details.

On a fundamental level, the beliefs of Hitler and Mussolini were thus different in kind. Mussolini's assumption that struggle was the father of all things, and his revolutionary and national myths, were scarcely cut from the same cloth as Hitler's political religion. Mussolini did not propose to rescue the world for good – but merely to establish the new Rome's dominant place in it. Nevertheless, the political and geopolitical programs the two leaders drew from their ideologies were rather more similar than the beliefs themselves.

By 1925–6, Mussolini's program was set in all essential details. Internally, he proposed to create a fanatical following for the national myth, while creating a new sort of Italian and consolidating his own unchallenged power as dictator. If Italy were to fulfil its destiny, Mussolini repeatedly insisted as early as 1919 and 1920, the national will had to be 'directed towards a common objective'. The war had undoubtedly accelerated the 'process of consolidation of the national consciousness', but given Italy's fragile traditions and short existence, *italianità* remained a 'privilege limited to a relatively small minority'.[27] Only a new elite could enforce the unity and discipline necessary for external self-assertion. Here the war itself was a help. It had divided the fittest nations, including Italy, from the unfit, and had divided the Italians themselves into those who 'had been there', and those who had not. The former, the 'lords of the trenches [*trincerocrazia*] would rule. But this vision soon proved a disappointment; the returning veterans were relatively democratic in their convictions, and disinclined to destroy the liberal system.[28] As for the early Fascists, Mussolini ruefully concluded in 1919 that 'their utter lack of respect for authority [*strafottanza*] and dynamism make it hard for them to form a bloc even with themselves'. By mid-1922, Mussolini had apparently concluded that the creation of national unity and of a new elite would take time; it would require 'future Fascist universities and ... Fascist schools' to rear the new imperial Italy. But Fascism would yet accomplish the task at which the Risorgimento had failed, the task of 'making Italians'.[29]

The full urgency of this task did not apparently dawn on Mussolini until the summer 1924 crisis following the murder of the Socialist deputy Giacomo Matteotti. The spontaneous revulsion of much of Italian opinion showed that whatever conversion to Fascism had so far taken place had been superficial. After he struck down the opposition in January 1925, Mussolini proclaimed his goal with a new openness. Fascism's 'totalitarian will' was 'to fascistize the nation, so that tomorrow Italian and Fascist, more or less like Italian and Catholic, will be the same thing'. That would give Fascism the right to call itself a revolution.

[...]

By the fall of 1925 Mussolini announced himself satisfied that dictatorship had overcome the old 'image of the Italian people, repeated abroad, ... of a small nation, disorderly, noisy, and fidgety'. But what Mussolini described as 'the weaknesses of the Italian character: ... shallowness, fecklessness, the belief that everything will go well', yet remained. These 'traditional defects' must give way to 'tenacity, perseverence, and methodical work'. The regime would create a 'new Italian', a 'Fascist Italian', out of the generations that had fought the war, and above all from the new legions under training in the Party youth organizations.[30] The regime must sweep away 'the sediments deposited in those awful centuries of political, military, and moral decadence that r[an] from 1600 to the rise of Napoleon', and complete the Risorgimento, which was 'only the beginning, the work of a tiny minority'. The final goal as Mussolini put it in 1934, was an Italian who knew (like Caligula) that being loved was second best: 'the most important thing [was] to be feared'. It was time to smash the old clichés Italians still labored under: 'No more mandolin players; [instead,] grenade throwers; no more exquisite manners; [instead,] the fist'. It was the eve of Italy's unprovoked attack on Ethiopia.[31]

The fist was also in store for the old elites and institutions at home. [...] He made no secret of his conviction that parliamentary democracy was a miserable nineteenth-century relic; this belief was yet another link between Mussolini the socialist and Mussolini the Fascist.[32] He openly proclaimed that he and his Party would entrench themselves 'and defend themselves against all comers'. And in the spring of 1924 he described the new Chamber of Deputies, despite its Fascist majority, as 'the last parliamentary experiment Italy [would] make'.[33]

Nor was he afraid to pronounce the word *dictatorship* with approval as early as November 1921. [...] The new regime was to be no mere personal dictatorship, but the inauguration of a new age in government.[34] Implicitly, the Duce's 'ferocious totalitarian will'[35] required the taming and ultimate removal of monarchy and papacy, as the political struggles of the 1930s were to show.

The method Mussolini chose was entirely consonant with the tradition of Oriani and of other post-Risorgimento yearners for a Great War to make Italy whole. Mussolini had already called in 1914–15 for war as a kind of revolution. All revolutions, he remarked in 1920, apropos of events in Russia, were 'fated to be imperialist'. War and revolution, he insisted in the same 1925 speech in which he celebrated the creation of the new generations in the laboratory, were 'almost always linked. Either war produces revolution or revolution leads to war'.[36] His regime, although he was careful not to alarm his conservative allies with the thought, sought to fuse the two.

In foreign policy, Mussolini's 1914 discovery of the nation and its mission led him naturally to celebration of its imperial destinies in terms familiar to readers of Oriani and of the nationalist leader Enrico Corradini. But Mussolini was more systematic than either in his synthesis of demographic expansionism and rudimentary geopolitics. His starting-point was inevitably the war, which even before its end had made Italy an 'imperial' nation, fully entitled to the Adriatic victory Slavs and Allies sought to deny. Italy also had the right to expansion in the Mediterranean, 'the sea of Rome'; the Italian people was 'prolific and hard-working'. Imperialism, Mussolini insisted unseasonably on the first day of January 1919, in the midst of his countrymen's Wilsonian enthusiasms, was 'an eternal and immutable law of life'.[37] At the March 1919 inaugural meeting of the *Fasci di Combattimento,* Mussolini proclaimed with statistics in hand that Italy's narrow, mountainous land and rapidly multiplying 40 millions entitled it to a greater share of the earth. Should the Allies of 1915–18 cheat Italy at the peace table, Mussolini threatened in the following weeks, Italy should join the Germans. From its position athwart Britain's Mediterranean communications it should shatter the British Empire in Africa and Asia.[38]

Mussolini took up with a vengeance Corradini's myth of the international class war. Italy should challenge the 'quintessentially plutocratic and bourgeois' alliance of French, British and Americans. The French, at least, were demographically exhausted. Italy would follow the Spain of Charles V and the France of Louis XIV and Napoleon as the 'dominant nation of the entire Latin world', thanks to its demographic dynamism and the 'virtues of our race [*stirpe*]'.[39] Versailles was transitory. Demographic equilibria were shifting. The 'immense wave' of Slavdom would wipe away the small states of central Europe, while the 70 or 80 million Germans would move west into France to rectify that decadent nation's regrettable 'imbalance between territory and population'. As for Italy, it was after Russia and Germany the 'most compact and homogeneous national bloc' in Europe. By 1950 it would have 60 million inhabitants, of which 15 or 20 million would be around the shores of the Mediterranean and across the Atlantic. Italy, 'to be free', must throw off its economic dependence on the Anglo-Saxons by achieving self-sufficiency in grain and energy: It could then 'become the dominating nation of the Mediterranean basin and discharge on the African shores of that sea the majority of its population and energies'. The areas Italy was destined to conquer were 'extraordinarily thinly settled' – an insight that would have come as a surprise to their inhabitants. But some 'overflowings of human masses [*straripamenti di masse umane*]' were 'inevitable and necessary', the 'fertilizing reversals of history'.[40]

Demography continued to furnish a major argument for expansion. But by the mid-1920s Mussolini had turned the argument in a direction unthought of by Corradini and other prophets of the imperialism of the prolific poor. Once in power, Mussolini discovered that pride in the 'riotous development' of Italy's population was misplaced.[41] Some areas of Italy, he recognized as early as mid-1923, were prey to 'demographic decadence', like the despised French. By 1927, after precise statistics had become available, Mussolini had become alarmed. In his marathon Ascension Day speech of May 1927, he surveyed the demographic decline of France and Britain, and insisted that the same decline – in other words, the usual demographic pattern of industrial societies – was a threat to Italy's future as well. Only fools claimed Italians were too numerous. 'Demographic potency' was the fundamental ingredient of national power: 40 million Italians were too few compared to the 40 million French, the 46 million British, the 90 million Germans, the 200 million Slavs, and the 540 million inhabitants of the British and French colonial empires. Italy, 'if it [were] to count for something', must 'approach the threshold of the second half of [the] century with a population no smaller than 60 million inhabitants'. The alternative was renunciation of Italy's mission: 'If we diminish in numbers, gentlemen, we will not found an empire, we will [instead] become a colony'. The tenacious resistance to 'the pernicious currents of contemporary civilization' by Basilicata, one of Italy's most miserably poor and populous regions, was thus an act of foreign policy.[42]

Mussolini's ensuing campaign to 'ruralize Italy, even if it takes billions, and half a century', was no more than a small part of a grand design that stretched far beyond the confines of the Italian state of the 1920s. It was an attempt to create the demographic conditions for Italy's Mediterranean primacy. The 'battle for grain' of 1925 and later years, which many historians have interpreted as a propaganda stunt or as largesse to the landed interests, was a conscious attempt to provide the economic prerequisites of Italy's 'freedom':

> In an Italy entirely reclaimed [*bonificata*], cultivated, irrigated, and disciplined, in other words a Fascist Italy, there is space for another ten million men. Sixty million Italians will make the weight of their numbers and their power felt in the history of the world.[43]

The geographic and strategic requirements of Italian freedom, and of empire, were as much on Mussolini's mind as the economic and demographic ones. The Great War had resolved the problem of Italy's land frontiers; the future now lay on the waters. Only Italy was a truly Mediterranean nation. French and Spaniards had Atlantic ports. Mediterranean preponderance (*predominio*) was therefore Italy's 'by right of its geographic configuration and the maritime traditions of its race [*stirpe*]'. The inland sea must become an Italian lake, 'expelling those who are ... parasites'. Asserting Italy's rights would require breaking 'the chains of hostility that surround[ed] Italy in the Mediterranean', and might also require 'the demolition of the British Empire'. The British guarded the principal exits from the Mediterranean at Gibraltar and Suez, and thus had a stranglehold over Italy's supplies of food and raw materials.[44] By 1926–7, Mussolini had apparently elevated this insight into a general law of geopolitics:

> A nation that has no free access to the sea cannot be considered a free nation; a nation that has no free access to the oceans cannot be considered a great power. Italy must become a great power.

The 'prisoner of the sea that was Rome's' must break that imprisonment in order to fulfil its historic mission.[45]

Hitler's vision had many similarities with Mussolini's, but was different in three fundamental ways. First, Hitler's unified, monocausal world view allowed him to derive everything from the central tenet of race. Second, the tenet's world-wide implications inevitably pushed any program drawn from it in the direction of world domination and biological Utopia, while Prussia-Germany's tradition of blood and iron and its barely thwarted 'grasp at world power' in 1914–18 made such a program inherently plausible to some Germans. Mussolini's nationalism, by contrast, merely aspired to Mediterranean mastery. [...]

From the beginning, Hitler showed greater theoretical rigor than Mussolini. Even the beer-hall agitator of 1920–1 conceived his internal goals, the 'nationalization of the masses', race purification, and creation of a pitiless national dictatorship, as a unified whole.[46] Germany's class, religious, and tribal cleavages must disappear, as they had in the euphoria of August 1914 and the trenches of the Great War. *Klassen-und Standesdünkel* [class and pride of place], religious mistrust, and Prussian-Bavarian enmity all weakened the Germanic Aryan race's struggle against the Jewish world conspiracy. And those internal divisions were themselves the product of racial mixing and Jewish parasitism. Class consciousness was a Jewish disease, a form of false consciousness that the Jews, that 'most national race of all the ages', deliberately and systematically spread, but did not share.[47]

The remedy was simple: a 'revolution of attitudes [*Revolution der Gesinnung*]' that would sweep away class distinctions and inculcate the 'blind, rock-hard, unshakable *belief* in the irresistible power of the German Volk' and in a better future. 'For this reason, the aim of the National Socialists from 1920 on was *not to become a class organization, but rather a Volk movement*'.[48] And hence Hitler's 'socialism': the term was more than mere demagogy, although Hitler did remark at one point that the movement's title of 'workers' party' was a consequence of the need to 'have the workers behind us'.[49] What Hitler meant by 'socialism' was not a society based on a nineteenth-century theory of political economy, but a new egalitarian style and unprecedented social mobility. The National Socialist revolution would not merely be one of *Gesinnung* [mind] or status.[50] It would liberate those Germans who until now had had no chance to rise. Ossified distinctions of birth, education, and wealth, according to Hitler, profited only the Jewish parasites. 'Make way for talent!' was a corollary of anti-Semitism, the chief social ingredient of National Socialism, and one of its most effective appeals. Hitler, the self-proclaimed and self-evident 'most capable man' of the Party, was simultaneously the prophet of the career open to talent, and its prize exemplar. [...]

The career open to talent inevitably had a negative side. By 1923 Hitler had come to the conclusion that those without talent – the requisite pedigree or physical attributes – must vanish. Germany would expel its Jews, if they were lucky, and take measures against the deformed, the mentally ill, syphilitics, and drunkards: 'The preservation of a nation is more important than the preservation of its unfortunates.' The *völkisch* state would see to it that 'only the healthy beget children'. By 1923–4, in connection with the evolution of his foreign-policy ideas, Hitler had also come to the conclusion that the healthiest of the healthy were the peasantry: 'The slums of the cities were responsible for nine-tenths, alcohol for one-tenth, of all human depravity.' The countryside, not the cities, had provided the 'healthier section of the Volk' that had crushed the 1919 red terror in Munich.[51] [...]

The final ingredient in Hitler's internal vision was of course a political revolution to accompany the revolution of attitudes, the career open to talent, and the repudiation of the last shreds of Judaeo-Christian morality. Germany, Hitler proclaimed as early as April 1920, needed 'neither monarchy nor republic, but the form of state that is the best for the [German] people. We need a dictator who is a genius.' He demanded 'a [man with an] iron skull, with muddy boots, perhaps, but with a clear conscience and a steel fist, who will end the blathering of these [Reichstag] drawing-room heroes, and give the nation a deed'.[52] Once Hitler had received 'dictatorial powers' from his own party, in the summer of 1921, his utterances on this score took on new authority. In a 'Germanic democracy', the best brain decided, not the 'sluggishness of the majority'. Hitler had already cast himself in the part. He might describe himself as a mere 'drummer' when flattering nationalist notables, but he also claimed for his movement the right to provide the 'strong man' Germany needed. As early as February 1922 he insisted the Party would lead Germany 'when the rotten edifice [of the Republic] finally collapse[d]'.[53]

Mussolini's example was a powerful help. Hitler apparently first took public note of the Duce in August 1922, and was soon proclaiming that Mussolini 'had shown what a minority can do, if a holy national will inspires it'. The Fascists had allegedly smashed 'Jewish-Marxist terror' and dragged a lethargic majority with them. The National Socialists, he now repeatedly proclaimed, aspired 'to take the Volk in hand'.[54] In the course of 1923 he sometimes veiled his claim to supreme leadership ('We must forge the sword; the almighty will give us the man for this sword'). But in predicting to the *Daily Mail* in October 1923 that if a German Mussolini came, 'people would fall down on their knees and worship him', Hitler could only have had himself in mind.[55] In his speeches at his trial after the November 1923 Putsch, he openly claimed political leadership of the *völkische* movement and of a nationalist revolution. His later outline in *Mein Kampf* of the constitutional implications of the Führer principle was no more than confirmation of views he had held since 1921–2 at least.[56]

Hitler's early sense of his vocation as Führer was never more apparent than in the foreign policy that accompanied and complemented his internal revolutionary goals. From very early, as with Mussolini, unity and leadership at home were the indispensable prelude to expansion abroad in fulfillment of the nation's mission: 'Nations are only capable of great advances when they have carried through the internal reforms that make it possible to project the entire race towards foreign policy goals.'[57] Still, unlike the 'prisoner of the Mediterranean', German traditions did not foreordain the direction of German expansion. Hitler was set on war from the beginning, and the Party's January 1920 program demanded 'land and soil for the nation', but it took until 1922 to work out whom to conquer.

Hitler had to start somewhere, and he began with the staid Wilhelmine program of naval and economic expansion he later denounced as naive and unworkable [...]

But by the end of December 1922, Hitler had developed a coherent vision, one he stuck to thereafter. His increasingly full-throated espousal of a German mission as '*Führer* of the Aryans' brought with it the need for a commensurate foreign policy. Even before the French occupation of the Ruhr in January 1923, which usually passes as the catalyst that impelled him to define his foreign program, Hitler's ideas had set. In a remarkable December 1922 conversation with an emissary of the then Reich Chancellor Cuno, Hitler outlined with only slight reticence his ideas on both internal and foreign policy.'[58] Internally he was tactically circumspect, in deference to his audience. The nationalist dictatorship needed to smash the Left could eventually give way to a monarchy; solution of the Jewish question need not involve violence. His other views were less restrained:

> In foreign policy Germany must adjust itself to a purely continental policy, while avoiding the harming of English interests. We should attempt the carving up of Russia with English help. Russia would provide soil enough for German settlers, and a broad field of action for German industry. Then, when [we] settle accounts with France, England would not get in the way.

Hitler also mentioned Italy as a possible ally; even before hearing of Mussolini's movement he had been alive to the chance of exploiting Italy's aspirations to 'predominance in the Mediterranean'. After discovering the Fascists, he had defied German nationalist orthodoxy by proclaiming in November 1922 and thereafter that the Italian alliance required an end to 'empty protests' over the South Tyrol which Italy had annexed in 1918.[59]

Hitler's December 1922 remarks included all the essential elements of the program he later outlined in the second volume of *Mein Kampf,* written in 1925–6: the forcible re-establishment of domestic unity; expansion at Russia's expense; a settling of accounts with France; England and Italy as allies, and the most un-Wilhelmine conception of isolating enemies and destroying them one by one. The order of the steps in this *Stufenplan* [step-by-step plan] remained problematic, however.[60] What the Ruhr occupation apparently did do for Hitler was to make neutralizing France his highest priority; eastern expansion could come only after that preliminary step. But that was a relatively minor change. The foundations of Hitler's program were in place. His subsequent elaborations of his vision in an essay of April 1924, in *Mein Kampf,* in his unpublished 'second book' of 1928, and in campaign speeches of 1928 and 1930, in which he unambiguously claimed world mastery for Germany, brought only two new elements. The first was Hitler's discovery of America – the recognition that the United States might prove his final adversary. In that contest, Hitler concluded, Germany's greater concentration of Aryan stock would carry it to victory.[61] The second novelty was the recognition, even more explicit than that of Mussolini, that foreign and domestic policy were inextricably linked:

> Domestic policy must secure the inner strength of a people so that it can assert itself in the sphere of foreign policy. Foreign policy must secure the life of a people for its domestic political development. Hence domestic policy and foreign policy are not only most closely linked, but must also mutually complement one another.

Translated into cruder terms, revolution was a prerequisite for expansion, and expansion for revolution. This insight was in its way as important a part of Hitler's program as his external *Stufenplan.*[62]

If the foundations of the world views of Hitler and Mussolini were rather different, the visionary programs the two developed thus had much in common.

Internal policy and foreign aggrandizement were intertwined. Both leaders developed a peculiar blend of demography and geopolitics. Both leaders hoped to proceed by stages: consolidation at home, then exploitation of the rivalries of other powers to gain freedom for conquest. But Hitler was relatively rigid in laying down the alliances and stages by which Germany would climb to world mastery. The early Mussolini never went beyond generic predictions that European turmoil would permit Italian expansion. With the partial exception of his tilt towards France in 1935, he remained uncommitted to a specific alliance structure until 1936 – and in this sense, if only in this sense, was more of a 'realist' than Hitler.

[...]

Unholy war

Mussolini's transition to active expansionism aroused less resistance than Hitler's; the Duce's chosen victims seemed less capable of defending themselves. Nevertheless, the decision to attack Ethiopia has found a variety of interpretations. Determinists have argued that the Depression and consequent need to reflate the economy prompted expansion. Another popular claim is that Mussolini sought to 'relaunch' a flagging regime and cement the loyalty of the younger generation by foreign adventure.[63] Renzo De Felice, while rejecting the economic argument and demonstrating convincingly that the regime was at the height of its popularity, has suggested that failure in transforming society at home impelled Mussolini into previously unsought imperial adventure. The decision for war, in all these views, was a choice for second best and Ethiopia no more than a target of opportunity that German revival impelled the frightened French to offer Mussolini. Finally, Jens Petersen has argued that what happened between 1932 and 1935 was that international alignments at last permitted Mussolini to implement a long-held expansionist program. German rearmament and French fear (to which one must add the Depression's severing of financial dependence on Washington) at last gave Mussolini his chance.[64]

Mussolini's repeated, almost monotonous references to the goal of empire from 1918 on support the last interpretation. But it was more than a foreign policy program that moved him to action. War, Mussolini insisted both as Socialist and as Fascist, was linked to revolution. Only war, whose uncivilizing effects he well remembered, could help break the old society's resistance to the new paganism, make Italy the 'militarist' nation he demanded,[65] and further undermine monarchy and Church. Foreign adventure was also internal forward policy, not the mere 'social-imperialist' defense of order at home characteristic of more staid authoritarian regimes.

The choice of Ethiopia was long overdetermined. Fascism, as part of its historic mission, had to avenge Adua, the humiliating defeat of its great precursor Crispi. Mussolini's interest in 'profiting from an eventual dissolution of the Ethiopian empire' dated from at least 1925, and concrete planning began in November 1932.[66] Once it had conquered East Africa, the 'prisoner of the Mediterranean' might hope to lever the British out of the Sudan and Egypt.[67] Finally and most importantly, Ethiopia was the one enemy Mussolini's flankers and the European powers would reluctantly permit him to conquer. The flankers also felt the shame of Adua, and assumed that the Italy that had stood up to Austria-Hungary could defeat a land-locked, half-tribal, half-feudal kingdom with perhaps a quarter of Italy's population. And the other powers were ultimately disposed to tolerate an Italian aggression outside Europe that did not directly touch their own possessions.

Mussolini nevertheless faced and overcame major obstacles in launching his Fascist imperial war. Internally, he had to sap the tenacious resistance of the army. That hierarchy remained wedded to its Alpine priorities and dubious of the advantages of empire; the Austrian crisis of July 1934 emphasized the need to keep Italy's guard up in Europe. Both Marshal Pietro Badoglio, the chief of the vestigial inter-service general staff, and General Federico Baistrocchi, the dynamic army chief of staff and undersecretary for war, were initially hostile to the project, which originated in the colonial ministry under Mussolini's aegis.[68] Once he had converted Baistrocchi and partially neutralized Badoglio by mobilizing navy and air force support, Mussolini still faced the king and a conservative Establishment that abhorred risk. The Duce complained in 1936 that the monarch bore no responsibility for victory: '*He* didn't want to go – I had to force him.' First-hand evidence of the king's attitude is lacking, but Mussolini's June 1935 complaint to his field commander in East Africa about 'grumblers and defeatists – more on high than below' suggests that king and Establishment were indeed recalcitrant.[69] Even Fascists wavered. The ex-secretary of the Party, Giovanni Giuriati, allegedly told the king that Mussolini's policy would lead to 'national disaster'. And Britain's apparent intention of fighting Mussolini in the Mediterranean if he went ahead produced warnings from Badoglio and the military of 'a disaster that would reduce us to a Balkan level'.[70] Even the Duce's son-in-law and future foreign minister, Galeazzo Ciano, temporarily gave way to despair after the League imposed sanctions.[71] Only the Church, which looked forward to civilizing the heretical Copts, and much of the public, which believed the regime's tales of Ethiopian and British provocations, and of an East African el Dorado, remained stalwart for aggression. Much later, Mussolini complained that many, many important people came to him and said, 'You have already done great things. Now [you should] pull in your oars.'[72]

Mussolini's knowledge of the British fleet's relative unpreparedness – on which he bet too heavily – and Whitehall's craven reluctance to force the issue allowed him to hold his course. But the attack on Ethiopia remained, in the words of overcautious advisors Mussolini later quoted, a gamble [*un'avventura*], a great gamble'.[73] The Establishment's reluctance may not have been entirely a consequence of Mussolini's external risk-taking. Defeat at the hands of the British, or stalemate at those of the Ethiopians, would risk far more than Italy's reputation and international position. It would risk the regime and, with it, the advantages the Establishment had secured through its forced compromise with Mussolini. Conversely, victory would excessively reinforce the regime and increase Mussolini's chances of receiving the blind obedience to which he aspired. And Mussolini lost no opportunity to make victory popular and Fascist, rather than military and dynastic. General Emilio De Bono, his original choice as commander in East Africa, was despite loyalty to king and army a man who owed his position to 'Fascist merits'.[74] The Militia mobilized, with army help, to provide specifically Fascist units whose combat performance the propaganda apparatus could then inflate. The new empire, Mussolini proclaimed to frenetic applause on 9 May, 1936, was a Fascist empire that 'bore the indestructible marks of the will and power of the Roman *fascī*. By implication, it owed nothing to the old order.[75]

Victory indeed had consequences. Mussolini, as 'founder of the Empire', could now impose on his subordinates, without being laughed at, the reverence he aspired to. His subsequent policy – Spanish intervention, the racial laws, the campaign against the bourgeoisie, the annexation of Albania, and the plunge into war in 1940 – was only possible thanks to domestic reinforcement through African victory, and the license for aggression which increasing German preponderance brought. Far from representing a falling off from the famous 'realism' that his propagandists and some historians have ascribed to him, Mussolini's later policies were simply ever more risky attempts to implement his program within his own lifetime. It was his mission to remake 'the character of the Italians through combat'. Revelation of a long-held vision, not the 'involution' of personality and will that some scholars have discerned, presided over Italy's road to the Second World War.[76]

African victory naturally did not remove all obstacles. Mussolini put the League of Nations's sanctions to good use in convincing the great economic interests that autarky – the breaking of Italy's remaining ties to the world market – was the only feasible course. And although autarky proved 'too tight a shirt' for the export industries, the increasing stream of armaments contracts helped ease the pain. Italy's massive dependence on imported energy and strategic raw materials made genuine autarky impractical, but furnished yet another argument for expansion. In both domestic and foreign policy, Mussolini moved with increasing self-confidence. He plunged into Spain apparently without consulting the king; when Baistrocchi objected and Badoglio grumbled, he sacked one and ordered the other to show public approval. Spain, however, provided anything but the expected easy victories, and the disaster at Guadalajara in March 1937 allowed the king to level veiled reproaches at Mussolini.[77] But the humiliation passed with the summer 1937 victories in the Basque country. By early 1938, the German example – Hitler made himself commander-in-chief of the armed forces on 4 February – prompted emulation. The Party, presumably on Mussolini's secret instructions, pushed through Chamber and Senate a bill creating both Duce and king 'First Marshals of the Empire'. This demotion of the monarch to Mussolini's level produced wrath at the Quirinal.[78] . Mussolini also promulgated in 1937–8 laws that formally wrote the Party into the constitution, and in January 1939 the Chamber of Deputies became the Chamber of Fasci and Corporations. Only the Senate remained as a relic of the liberal-monarchical past, and it owed its considerable staying power to its life tenure and royal appointment.

Mussolini and his entourage began looking forward with increasing anticipation to the removal of the king, perhaps even as early as the end of the Spanish war. It was only right, the Duce commented cynically in 1936 when exempting the king's foreign assets from the nationalization that League sanctions made necessary, to leave him 'a well-protected nest-egg'. The fate of monarchies was frequently an uncertain one.[79] The Duce's private remarks suggest an ever-growing resolve to smash the internal and foreign-policy restraints the monarchy still imposed.[80]

The military, like the monarchy, also failed to show the necessary enthusiasm for Mussolini's increasing risk-taking. Although he had achieved *de facto* direction of the armed forces during the Ethiopian war, Mussolini remained a prisoner of their institutional structures. Major surgery, such as the 1933 and 1936–7 plans for a tri-service defense ministry that would restrict the services' autonomy, was impossible without disturbing the interservice balance and tampering with the monarchy's prerogatives.[81] Both the rigidity of service promotion procedures and the caste resistance of the senior generals inhibited the injection of fresh and necessarily Fascist blood into the higher reaches of the military. In strategic planning, Mussolini had his way for a while. In 1937 and 1938 the army, under Baistrocchi's successor Pariani, made grandiose plans, with navy cooperation, for an assault on Egypt from Cyrenaica. But after the shock of Munich Badoglio reasserted his prerogatives, and killed the plan. If France were also hostile, Italy was too weak to seize Suez. Badoglio's refusal ' to permit planning 'that [did] not correspond to the situation' meant that when the situation changed, Italy had no plans. In the event, Mussolini had to trick his generals and admirals into war in 1940 with the assurance that they need not fight.[82]

Less dangerous for Mussolini than the recalcitrance of monarchy and military, but still inconvenient, was the Church. The Vatican, despite its compromise with Mussolini, made difficulties about what Pius XI denounced as 'pagan state idolatry'. Naturally, the Church overwhelmingly supported the Ethiopian campaign and Mussolini's allegedly anti-Bolshevist intervention in Spain. It evinced qualified approval even of the annexation of Albania.[83] But when Mussolini's concern with the 'purity of the race' came home from the colonies, and in deference to the Germans attacked Jews as well as blacks, the Vatican became uneasy. The Church was not averse to religious discrimination, and avant-garde Jesuits urged segregation of the Jews, but the pseudo-biological provisions of the 1938 racial laws included Catholic converts.[84] At the same time, the German alliance and the increasing risk of general war added to the Church's reservations about the regime. War – apart from the predictable loss of life and destruction – would either result in Axis defeat, endangering Italy and the Lateran pacts, or a victory that would bring pagan racist revolution in earnest. Hence the papal protests and peace messages against which Mussolini increasingly railed between 1938 and 1940.

The upper-middle classes, too, began to distance themselves subtly from Mussolini as he moved to implement his vision. It required the shock of defeat to consummate the divorce Italian-style between the regime and what Mussolini described as a bourgeoisie riddled with 'cowardice, laziness, [and] love of the quiet life'. But the origins of that divorce lay in Mussolini's post-Ethiopian activism both at home and abroad. Italy's forced 'non-belligerence' in September 1939 was thus not an example of Mussolini's purported realism, but rather the Establishment's last victory over the regime's expansionism. The pope and Badoglio, Ciano and the diplomats industrialists and king all coalesced to hold back Mussolini and the Party enthusiasts. But the victory was a Pyrrhic one. Mussolini remained in control of the machinery of government. Only a coup, which the king briefly contemplated in March 1940, could remove him. When the king failed to move, the members of the quasi-coalition of 'moderates' remained prisoners of their separate bargains with the Duce, and of their own cautiously expansionist appetites.

The great German victories in the West in May 1940 enabled Mussolini to activate that expansionism with the promise that Italy need not fight. He himself sought instead a swift but decisive conflict that would free Italy from its Mediterranean imprisonment and give him the prestige to crush his flankers. That was why the regime insisted – contrary to common sense, which dictated the mobilization of all strands of Italian nationalism – that this war was *la guerra fascista*. It was a war of internal as well as foreign conquest. And when Italy's independent war ended in the winter of 1940–1 in disaster at Taranto, in the Albanian mountains, and in the sands of Beda Fomm, Mussolini's revolutionary project died with it.[85] The regime survived until the 'moderate' Fascists revolted against Mussolini, and the king and generals overthrew him in July 1943. But the crushing defeats of 1940 and Italy's humiliating new status as first satellite of the Reich had broken the prestige Mussolini needed for internal transformation. In the end, the flankers, emboldened in defeat, repudiated the regime in the name of the same Italian nationalism, and interests, that had once led them to support it.

Hitler fortunately also failed, but his failure was less humiliating and infinitely bloodier than Mussolini's. Hitler had written in *Mein Kampf* that Germany would 'either be a world power, or cease to be'. He almost achieved the first, and barely failed at the second. His starting-point in blending revolution and territorial expansion was his discovery in November 1937 that Germany's growing if foreseeably temporary preponderance in armaments had not convinced Blomberg, Fritsch, and Neurath that Germany could, should, and must fight. Their lamentable lack of faith emerged from the alarmed protestations at the 5 November 1937 Reich Chancellory conference at which Hitler revealed for the first time that he intended to seize Austria and smash Czechoslovakia, situation permitting, as early as 1938. Fritsch and his subordinate Beck did not merely object to the risks involved, but above all to Hitler's implicit claim to be Germany's sole font of strategic leadership. Regrettably, the first civilian since Bismarck to impose on the army both civilian control, and Clausewitz's heretical notion that war was a tool of politics, turned out to be Hitler.

The dictator confirmed his 5 November prediction of war two weeks later in a speech to Party officials: new tasks awaited Germany, 'for the living space of our Volk is too narrow'. And he again stressed the identity of foreign and domestic policy. Just as the National Socialists had 'led the nation upwards' internally, so they would achieve for Germany abroad 'the same rights to existence as other nations'.[86] Two months later, he dismissed both Blomberg and Fritsch, and for good measure, Neurath and the ambassador to Italy, Hassell. [...]

In the aftermath of the 4 February coup, many high officers seethed with indignation at the preposterous accusations against Fritsch, but foreign policy came to Hitler's aid. Political developments in Austria allowed him to distract the army with a job to do: the Anschluss. The resulting personal triumph allowed him to brush off Army pressure for Fritsch's reinstatement, while the public, consulted in the first plebiscite since the Rhineland coup, returned an overwhelming vote of confidence. Foreign policy had first demanded domestic upheaval, then blessed it with success.

But obstacles remained [...] Throughout the summer, as preparations to attack Germany's next victim, Czechoslovakia, went forward, Hitler gave vent to a stream of complaints against the generals. Most of them 'had rejected [his leadership], and continued to reject it'. They 'as yet did not understand the meaning of the new age', and were far inferior in élan to his trusty Gauleiters.

Delays in the army-supervised construction of the *Westwall* fortifications led him to threaten to turn the job over to Martin Bormann, 'whom he could at least rely on'.[87] Fritz Todt, another Party luminary, actually got the job. And several months later, Hitler apparently intimidated a reluctant Admiral Raeder with the not entirely incredible threat that if further delays slowed the gargantuan naval program, he would turn procurement over to Todt.[88]

The real issue of the summer, however, was what Hitler characterized as '*Angst* and cowardice in the army': the refusal of Beck and the hesitation of other senior officers to accept his strategic leadership and the risks the Czech enterprise would involve. Fortunately for Hitler, Beck was relatively isolated both in his high assessment of the risk of general war and his dogged insistence on the co-responsibility of the army chief of staff for strategic decisions. Nevertheless, Hitler felt obliged to harangue his top commanders twice in mid-August to counteract Beck's influence and steel their nerves for the coming struggle. Conveniently for Hitler, Beck cracked under the strain of isolation and resigned. His successor Halder plotted in secret, but made no attempt at open contradiction.[89] Even more fortunately for Hitler, the West surrendered Czechoslovakia without fighting. Bloodless triumph cut the ground from under doubters and plotters. Munich also raised Hitler higher in the public esteem than ever before – the German people had nationalist triumph without war.[90]

The crisis had other effects besides strengthening Hitler internally. He had passionately sought war against the Czechs, both to steel the young, and to test the newly minted Wehrmacht. Only at the last moment had he accepted a negotiated surrender of the Sudetenland, On the evening of 27 September, Hitler had watched motorized units on their way to the border roll through central Berlin, as he had ordered. The public stood, silent and sullen; no cheers or 'German greetings' honored the Führer's appearance at the Reich Chancellory balcony.[91] The delirious scenes of August 1914 did not repeat themselves. After the euphoria of the Anschluss this may have come as a shock. The unfeigned enthusiasm of German crowds for Chamberlain added insult to injury.[92] Hence Hitler's post-Munich rage at the British ('we will no longer tolerate the supervision of governesses') and his diatribe to German press representatives on 10 November demanding indoctrination that would 'free the Volk of doubts that make it unhappy' and inculcate '*fanatical* belief' in final victory. The nation must stand like 'formed-up troops' behind his decisions. The 'intellectual strata' – by which he meant those educated Germans, including officers, who still refused to accept him on faith – were unfortunately still necessary: 'otherwise one could exterminate them, or whatever.'[93]

Hitler could have been under no illusion that propaganda alone would consolidate internal unity behind him. As he harangued the press, the SS and police were supervising the cleanup of the debris from synagogues and Jewish shops burned out in the *Kristallnacht* pogrom. Hitler had inspired that action as a hint of things to come and as a salutary release for Party radicalism, but he was too shrewd a judge of public and elite opinion to associate with it openly. Generals were still heard to mutter about hanging 'this swine, Goebbels', who was ostensibly responsible.[94] The time of the Jews was nevertheless coming, Hitler hinted in his 30 January 1939 Reichstag speech. That of the churches, he had said privately the previous August, had not yet come; he still had 'too many other problems'.[95]

Yet as his insistence on his cyclopean building program and his acceleration of the already breakneck pace of naval construction suggest, Hitler had already left the confines of the inter-war German state far behind (symptomatically, Germany proper now became the *Altreich* [old realm]). The immense Nazi eagle with a globe in its claws that Hitler ordered to crown his gigantic Berlin great hall was no mere ideological metaphor. Germany, he told a group of senior officers in early February 1939, was bound for world mastery; the triumphs of 1938 were not the end of the road but the beginning. Germany could best preserve the reputation and prestige acquired since 1933 by 'without letup exploiting every opportunity, however small, to move immediately towards a new success'.[96] He would tolerate no more 'warning memoranda' – an apparent reference to Beck's attempts to thwart him the previous summer. The alleged 'hot-house intellectualism' of the general staff since Schlieffen's day was outdated; he demanded 'believing officers' with 'trust and blind confidence'.[97]

The next major success, Hitler decided shortly after his bloodless absorption of rump Czechoslovakia in mid-March, must come in war against Poland. The origins of that war, which contrary to Hitler's intentions eventually became a world war, have inevitably provoked vast controversy. But until Tim Mason's work on the regime's relationship with the industrial workers, few scholars have had much to say about the internal ramifications of Hitler's decision. Mason has opened the question up by suggesting that Hitler took the plunge largely to escape the economic and political crisis rearmament had created. Conquest was 'an end in itself', an improvised defensive 'flight forward' to escape intolerable domestic problems. The argument is not overly convincing.[98] Hitler had passionately wanted to fight in 1938, before the crisis reached full intensity. Politically, the regime was hardly on its last legs, either in the public or in the official mind. Mason's arguments for social and political crisis echo with the liturgy of the class smuggle, but fail to address at least some of the evidence. The Ruhr miners, on whose efforts all of German industry relied, had a lower absentee rate in 1938 than in 1929, and later showed remarkable aptitude for supervising slave labor.[99]

As for the economic crisis, the evidence does not suggest that anyone except a narrow circle recognized it as such. Hitler merely argued, in prodding his generals toward war, that Germany could hold out only 'for a few more years'.[100] This was less a prediction of imminent catastrophe than a ploy to egg the reluctant onward by reminding them of difficulties that they had helped him create. Mason has also claimed in support of his thesis on Hitler's remarks in both 1937 and 1939 that Germany faced a choice between expansion and degeneration. But those remarks were Hitler's standard justification, fixed since 1921–2, of the need for *Lebensraum*.[101] The economic strains of 1938–9 were for him no more than confirmation of that insight.

But the foremost difficulty with Mason's theory is that it isolates the events of 1938–9 from those preceding, and thus interprets as cause a phenomenon that is first of all effect. As Jost Dülffer has pointed out, the internal crisis was a consequence of Hitler's ever-increasing demands on the economy for armaments and for the immense building program.[102] Those demands led directly to war, with no need for an intervening *deus ex machina* in the form of internal crisis. Only war could transmute armaments into *Lebensraum* and world mastery. Only war, along with the new Reich's cyclopean monuments and incessant propaganda, could fully nationalize the masses. The 1938–9 crisis was above all a symptom of Hitler's offensive forward thrust towards war and revolution, rather than a driving force behind it.

As for the timing of the attack on Poland, three considerations were decisive. First and least important was the pact with Stalin, which secured Germany's rear and checkmated the remaining doubters among the generals. Second came a broader consideration, which Hitler repeatedly emphasized in his 1939 harangues to his military leaders. Rearmament had created a brief window of opportunity for Germany; after 1941–2 that window would close as the other powers caught up. Finally, of course, came Hitler's ever-growing obsession with the short time left to him personally; as he told his generals 'in all modesty' in November 1939, he alone possessed the nerve *(Entschlusskraft)* to fulfill Germany's mission.[103]

He lost no time putting war to use. Within the Reich, he secretly ordered the killing of the congenitally ill and insane in state institutions. Poland offered an even greater opportunity to implement his internal programs for Germany – using Poles as 'laboratory rabbits'. As Heydrich crudely explained to the army, 'we want to spare the little people, but nobility, clergy, and Jews must be killed'.[104] The generals recoiled in pious horror, then sheepishly yielded responsibility for the occupied territories.

The generals did make a brief stand on the sole issue they could not evade: Hitler's demand, made immediately after Poland's collapse, for an immediate offensive to smash the French and British. The military's resistance, which included yet another hesitant Putsch conspiracy in which Halder again took fleeting interest, was the last twitch of the organized German Establishment. It was short-lived. This time, no one dared openly question Hitler's strategic judgment as Beck had done; instead, the generals took refuge in technical arguments that inevitably lost force as army readiness improved and French ineptitude and demoralization became apparent. Hitler's tirades terrorized Brauchitsch and Halder, and the repeated weather postponements of the attack allowed the generals to prepare it with even more of the thoroughness that was their trademark. The pathetic April 1940 showing of the British and French in Norway did the rest. When army and Luftwaffe crossed the western borders on 10 May, the doubters had long fallen silent or joined the ranks of the converted.

In mid-January, even before the Wehrmacht rolled, Hitler had made clear to some of his associates the internal consequences of victory: 'The war is in this respect, as in many other matters, a favorable opportunity to dispose of it (the church question) root and branch'. In the ancient world entire peoples had been liquidated, and the Soviet Union was setting the example in the present. But the old German 'proclivity for mysticism' still thwarted him:

> If he did nothing now against the rebellious parsons, then it was not least out of concern for the Wehrmacht. There they ran to the field chaplains, and a trooper who was brave with the good Lord was always more useful to him than one who was cowardly without Him. But here the indoctrination of the SS, which was now proving in war that ideologically schooled troops could be brave even without the Lord, would outline the necessary development.[105]

In conversation with Rosenberg, his religion expert, Hitler foresaw the possibility of smashing the churches by force ('ein harter machtpolitischer Eingriff') – but this could take place only when Germany was 'fully independent internationally'; 'otherwise the resulting blaze of internal political controversy could cost us our existence'.[106]

The Wehrmacht's crushing victory over France in May–June 1940 did not secure the full measure of freedom Hitler sought, but he now commanded the confidence of the military elite as never before or after. Symptomatic of that confidence was the pleasurable anticipation with which many senior generals prepared to tackle the next intriguing military problem Hitler set them: the destruction of the Soviet Union and the physical elimination of its 'Jewish-Bolshevik intelligentsia'. [...] The public, sullen during the phony war, suddenly went 'berserk with success'; in the words of one jaundiced eyewitness, after the French collapse Germany's cafes were full of 'beer-soaked old pinochle players dividing up continents over their steins'.[107]

Nevertheless, Hitler still lacked the prestige to impose his vision in its entirety inside Germany. The attack on the Soviet Union was thus more than merely a response to Churchill's incomprehensible obduracy and to United States support for Britain, or another momentous step in Hitler's foreign policy *Stufenplan*. It was also a further mighty thrust towards the internal barbarization of Germany itself. *Lebensraum* and foreign policy 'freedom' would enable him at last to crush that 'reptile', the churches.[108] The war of racial annihilation in the East would harden German youth to destroy the old society at home, while the lavish rewards of victory would still whatever unquiet consciences remained.

But even while the Wehrmacht struck deep into Russia, the Bishop of Münster, Count Galen, raised his voice publicly against the euthanasia program, and the regime had to suspend it. Hitler raged in private. This, too, would appear on the churches' final bill. He had, he noted privately in October 1941, also had to put up with the Jews for a long time; now, though he left it unsaid, extermination had begun.[109]

That last foundation of his program was indeed all that remained once the Wehrmacht failed to take Moscow in November–December 1941. In Jodl's words, 'long before anyone else in the world, Hitler suspected or knew that the war was lost', and that suspicion drove him to give the Final Solution an ever higher priority, a priority that soon eclipsed the fighting of the war itself.[110] Internally, SS and Party vied in radicalism, while furtive half-knowledge of Germany's Eastern crimes and of coming retribution bound the public to the regime to the end. What remained of the Establishment had lost in 1938–40 all capacity to put the brakes on Hitler. The final despairing gesture of some of its members, the botched bomb plot of 20 July, 1944, if anything strengthened the regime. Barbarous revenge ended the history of Prussia, while miraculous survival fleetingly refurbished Hitler's defeat-tarnished charisma.[111] Hitler's revolution, unlike that of Mussolini, had at least made itself irreversible from within. And the temporary allies who met across the rubble of Greater Germany could not restore Bismarck's Reich, even had they wished it.

Conclusion

From the perspective of results, Mussolini's claim that Italy and Germany were 'congruent cases' was something of an exaggeration. It also cannot erase the many differences between the societies over which the two regimes arose, and between their myths, traditions and institutions. The degree of freedom of action the regimes achieved was markedly different because of these underlying conditions, and not merely because of the frequently invoked but partly illusory gap in ruthlessness and dynamism between the dictators. The two leaders' visions, despite the differences between their underlying ideologies, were indeed congruent in their mixture of demography and geopolitics, if not in Hitler's racialist teleology. Above all, the relationship between foreign and domestic policy in the two regimes was similar. Foreign policy was internal policy and vice versa; internal consolidation was a precondition of foreign conquest, and foreign conquest was the decisive prerequisite for a revolution at home that would sweep away inherited institutions and values, Piedmontese-Italian and Prusso-German military castes, the churches with their claim to deep popular loyalties and their inconvenient if not always operative Christian values, and, last but not least, the putatively decadent and cowardly upper-middle classes.

In the end it is this identity of foreign and domestic policy that distinguishes these two regimes from the other types of political gangsterism prevalent in this century of war and mass murder. Most twentieth-century revolutionary regimes have sought to destroy either the social order or the international one. Despots that come to power through revolutionary civil war in relatively primitive societies – Lenin, Stalin, Mao, Pol Pot – can have millions shot or starved without need of territorial aggrandizement, though they scarcely despise it. Ideology may dictate expansion, but in practice foreign conquest is a bonus, not the indispensable prerequisite for internal transformation. As for despots who inherit more organized nations, they usually expand partly to defend existing privilege. Brezhnev's troopers did not swoop down on Kabul, or the Argentine navy on the Falklands, to undermine order at home. Only Mussolini and Hitler simultaneously sought to overthrow their societies and their neighbors. In this sense, reason, not faith unites their two regimes.

Notes

[1] I thank the Woodrow Wilson International Center for Scholars and the John Simon Guggenheim Memorial Foundation for generous support during the research and writing of this piece, which attempts to summarize the argument of a book in progress. My thanks also to Hans W. Gatzke, Michael Geyer, Isabel V. Hull, Adrian Lyttelton and Williamson Murray for helpful comments and suggestions. Initial quotations: Strunk minute, 31 January, 1936, US National Archives, microcopy T-454/56/000226; Hitler, *Monologe im Führerhauptquartier 1941–1944*, Hamburg, 1980, p.43.

[2] Nolte, *Three Faces of Fascism*, New York, 1966, pp.20–1; Gilbert Allardyce, 'What Fascism is not. Notes on the deflation of a concept', *American Historical Review*, 84, 1979, 367–88; see also Berndt Martin, 'Zur Tauglichkeit eines übergreifenden Faschismus-Begriffs', *Vierteljahreshefte für Zeitgeschichte* (henceforth VfZG) 29, 1981, 48–73.

[3] 'The doctrine of fascism', p.47, in Adrian Lyttelton (ed.) *Italian Fascisms from Pareto to Gentile*, New York, 1973.

[4] See particularly A.J.P. Taylor, *The Origins of the Second World War*, New York, rev. paperback edn, 1966, pp. 70–2, and Norman Stone, *Hitler*, Boston, Mass., 1980, pp. 16, 67. Hans Mommsen, 'National Socialism', in *Marxism, Communism, and Western Society*, New York, 1973, 6: 67, finds Schumpeter's 'aimless expansion' the best description of National Socialist policy. Gerhard Schulz, *Aufstieg des Nationalsozialismus*, Frankfurt, 1975, p. 218, argues on the basis of a *Mein Kampf* passage (p. 170 of the English edition, trans. Ralph Manheim [New York, 1971] [henceforth MK]), that Hitler was a mere '*Machiavellist*' who did not care whether his ideology was 'true or false' (see also pp. 212–13). But the *Mein Kampf* passage actually establishes only that Hitler thought Marxism 'false'; he viewed his own theoretical task as the establishment of 'absolute truth' (MK, p. 210).

[5] See De Felice, *Mussolini il duce*, Turin, 1974, 1, 496.

[6] Pareto, elites: *OO*, 1: 6–7, 73–5, 128 (1904–08); 3: 26 (1910); Marx and Darwin: 2: 9–10 (1909); Oriani: note 9 below. For Pareto and Marx, see especially Gregor, *The Young Mussolini and the Intellectual Origins of Fascism*, Berkeley, Calif., 1979.

[7] I have throughout endeavored to use the term *revolution* in as neutral a fashion as possible, without assuming that revolutions (violent attempts to achieve rapid, fundamental changes in dominant values and myths, political institutions, social structures, leadership and government policies) are of necessity 'progressive'. I have also applied the term to relationships between states, to mean an attempt to achieve violent, fundamental change in power relationships and the distribution of territory. The widespread assumption that only the Left makes revolutions contains a hidden but indefensible teleology, and when applied to the twentieth century falls foul of the obvious confusion between political extremes: was Stalin 'Left' or 'Right'? (See, in general, Eugen Weber, 'Revolution? Counterrevolution? What Revolution?', *Journal of Contemporary History*, 9, 1974, 3–47; Perez Zagorin, 'Theories of revolution in contemporary historiography', *Political Science Quarterly*, 88, 1971 23–52, and 'Prolegomena to the comparative history of revolution in Early Modern Europe', *Comparative Studies in Society and History*, 18, 1976, 151–74.

[8] Barbarous socialism: *OO*, 3: 66 (1910); 'I am a primitive', 4: 183 (1912); paganism (Nietzsche): 1: 174ff.; new civilization: 3: 87 (1910); revolutionary elite: 1: 128 (1908), 3: 26 (1910).

[9] Nationalism: *OO*, 2: 75 (1909); 3: 266–7 (1910); 6: 58–60 (20 January 1920); Oriani: 38: 456; 2: 128 (1909). Gentile, *Ideologia*, p. 37, assumes Oriani's nationalism, and hence Mussolini's, was cultural – a charitable interpretation that ignores both ideologues' thirst for blood.

[10] *OO*, 6: 429 (10 November, 1914); 7: 70 (11 December 1914); 7: 197 (14 February 1915); 7: 418 (24 May 1915); 7: 394 (16 May 1915).

[11] ibid., 7: 57 (29 November 1914).

[12] The war and Italy's mission: ibid., 11: 86 (19 May 1918); 13: 147 (24 May 1919); 18: 200 (24 May 1922); 21: 443 (4 November 1925); 23: 248 (4 November 1928); beacon of civilization: 12: 77 (20 December 1918); 16: 128 (25 January 1921).

[13] ibid., 14: 22 (24 September 1919); also 15: 70, 16: 106, 17: 148; Rome: 15: 217-18 (24 September 1920).

[14] ibid, 16 159 (6 February 1921); 18: 144 (6 April 1922).

[15] ibid., 17: 18 (30 June 1921); see also 18: 69, 71; 16: 142 (2 February 1921).

[16] ibid., 21: 389 (24 September 1925); 22: 109 (7 April 1926); 22: 187 (early August 1926); 22: 12 (18 November, 1925); 22: 135 (23 May 1926); also, in general, Michael Ledeen, *Universal Fascism*, New York, 1972.

[17] Hitler, *Sämtliche Aufzeichnungen 1905–1924*, ed. Eberhard Jäckel and Axel Kuhn, Stuttgart, 1980 (henceforth HSA), p. 89 (16 September 1919); a dearth of sources has so far prevented convincing reconstruction of Hitler's views before 1919.

[18] HSA, p. 301 (26 January, 1921); MK, p. 339.

[19] On the eschatological core of Marxism, see Robert C. Tucker, *Philosophy and Myth in Karl Marx*, London, 1961, and Leszek Kolakowski, *Main Currents Of Marxism*, vol. 1, Oxford, 1978.

[20] Common practice is to ascribe canonical status to *Mein Kampf* (1924–26). The early sources in HSA show that all decisive elements in *Mein Kampf* had emerged by the end of 1922.

[21] *Monologe*, p. 49 (July 1941); see also p. 262.

[22] HSA, pp. 137–8, 145–6, 184–204 (31 May, 11 June, 13 August 1920); HSA, pp. 119–20 (6 April 1920): '... es beseelt uns die unerbittliche Entschlossenheit, das bel an die Wurzel zu packen und mit Stumpf und Stiel auszurotten (lebhafter Beifall)'.

[23] Jewish world domination: HSA pp. 195, 220, 254, 273, 464, etc.; uniting all Germans: pp. 106, 126, 128, 180, 242.

[24] HSA, p. 354 (19 March 1921); Hitler borrowed from a nineteenth-century tag: 'und es mag am deutschen Wesen / einmal noch die Welt genesen'.

[25] HSA, pp. 620, 623, 631, 698, 779 (12 April 1921; 28 September 1922; 3 January 1923); see also p. 694.

[26] MK, pp. 383-4, 288.

[27] See particularly *OO*, 13: 147–8 (24 May 1919); 16; 20 (20 November 1920).

[28] ibid., 8: 272, 10: 140 (22 December 1916; 15 December 1917); on the veterans' movement, see Giovanni Sabbatucci, *I combattenti nel primo dopoguerra*, Bari, 1974.

[29] *OO*, 14: 71 (18 October 1919); 18: 331 (2 August 1922); 20: 284 (24 May 1924); the Risorgimento as failed revolution was a favorite theme of Mussolini as well as of Gramsci.

[30] ibid., 21: 426 (28 October 1925); 22: 23, 100, 117, 246 (5 December 1925; 28 March, 15 April, 28 October 1926); 23: 78-9 (17 December 1927).

[31] ibid., 24: 283 (27 October 1930); 44: 91 (29 October 1934): 'Sonatori di mandolino, no; lanciatori di bombe, gente cortese, no. Cazzottatori'.

[32] ibid, see 17: 18, 268-9 (30 June, 22 November 1921); 18: 66ff. (25 February 1922).

[33] ibid., 19: 196 (March 1923); 20: 295 (27 May 1924).

[34] ibid., 17: 268 (22 November 1922); 20: 80 (1 November 1923). De Felice's contention (*Mussolini il fascista*, 1: 537-8 (see also pp. 465, 591, 594, 602, 618, and 2: 9-10, 34-5, 67, 128-9, 342) that Mussolini did not seek a one-party dictatorial regime before late 1925 does not fit the evidence.

[35] *OO*, 21: 362 (22 June 1925).

[36] ibid., 14: 292, 21: 363 (7 February 1920, 22 June 1925).

[37] ibid., 10: 434–5 (7 April 1918); 11: 91–;2 (28 May 1918); 12: 77, 101 (20 December 1918, 1 January 1919).

[38] ibid., 12: 323 (23 March 1919); 15: 184-5 (5 September 1920); 13: 71, 76 (20, 23 April 1919).

[39] ibid., 13: 109, 147-9 (9, 24 May 1919).

[40] All from ibid., 16: 105-6 (8 January 1921): 'Per essere liberi'.

[41] Demography (among others): ibid., 16: 335, 18: 180, 19: 191, 20: 74, (1921–3) and particularly 21: 97 (4 October 1924); 'decadence' in some areas of Italy: 19: 285 (22 June 1923).

[42] French decadence: see especially ibid., 38: 396 (22 June 1923); the rest from 22: 364-7 (26 May 1927) (the 'discorso dell'Ascensione').

[43] 'Ruralize Italy': ibid., 40: 298 (24 March 1927); the rest from 23: 216 (September 1928). De Felice's assumption that Mussolini's foreign and domestic programs were mutually exclusive alternatives *(Mussolini il fascista,* Turin, 1968, 2: 359-60; *Mussolini il Duce,* 1: 179; *Mussolini il Duce,* Turin, 1978, 2: 155) fits neither Mussolini's words nor the regime's actions.

[44] In order: *OO,* 13: 143 (22 May 1919); 15: 289-90 (20 August 1920); 16: 300-01 (3 May 1921); 18: 439 (4 October 1923); 15: 37 (15 June 1920) (see also 15: 29, 18: 459); 18: 432 (1 October 1922); 21: 273 (2 April 1925).

[45] Block quotation from Emilio Canevari, *La guerra italiana,* Rome, 1948-9, 1: 212 note; 'prisoner': *OO,* 24: 234 (17 May 1930); also *I documenti diplomatici italiani,* 7th series (Rome, 1953–), 8, no. 323. For more on this geopolitical vision, see MacGregor Knox, *Mussolini Unleashed, 1939–1941,* Cambridge, 1982, particularly pp. 38–40.

[46] For the phrase, MK, p. 336; for some of the background, George L. Mosse, *The Nationalization of the Masses,* New York, 1975.

[47] HSA, pp. 136-8, 145-6, 151 (31 May, 11 and 24 June 1920).

[48] ibid., pp. 239, 255, 156 (24 September, 26 October, 3 July 1920).

[49] ibid., p. 105 (16 January 1920).

[50] David Schoenbaum, *Hitler's Social Revolution,* New York, 1966.

[51] ibid., pp. 646, 1023, 1026, 1116 (22 June 1922; before October 1923; 28 February 1924); MK, p. 403.

[52] HSA, pp. 126, 127 (27 April 1920), also p. 443; 'iron skull': p. 333 (6 March 1921).

[53] ibid., p. 438 (14 July 1921); p. 622 (12 April 1922); pp. 643 and 643, note 6; also pp. 753–4 (29 May, 4 December 1922): Wir brauchen einen starken Mann, und den werden die Nationalsozialisten bringen'; p. 565 (2 February 1922).

[54] ibid., pp. 683, 726, 704, 711 (17 August, 9 and 22 November, 25 October 1922); see also pp. 795 ('heads will roll'), 806, 950. As early as February 1921, Hitler had claimed that the movement's swastika flag was the only appropriate one for a future 'germanic state of the German nation' (p. 323).

[55] ibid., pp. 966, 1027.

[56] ibid., pp. 1007, 1128, 1188, 1210; MK, pp. 449-50. For a different view, see Albrecht Tyrell, *Vom 'Trommler' zum 'Führer',* Munich, 1975. Tyrell's stress on the role of Hitler's surroundings and followers in creating the Führer role is well taken. But Tyrell also reads Hitler's comparative modesty between 1919 and 1921-2 as self-doubt, and ignores the more plausible possibility of tactical reticence.

[57] HSA, p. 269 (30 November, 1920).

[58] Conversation with Eduard Sharrer, ibid., pp. 770–5; for the importance of the document, see pp. 34ff. of Geoffrey Stoakes, 'The evolution of Hitler's ideas on foreign policy, 1919-1925', in Peter D. Stachura (ed.) *The Shaping of the Nazi State,* New York, 1978.

[59] HSA, pp. 118, 122, 168, 728 (29 March, 17 April, 1 August 1920; 14 November 1922); Jens Petersen, *Hitler-Mussolini,* Tübingen, 1973, pp. 65-8.

[60] For Hitler's insistence on the need to proceed by stages, see MK, pp. 249–50, and Calic, *Ohne Maske*, pp. 50, 93; for the *Stufenplan* metaphor, Andreas Hillgruber, *Hitlers Strategie,* Frankfurt, 1965; Klaus Hildebrand, *Deutsche Aussenpolitik 1933-1945,* Stuttgart, 1971; and Jost Dülffer, *Weimar, Hitler und die Marine,* Düsseldorf, 1973.

[61] For the chain of utterances that links the Hitler of 1924 with that of 1933, Jochen Thies, *Architekt der Weltherrschaft,* Düsseldorf, 1976, pp. 41–61, and Dülffer, *Marine,* pp. 204–20.

[62] Adolf Hitler, *Hitler's Second Book,* New York, 1961, p. 34; similarly, pp. 24, 46–7, 79, 210. See also Martin Broszat, 'Betrachtungen zu "Hitlers Zweitem Buch"', VfZG 9, 1961, 422; the only systematic attempt to interpret Hitler's later policies in these terms is Dietrich Orlow, *The History of the Nazi Party,* vol. 2, Pittsburgh, 1973.

[63] Franco Catalano, *L'economia italiana di guerra,* Milan, 1969, p. 7; Giorgio Rochat, *Militari e politic nella preparazione della campagna d'Etiopia,* Milan, 1971 pp. 105–7.

[64] *Mussolini il fascista,* p. 359; *Mussolini il duce,* 1: 179, 466–7; Petersen, 'Die Aussenpolitik des faschistischen Italien als historiographisches Problem', VfZG, 22, 1974, 417–57.

[65] *OO,* 26: 308 (24 August 1934) (the 'discorso del carro armato').

[66] See Rochat, *Militari e politici,* pp. 26-33.

[67] Pompeo Aloisi, *Journal (25 juillet 1932-14 juin 1936),* Paris, 1957, p. 382 (8 May 1936).

[68] For details, Rochat, *Militari e politici,* chs 1, 2.

[69] Luigi Federzoni, *L'Italia di ieri per la storia di domani,* Milan, 1967, p. 233 (also Attilio Tamaro, *Venti anni di storia* [Rome, 1953–54], 3: 217, note 98a); *OO,* 42: 107 (26 June 1931.

[70] Badoglio to Mussolini, September 1935, in Rochat, *Militari e politici, p.* 229.

[71] Alessandro Lessona, *Memorie,* Florence, 1958, pp. 239–40.

[72] *OO,* 44: 325 (17 April 1943).

[73] ibid.

[74] His replacement in November 1935 by Badoglio was consequently an internal setback for Mussolini – but winning on the battlefield obviously had immediate priority.

[75] *OO,* 27: 268–9 (9 May, 1936).

[76] Mussolini's words: Galeazzo Ciano, *Diario 1937–1943,* Milan, 1980, 13 November 1937. For the involution thesis, which resembles the folk wisdom of the day ('… se dopo l'Etiopia, si fosse fermato. …'), De Felice, *Mussolini il duce,* 2, ch. 3.

[77] Knox, *Mussolini Unleashed, p.* 30.

[78] De Felice, 'Mussolini e Vittorio Emanuele III Primi Marescialli dell'Impero', in Università degli Studi di Messina, *Scritti in onore di Vittorio De Caprariis,* Rome, n.d., pp. 347–68.

[79] De Felice, *Mussolini il duce,* 2: 16 (in general, pp. 14–21).

[80] See particularly ibid., p. 40, and Giuseppe Bottai, *Diario 1935–1944,* Giordano Bruno Guerri (ed.), Milan, 1982, entries for 23 June, 12 July and 13 June 1938.

[81] Knox, *Mussolini Unleashed, pp.* 17–18.

[82] ibid., pp. 18-19, 58, 119-23.

[83] ibid., p. 11.

[84] See De Felle, *Storia degli ebrei italiani sotto il fascismo,* Turin, rev. edn, 1972, pp. 204–5, 286–87.

[85] Knox, *Mussolini Unleashed,* chs 3 and 6, and Conclusion.

[86] Domarus, *Hitler, p.* 760 (21 November 1937).

[87] Engel, *Heeresadjutant,* pp. 20, 26, 32 (20 April, 25 June, 18 April 1938).

[88] 88 Dülffer, *Marine, pp.* 500–1, 512, 541.

[89] Müller, *Heer,* chs 7, 8; Williamson Murray, *The Change in the European Balance of Power, 1938–39,* Princeton University Press, forthcoming, chs 5–7.

[90] Ian Kershaw, *Der Hitler-Mythos,* Stuttgart, 1980, p. 123.

[91] See Telford Taylor, *Munich,* New York, 1979, p. 877.

[92] See the editors' remarks in *'Es spricht der Führer',* pp. 230–1.

[93] 'Governesses': speech at Saarbrücken, 9 October 1938, Domarus, *Hitler,* p. 956; the rest from *'Es spricht der Führer',* pp. 283, 281–2.

[94] Fedor von Bock, quoted in Müller, *Heer,* p. 385.

[95] Domarus, *Hitler, p.* 1058; Engel, *Heeresadjutant,* p. 30 (6 August 1938).

[96] All from Thies, *Architekt der Weltherrschaft, p.* 116.

[97] Quoted in Müller, *Heer,* p. 383.

[98] See Mason, Innere Krise und Angriffskrieg 1938/1939', pp. 158–88 in F. Forstmaier and H. E. Volkmann (eds), *Wirtschaft und Rüstung am Vorabend des Zweiten Weltkrieges,* Düsseldorf, 1975; also his *Arbeiterklasse und Volksgemeinschaft,* pp. 119ff. For the criticisms, Jost Dülffer, 'Der beginn des Krieges 1939: Hitler, die innere Krise, und das Mächtesystem', *Geschichte und Gesellschaft,* 2, 1976, 443–70, and Ludolf Herbst, 'Die Krise des nationalsozialistischen Regimes am Vorabend des Zweiten Weltkrieges und die forcierte Aufrüstung, 'ZfZG, 26, 1978, 347–92 (see particularly pp. 376–82). For public opinion, see Kershaw, *Mythos,* pp. 123-5, which suggests that only fear of war marred the popularity Hitler had achieved through foreign success in 1938-39.

[99] John Gillingharn, 'Ruhr coal miners and Hitler's war', *Journal of Social History,* summer 1982, 637-53.

[100] Hitler speech summary, 22 August 1939 (probably from stenographic notes by Canaris), *Akten zur deutschen auswärtigen Politik,* Serie D, (Baden-Baden, Frankfurt, 1950-) (henceforth ADAP,D) 7: 168. A second version, written that evening by Admiral Boehm, suggests even less urgency: 'perhaps 10-15 years'. Mason prefers the Lochner document (ADAP,D, 7: 171–2 note), which ascribes to Hider a lament that 'the Four-Year Plan [has] failed and we are finished, without victory in the coming war'. But the Lochner version will not bear much weight; its provenance, its divergences from all other accounts, and its piquant fabricated details (a Goering war-dance on the conference table) mark it as an Abwehr/resistance concoction for Western consumption. (On the sources, see Winfried Baurngart, 'Zur Ansprache Hitlers vor den Führern der Wehrmacht am 22. August 1939', VfZG 16 (1968): 120–49).

[101] Mason, Innere Krise', pp. 182–4.

[102] Dülffer, 'Beginn des Krieges', p. 464.

[103] ADAP,D, 7: 168 (22 August 1939) and 8: 348 (23 November 1939).

[104] Müller, *Heer,* p. 427.

[105] All from Engel, *Heeresadjutant,* pp. 71–2 (20 January 1940); see also p. 52 (8 July 1939)

[106] Rosenberg, *Tagebuch*, p. 98 (19 January 1940).

[107] Friedrich Percyval Reck-Malleczewen, *Diary of a Man in Despair*, New York 1970, pp. 109, 103.

[108] 'Reptile': *Monologe*.

[109] ibid., p. 108 (25 October 1941). Hitler frequently remarked that the ideal solution would be to let the churches die out naturally (ibid., pp. 40–1, 67, 82–5), but he clearly intended to help them along (see especially ibid., p. 272).

[110] Jodl memorandum, October 1946, in Percy Ernst Schramm, *Hitler: The Man and Military Leader*, Chicago, 1971, p. 204; Hillgruber, *Hitlers Strategie*, pp. 551–4 and note 84; Hildebrand, 'Weltmacht oder Niedergang: Hitlers Deutschland 1941–1945', in Oswald Hauser (ed.) *Weltpolitik II 1939–1945*, Göttingen, 1975, pp. 308-13.

[111] See Kershaw, *Mythos*, pp. 186-91.

(*Journal of Modern History*, no. 56, pp.1, 4–6 and 43–57, Chicago, University of Chicago Press)